Prisone

CHRISTOPHER CLARK

Prisoners of Time

Prussians, Germans and Other Humans

ALLEN LANE
an imprint of
PENGUIN BOOKS

ALLEN LANE

UK | USA | Canada | Ireland | Australia
India | New Zealand | South Africa

Allen Lane is part of the Penguin Random House group of companies
whose addresses can be found at global.penguinrandomhouse.com

First published 2021
001

Copyright © Christopher Clark, 2021

The moral right of the author has been asserted

Set in 10.5/14pt Sabon LT Std
Typeset by Jouve (UK), Milton Keynes
Printed and bound in Great Britain by Clays Ltd, Elcograf S.p.A.

The authorized representative in the EEA is Penguin Random House Ireland,
Morrison Chambers, 32 Nassau Street, Dublin DO2 YH68

A CIP catalogue record for this book is available from the British Library

ISBN: 978-0-241-51904-2

To my friend Richard Sanger,
Toronto poet and playwright

'The Snowball'

It was the history teacher's car
Letting off steam at the intersection.
Walking home through the snow
With a pack of friends, the stop sign
Still recoiling from a bull's eye,
I reloaded quick and let go—

Oh how the whole world soared
For one brief and joyous moment,
Soared too high for its own good . . .
Then came Sarajevo, the war, the trenches,
They told the Archduke not to go
But he, like a fool, up and went.

The car started off. We hightailed it,
Leaving a small disturbance
Raised in his rearview mirror
And him to put the two together,
His second-hand powder keg,
My snowball loaded with the weight of events.

Richard Sanger

Contents

Preface

Out of the Present into the Past

In early nineteenth-century New Orleans, the months when yellow fever was in town were known as the *tiempo muerto*, the dead time. People who could afford to left the city. The dead could be seen everywhere, in parks, on open barrows, or floating down the Mississippi. The disease known as COVID-19 is less lethal than yellow fever, which, in a bad year, might kill as much as a tenth of the population. In 2020, the bodies piled up in smaller numbers and out of sight, unless you happened to be working in a hospital, morgue or crematorium.

But the phrase *tiempo muerto* does capture something of the pandemic season of 2020. The great deceleration of all things felt like a reversal of modernity's inner logic. Flights, speeches, conferences, ceremonies and meetings were cancelled. Time ceased to rush like water in a fast river. It pooled around each task. The future became hazy. For a seasoned professor confined to his house it was a good time to be writing a book and compiling a volume of essays. For young people in the academic sector, on the other hand, there were no final exams, no conferrals of degrees and no celebrations with friends and relatives. The thresholds they had striven towards, rites of passage marking the transition from one phase of life to the next, had melted away. For them, it was as if the future had been switched off.

In order to collect my own thoughts and to signal to the wider world that historians were still thinking, even as the world around them was shutting down, I began a series of podcast conversations with colleagues whose aim was to explore how reflecting on the past can help us to reflect on our present predicaments. These discussions, broadcast under the title *The History of Now*, generated suggestive and contradictory insights.

The raw terror of earlier encounters with epidemic disease was one interesting theme. In early modern Venice and Florence, Jane Stevens Crawshaw and John Henderson reported, fear was seen as a threat in its own right, because it was believed to heighten the vulnerability to infection. The public health authorities tried to counter it by dealing with the public in a calm and compassionate way. But the opposite problem also presented itself. When passing health inspectors discovered a gaggle of young Florentines blithely partying at the height of a sixteenth-century plague epidemic, they went to a nearby grave-yard, brought back the corpse of a young woman who had recently died and threw it into the midst of the revellers, shouting: 'She wants to dance too!'

It was a striking feature of the COVID-19 pandemic, Samantha Williams, Romola Davenport and Leigh Shaw-Taylor observed, that although our capacity to amass and communicate scientific know-ledge was incomparably greater than that of our predecessors, our ability to actually fight and treat the disease (at least until the emer-gence of a dependable vaccine) was less well developed, with the result that we tended to fall back on techniques already employed by medieval and early modern cities: quarantine, lockdown, social dis-tancing, masks and the closure of public facilities such as shops, markets and churches. Then, as now, the political authorities had to balance the threat to life against the threat to incomes and economic vitality. In commercial cities such as New Orleans, Istanbul, Bombay and Hamburg, that was an impossible balancing act.

The measures adopted by political authority to meet the challenge of contagious disease always go to the heart of the social contract between the rulers and the ruled, Peter Baldwin told me. Where the danger was evident and the policies plausible and transparent, social conformity with counter-epidemic measures tended to be high. But where trust in the authorities was lacking, the effort to suppress con-tagion by ordinances limiting movement and economic activity could trigger protests and riots, as in today's United States, or, as Shruti Kapila observed, in late-nineteenth-century plague-struck Bombay, where measures enacted by the British triggered an uprising that cul-minated in the assassination of the city's plague commissioner and his assistant. 'Plague is more merciful to us,' wrote the Indian nationalist

Bal Gangadhar Tilak, 'than its human prototypes now reigning the city.'

The habit of assigning a moral meaning to pestilence is as old as the written record of its effects. In the Mosaic Bible, disease is often presented as something willed by God. 'For now,' says the God of Exodus (9:15), 'I will stretch out my hand that I may smite thee and thy people with pestilence.' From this it followed that epidemics must be signs of divine disfavour requiring acts of propitiation by humanity. The towns of medieval and early-modern Europe, Chris Briggs told me, often flanked their public health measures with regulations forbidding prostitution, gambling, card playing and general frivolity, on the grounds that these would further provoke an already vexed deity. The habit has persevered: think of the businessman and bed accessory tycoon Mike Lindell, CEO of MyPillow® Inc., who appeared at a White House press conference alongside Donald Trump and presented an off-piste monologue in which he declared that the current COVID-19 pandemic was God's way of punishing an America that had 'turned its back on God'. Americans should get back to reading 'the book' with their families.

There has always been an alternative view, of course. In his account of the ancient Athenian plague epidemic, the historian Thucydides noted archly that the pious and the impious died of the disease in equal numbers. In the Book of Job, Jonathan Lamb reminded me, disease is not a punishment, but the consequence of a dark wager between God and Satan. Jealous of Job's loyalty to God, Satan tempts the deity to let him test this virtuous man by visiting disease and death first on his cattle, then on his wife and children and finally on Job himself, who passes through these horrors in a state of the profoundest confusion, because he has no way of understanding why he is being tormented. The need for moral understanding remains strong. Even in the relatively secularized environment of the present-day West, there is an urge to mitigate the meaninglessness of suffering and death by speculating hopefully on the notion that the pandemic will leave us more attentive to the ecological fragility of our world and more sensitive to the bonds of solidarity and interdependence that connect us with our fellow citizens.

It is easy to imagine that contagious diseases fan out evenly across human populations, like billiard balls rolling across a table. But in fact their trajectory is highly uneven, because it is nearly always mediated by structures of social inequality. In the towns of early modern Europe and the Ottoman Empire, Nükhet Varlık pointed out, the wealthy could flee from crowded cities to rural retreats where infection was less likely. In the plague years of early modern Cambridge, the highest mortality rates were seen in the suburban areas between Jesus College and Barnwell, where college servants and the labouring poor lived. Kathryn Olivarius told me that in New Orleans, new immigrants, especially Irish and Germans, tended to die in the greatest profusion from yellow fever, because they occupied cheap rooms in crowded tenements, where rates of infection were high. In colonial America, Sarah Pearsall reported, epidemic disease killed fastest in populations that were already immuno-suppressed by malnutrition. Eighteenth-century Native Americans displayed heightened vulnerability to smallpox, Pearsall observed, because forced displacement had already degraded their nutritional standards.

Today, there are signs in the United States and many other countries of a stark variation in mortalities that correlates with income and levels of community health. Even in the most prosperous parts of the world, the pandemic has intensified social awareness. Attention focused on carers, nurses, social workers, paramedics and delivery drivers – fellow citizens whose work is not usually handsomely rewarded, but whose importance was now suddenly conspicuous. People got to know their neighbours, brought food, shopping and medications to vulnerable men and women locked down in their homes, and lined up along their streets to applaud health workers (at least until the government began telling them to do so, at which point enthusiasm dwindled). Here, too, there were parallels with the past. Even during visitations of the bubonic plague, a pitiless and terrifying disease with a far higher lethality than COVID-19, medieval English communities displayed high levels of social solidarity. In Venice and Florence, the authorities rolled out elaborate provisions – furlough payments, free food deliveries (including a litre of wine per day), tax and rent freezes and efforts to get people back into work once the disease had passed. The smallpox epidemics of colonial America triggered stupendous feats of caring, mainly by women, who often took in and raised the children of dead neighbours, friends and relatives. Far from breaking the bonds of social solidarity and unleashing anarchy, the encounter with epidemic disease heightened social cohesion and reinforced ethical norms.

During the lockdown, I happened to be reading Heinrich Heine's *Französische Zustände*, a series of articles written during his sojourn in Paris in 1832. In the midst of a piece composed in April of that year, I found the following parenthesis, inserted some years later:

> At this time I was often disturbed, most of all by the horrific screaming of my neighbour, who died of cholera. In general, I must point out that the conditions at that time had a regrettable impact on the pages that follow . . . It is very disturbing when the sound of death sharpening his sickle rings all too sharply in one's ears.

Heine had seen people dragging through the streets the mutilated corpse of a man lynched by a crowd because he had been found to be carrying a white powdery substance, believed to be a cholera-spreading toxin (in fact the powder turned out to be camphor, thought by some to protect against the disease). He had seen white bags full of corpses piled up in the spacious hall of a public building and watched the corpse wardens counting off the bags as they passed them to gravediggers to be loaded onto wagons. He remembered how two little boys with sombre faces had stood beside him and asked him which bag their father was in. A year later, the misery and fear were forgotten. This same hall was full of 'cheerful little French children jumping about, the chattering of pretty French girls, who laughed and flirted as they went about their shopping'. The cholera months had been 'a time of terror', more horrifying even than the political Terror of 1793. Cholera was a 'masked executioner who made his way through Paris with an invisible mobile guillotine'. And yet its passing seemed to leave no trace on the frivolous vitality of the city.

I began to think about the place of epidemic catastrophes in history. There exist many wonderful studies of the impact of epidemic disease: Richard Evans's classic *Death in Hamburg* on the nineteenth-century cholera crises, Laura Spinney's *Pale Rider* on the Spanish flu pandemic of 1918–19, Elizabeth Fenn's *Pox Americana* and Kathryn Olivarius's study of yellow fever in antebellum New Orleans, to name just a few.

But it was striking how little trace even the most horrific encounters with deadly pathogens had left on mainstream historical narratives and on public memory.

In one of our podcast conversations, Gary Gerstle remarked that he had been thinking all his adult life about the impact of war on American governance and yet had never written a single word about the flu pandemic of 1918–19 that killed more Americans than the First World War. How many Americans today remember that more compatriots died of smallpox during the American Revolutionary Wars than as a consequence of armed conflict?

This seemed to be a problem specific to modern history – the Black Death, Miri Rubin reminded me, was one of the central themes of medieval studies, and the early modernists, too, were alert to the importance of epidemic disease. The Spanish conquest of the Americas, Gabriela Ramos remarked, might not have happened as it did, were it not for 'invisible allies' in the form of diseases endemic to peninsular Spain, but unknown in Mexico and Andean America, whose inhabitants, immunologically naïve to these pathogens, were all but wiped out by them. Only in the modern era did epidemic disease seem to have been moved to the margins of visibility. Sarah Pearsall proposed that this had to do with gender: since the lion's share of caring during epidemic crises fell to women, she argued, the topic forfeited its claim on the attention of male historians. Commenting on the near-invisibility of the flu pandemic in many accounts of the US contribution to the First World War, Gary Gerstle suggested that an historiography oriented towards the struggle and destiny of nation-states was more attuned to the kinds of suffering and sacrifice that take place on battlefields than on those that unfold in hospital wards when mortalities surge.

And perhaps, Laura Spinney remarked, there is something inherent in the character of an epidemic that resists our efforts to integrate it into grand narrative. Historians, and humans generally, are addicted to human agency, they love stories in which people bring about or respond to change. They think in terms of long chains of causation. But an epidemic occurs when a non-human agent erupts without warning into the human population. A narrative centred on humans, Sujit Sivasundaram suggested, will never be capable of making sense of a phenomenon like COVID-19, whose unliving pathogen crossed the boundary between the animal and the human worlds. What was needed was a different way of telling history, one that made space not just for the disruptions wrought by humans, but also for the sentient agency of pangolins and civet cats and the non-sentient energy of atmospheric systems and the physical environment.

For the most part, humans have preferred accounts of disease that stress either divine agency (this is a scourge from God or the gods) or human causation. In the fourteenth century, Jews were suspected of poisoning wells; in sixteenth-century Milan, suspicion focused on *untori*, plague 'anointers', strangers from other Italian towns who were believed to be smearing church altars with a pestilential paste; in nineteenth-century Paris, crowds sprang upon men believed to be 'poison-mixers'. President Donald Trump spoke of 'the Chinese virus' and bantered with his supporters about 'Kung Flu', while theories proposing that COVID-19 was concocted in laboratories by Chinese, American or Russian scientists were rife on the internet. One of the most virulent conspiracy theories worldwide claimed that the COVID-19 virus was spread by 5G phone masts. A curious variant, widespread in Brazil, Pakistan, Nigeria and Argentina, proposed that Bill Gates had personally engineered the current pandemic in order to implant microchips in humans along with a vaccine, so that they could be 'controlled' via 5G telephone networks.

We have learned so much and we have learned so little. Watching President Donald Trump flounder day after day in front of the cameras as he recommended untested therapies to the public like a snake-oil salesman from the Old West, contradicted his own medical experts and tried to blame the virulence of the disease on the poor governance of Democrat governors and mayors, I found myself thinking of Wilhelm II, Germany's last and most incompetent Kaiser. The two men were strikingly similar. Both exhibited a tendency to blabber about whatever preoccupation happened to be on their minds at any given moment. A short attention span, extreme irritability, a tendency to drift into incoherence under pressure, anger-management issues, a hectoring, bullying demeanour, coldness and lack of empathy, egregious boastfulness, crackpot plans, sarcastic asides and off-colour jokes were common to both. It was Wilhelm II

who said to a group of advisers: 'All of you know nothing. I alone
know something,' but no one would be surprised to hear these words
on the lips of Donald Trump. Both men denounced domestic protest-
ers as anarchists and troublemakers and both insisted on tough
repressive measures against them. Both were preoccupied by zero-
sum scenarios of conflict in which one country's victory must be
another's defeat. Like Trump, the Kaiser was completely incapable of
learning from his own mistakes.

We all saw the strained expressions on the faces of the experts and
staffers standing around the president as he veered off the text prepared for him into narcissistic speculations that appeared completely
decoupled from reality. In 1907, exactly the same phenomenon was
captured in a famous caricature by Rudolf Wilke published in the
satirical journal *Simplicissimus* under the title 'During a speech by the
Kaiser'. A group of generals listen to a speech unfold in three phases.
During the first, 'The Fine Opening', the gentlemen look on, calm and
attentive. Then comes 'The Awkward Bit' – the Kaiser is off-message,
the generals stroke their beards, adjust their monocles and look awk-
wardly at the decorations. At last comes 'The End': Hurra – hurra –
hurra!!' The speech is over, to everyone's great relief.

The point of these reflections is not that they make William II look
any better, because they do not. It is rather that the extraordinary
spectacle of the Trump presidency could be said to have changed the
frame of reference. There was a time when the Kaiser looked like a
uniquely German disaster. The domineering demeanour, the empty
posturing, the absurdly affected countenance at public occasions, the
impulsiveness, the self-absorption – all looked like the symptoms of a
peculiarly German malaise. In a brilliant study of the Kaiser's court,
John Röhl described eloquently the 'Byzantinism' of the Kaiser's
entourage, the toadying, forelock-tugging deference to the 'All-Highest
Person'. Everything that was wrong with Germany seemed to be on
display here. The Trump presidency has not overturned that narrative,
but it has unsettled it. We all remember cringing at that televised
meeting in the cabinet office of the White House in June 2017, at
which cabinet members newly appointed by Trump vied to outdo
each other in gushing expressions of praise and fealty to the president.
No one *chose* Wilhelm II – he was thrust upon the Germans by the

inflexible logic of dynastic inheritance. The Trump presidency revealed that even a powerful and self-confident democracy rooted in liberal values can bring forth atavistic enormities.

What we will learn from the pandemic remains to be seen. As I write these words it is still unclear how quickly and how fully economies across the world will recover from this crisis. The encounter with a pandemic is not new, but the measures enacted to counter its propagation are. As Adam Tooze remarked in one of our podcasts, the velocity and volume of the economic shutdown are completely unprecedented. The crises of 1929 and 2007–8 were different from each other, but both were triggered by internal malfunctions of the global system. This pandemic crisis, by contrast, is an exogenous shock, a fast-freeze of the real economy by government fiat. The speed of the freeze was important, because it meant that stakeholders had almost no time to adjust their behaviour to changing conditions. Whether a partially frozen world economy can be thawed and primed back into rude life remains to be seen. We have never been here before.

The essays in this book were chosen because they address themes that have informed my work since I became a student of modern European history: religion, political power and the awareness of time. The history of religion has always interested me because religious traditions situate human endeavour within the largest possible compass. Political power connects culture, economy and personality with decisions that affect great numbers of people. And the study of time, not as the limpid plasma through which history moves, but as something constructed and shaped by narratives, religious and secular, has always interested me, because it exposes one of the deepest ways in which those who wield power manipulate our awareness, our sense of history. Most of the essays are the product of repeated redactions and elaborations. They are all *essays*, in the sense that they are all exploratory chains of thought, rather than watertight exercises in historical argument. Some of them stem from public lectures, others from review pieces. Only two of them ('From Prussia with Love' and 'The Life and Death of Colonel General Blaskowitz') are supplied with source notes, because they draw extensively on archival sources. I have included two short pieces in which I discuss the work of a colleague, in order to show the work of others illuminates our path, both as historians and as people. I have not attempted to 'update' any of the essays – readers will note that the final one, 'Uncertain Times', though contemporary in focus, dates from that far-off epoch before COVID-19. There seemed to me to be a risk that in making it more up-to-date, I might make it less fresh. The essays in this book, like their author and the protagonists who appear in them, are prisoners of time.

The Dream of Nebuchadnezzar: Thoughts on Political Power

I want to begin these thoughts with the Book of Daniel. Chapter 2 of this book opens with a scene involving King Nebuchadnezzar II of the Neo-Babylonian Empire, who reigned from 605 BC until 562 BC – forty-three years in all. Today Nebuchadnezzar is mainly known for two things: building the Hanging Gardens of Babylon – one of the wonders of the ancient world – and for besieging Jerusalem and destroying its temple, inaugurating the so-called 'Babylonian Captivity' of the Judeans.

Chapter 2 of the Book of Daniel recalls a morning in the second year of Nebuchadnezzar's reign, after the sacking of Jerusalem. The king wakes up disturbed by a dream. He can't find rest. He summons his wise men, 'the astrologers, and the sorcerers, and the Chaldeans'. They appear. They ask him to describe the dream. He can't. 'The thing is gone from me.' It seems the king has forgotten his dream. At this point the mood in the room plummets. The wise men (who are now not feeling very wise) try as gently as they can to break the news that their transferable skills, impressive as they are, do not include reading the minds of sleeping kings: 'it is a rare thing that the king requireth, and there is none other that can shew it before the king, except the gods, whose dwelling is not with flesh.' In other words: 'Sorry boss, this is way above our pay grade.' The wise men are presumably feeling apprehensive at this point, and with good reason, because a moment later the king says: 'If ye will not make known unto me the dream, with the interpretation thereof, ye shall be cut in pieces, and your houses shall be made a dunghill.' The conversation continues, but the thrust of the king's position is already clear. The wise men are a waste of space. This empire has had enough of experts. In his rage, the king orders that every wise man in Babylon be executed.

The king's execution order stirs consternation. Among those who are shocked to learn of it is a young Jewish captive, in effect a prisoner of war, by the name of Daniel – a man of noble birth who had lived through the siege and destruction of the city of Jerusalem. Daniel was one of a group of handsome and intelligent young Israelites from good families who had been brought back from the defeated city to be taught the literature and language of Babylon and serve in the monarch's court. So Daniel, too, was among those 'wise men' who faced execution if the king's decree were to be carried out. The book records that Daniel speaks to one of the palace guards. He asks what's up with the king. The guard explains. Daniel wants to know if he can get some face-time with the monarch (I'm translating freely from the Aramaic here). The guard agrees to fix a meeting. Daniel goes to the friends he shares his apartment with: Hananiah, Mishael and Azariah. Guys, he says, let's pray to God for insight. Let's 'desire mercies of the God of heaven concerning this secret'.

The next morning, Daniel goes to the king. We have to imagine that the king is initially sceptical: if the wise men of Babylon have collectively failed in this task, what should Daniel hope to accomplish? But to the king's astonishment, Daniel describes the dream, or, rather, he describes *a* dream, a dream that he hopes the king will accept as his own. He frames it not just as an alarming nocturnal experience, but as a prophetic revelation: 'O king, thy thoughts came into thy mind upon thy bed, what should come to pass hereafter: and he that revealeth secrets maketh known to thee what shall come to pass.' And then comes the dream itself. The king, Daniel says, had beheld a colossus: 'This great image, whose brightness was excellent, stood before thee; and the form thereof was terrible.' Its head was of gold, as brilliant as the sun. Its breasts and arms were of silver. Its belly and thighs were of bronze. Its feet were part of iron and part of clay.

But what does it mean, the king asks. One can only suppose that Daniel felt tremendous relief at this point. After all, he had no way of knowing whether the king would accept the dream Daniel had proposed to him. Daniel begins his exegesis of the dream he has put into the king's head: 'Thou, O king, art this head of gold.' For 'wheresoever the children of men dwell, the beasts of the field and the fowls of the heaven hath he given into thine hand, and hath made thee ruler over them all'. At this point, one has to admit, Daniel is handling the situation brilliantly. He flatters the king, first, by suggesting that he is the privileged receiver of mysteries divulged by the hidden master of all secrets and second, by implying that this divine authority underwrites the king's power. The king wants to know more: what are the silver breasts, the belly of bronze, the iron thighs, etc. for? Daniel explains: after the golden age of Nebuchadnezzar, whose lustre will never be outshone, will come a lesser age of mere silver, and then an even lesser age merely of bronze. And then will come a really quite crap age of iron and clay when men shall fight men and kings shall fight kings. 'And in the days of these kings shall the God of heaven set up a kingdom, which shall never be destroyed.' There are other details to the dream and to Daniel's exegesis that I shall not deal with here.

The king's reaction to all of this is quite extraordinary: 'Then the king Nebuchadnezzar fell upon his face, and worshipped Daniel, and commanded that they should offer an oblation and sweet odours unto him.' The mass execution of the wise men is cancelled. There are some further complications in this story: Nebuchadnezzar's mood swings get a lot worse – he spends a seven-year period in a state of mental anguish living with beasts in caves and fields. In the early nineteenth century, William Blake captured this phase of his life in an unforgettable print, naked, dirty and crawling on all fours, Nebuchadnezzar stares at the viewer in swivel-eyed mania (Fig. 1). The Book of Daniel, a very eccentrically structured text, records various further dreams and visions, and Daniel gets into some hot spots, most famously an intimidating encounter with some lions in a den.

But if we reflect on the opening scene in which Daniel narrates and interprets the dream, we find in it a beautiful and subtle fable on power. The story tells us that the most powerful man in the world is powerless before his night terrors. He summons the holders of bureaucratic power, the experts, the custodians of privileged knowledge. But they fail to come up with a solution, and as a result they forfeit their power

Figure 1. The anguish of a once mighty ruler: *Nebuchadnezzar* by William Blake (*c.* 1795–1805) (*Tate Gallery*)

and even, potentially, their lives. And into this fraught constellation steps someone with no power at all: a rightless young alien, a prisoner of war, a captive from a sacked city. The jury is still out on whether God actually told Daniel the king's dream, or whether the young man didn't simply possess the human insight required to understand the true nature of the king's predicament. Later in the book there are verses thanking God for lending Daniel a helping hand. But this is an interpolation. The story itself suggests something different, namely that the young man understood how to read the situation in which the king found himself. What could a man as powerful as Nebuchadnezzar possibly fear, other than his own mortality? And how better to reconcile him with that terrible certainty than to establish his eternal primacy over the rest of human endeavour? At the same time, Daniel imparted to the king something he had himself experienced as the son of a destroyed city, a piece of wisdom, namely, that power is *always temporary*. And his reward for this wisdom is to see the greatest king in the world abase himself before him.

4

It is hard to overstate the importance of Nebuchadnezzar's (Daniel's) dream for the theme of this essay. Because the colossus of the dream, presented by Daniel as prophecy, became a way of imagining world history as the unfolding of something foreordained, a narrative sanctioned by biblical prophecy. Until well into the early modern era, it was conventional to think of world history as an eschatological sequence of hegemonies based on Daniel's dream, starting with the Babylonians, then moving on to the Persians (with the optional addition of the Medes), the Greeks and the Romans. I will return to this idea in a moment.

Power is at once the most ubiquitous and the most elusive theme of historical writing. Questions of power lie at the centre of most historical narratives, but the concept is rarely interrogated or analysed. There are studies that aim to clarify the differences between various types of power, but they tend to be written by sociologists or political scientists rather than historians and no consensus on definitions has been reached. Even in the field of political and diplomatic history, pre-eminently concerned with the exercise of power, the term is almost always deployed as a transparent signifier whose meaning requires no separate elucidation. By contrast with 'gender' and 'culture', 'power' has never provided the focal point for the kind of sub-disciplinary formation that might have licensed a concerted theoretical and comparative engagement with the problem of power across the full spectrum of historical practice. Look up 'power studies' on the internet and you will find pages focusing on the strategic and conceptual study of air and space power or the protection of personnel and equipment through safety training, or the optimization of electrical grid performance.

Why is this so? The reason may lie partly in the nature of power itself. It is, as the historian of the Middle Ages Thomas N. Bisson has put it, 'so conceptually vast and so inscrutably inflated, that one instinctively seeks to pluralize the word'. Power is not an identity that can be said to inhere in groups or individuals; rather it expresses a relational state of affairs. Power is thus neither a substantive entity, nor an institution, nor even a possession, but rather an attribute of the relationships within which it is exercised. It was in recognition of this feature of the phenomenon that Michel Foucault, the most influential post-war theorist on power, refused to treat it under a separate rubric, choosing instead to embed his reflections in an analysis of specific institutional and disciplinary contexts and practices.

From this flows the difficulty of power as an object of synoptic historical contemplation, for the relationships within which it makes itself felt are as varied as the entire field of human experience. As a purely relational concept, it is often difficult to localize. This may help to explain the perennial debates that are fought across academic history over the extent of the power wielded by specific sovereigns and regimes. At the very least, they suggest a persistent uncertainty about how and where power arises and resides in complex systems and whether its exercise depends more upon coercion or the consent of those over whom power is supposedly wielded.

The bundling of meanings in and around the term 'power' is a further difficulty. 'Power' and 'influence', though used interchangeably, are not necessarily synonymous. I remember seeing a colleague walking in Cambridge and being amused at the words emblazoned on the T-shirt of her three-year-old daughter: 'I may be small, but I'm very influential'. The international relations theorist Robert Keohane found the same imbalance in what he called 'the big influence of small allies'. 'Like an elephant yoked to a team of lesser animals', he wrote, the United States is tied by various international agreements to an array of smaller and weaker allies. 'These are the badgers, mice and pigeons of international politics and in many cases they have been able to lead the elephant.' The boundaries between power and authority are often blurred, despite the long European tradition of theorizing the relationship between secular and priestly authority in terms of the distinction between *potestas* and *auctoritas*. Making sense of power has thus often involved disentangling the different kinds of asset that may be invoked to sustain it.

So I shall make no attempt here to chart chronologically the evolution of historical 'power studies' (since no such thing exists). I'm not going to categorize the various ways in which historians have deployed the term or tried to define it. Rather, I want to look very briefly at some of the configurations in which the operations of power have attracted the attention of historians: the powers and superpowers of the international system, power and personal dominion, the power of states, the ultra-concentration of power in the totalitarian regimes of the twentieth century, its place in pluralist democratic systems and its supposed diffusion in the era of 'late capitalism'.

The sources that historians use are themselves often artefacts of power. Many of the archives historians labour in are the fossilized remnants of once-powerful bureaucracies, and historians themselves are not immune to the attractions and repulsions of power. Bearing this in mind, I close with some brief thoughts about the operations of power upon the writing of history.

THE POWER OF THE POWERS

The book of Daniel laid the foundation for a way of thinking about the history of the world as the unfolding of a prophesied sequence of empires. The age of the Babylonians was followed by that of the Medes and Persians. Then came the Greeks and then the Romans, whose reign many Europeans believed had outlasted antiquity in the form of the Holy Roman Empire of the German Nation. This sequential template remained hugely influential well into the early modern period and still wields profound influence in the world of rapture websites. The term 'rapture' refers to an eschatological doctrine positing that the history of the world will end with a seven-year period of tribulation, before or after which Christians will be seized away into the heavens to join Christ.

In other words, Daniel's prophecy imagined world history, before it had even happened, as a sequence of powers, a sequence of hegemonies. The grip of this vision began to weaken only when the Saxon political theorist Samuel von Pufendorf, along with various other scholars, began to argue in the seventeenth century that the era of the Romans was long over. Pufendorf denied that the Holy Roman Empire was the continuation (in the prophetic or any other sense) of the ancient Roman Empire and so challenged the hold of revelation upon history. For Pufendorf, what mattered about history was not the diachronic sequence of empires, but the synchronic relations between them – expressed in alliances, conflicts and wars. The relations among powers, Pufendorf argued, were inherently chaotic and unpredictable, since the interests of each territorial state constantly changed in accordance with shifts in the balance of power among them. The idea of powers jockeying for supremacy, or at least security, within a competitive multi-state system helped to establish 'human history' as an autonomous discourse, distinct from the *historia divina* underwritten by prophecy.

Once it was separated from prophecy, the history of powers could unfold under the rubric of disruption and change. 'Fragility and instability are inseparable from the works of men,' wrote Frederick II of Prussia in 1751. This was just as well, the king thought. For if there were no great upheavals, 'there would be no great events'. The arc of ascendancy and decline traced by the great powers of world history reminded the king of the regular motion of the planets that, 'having traversed the space of the firmament for ten thousand years, find themselves at the place from which they departed'. The study of the careers of great states was thus a study in the mutability and elusiveness of power. The hegemony of any one state was always temporary. The mighty empires of the ancient near east and of Greece and Rome were now mere ruins. Today's great potentate was tomorrow's Ozymandias. The Spanish Habsburg hegemon of the sixteenth century, with its bullion and mercenary armies, made way for the Dutch Empire of the Golden Age; the hegemony of late seventeenth-century France made way after long and bitter struggles for the British Empire of the nineteenth, a vast naval enterprise sustained by industrial might and unparalleled financial resources. But British imperial hegemony was also temporary; it would not outlive what Henry Luce famously called the 'American century'.

The habit of imagining history as a succession of empires has been hard to shake. And from this arises one of the central questions posed by US political scientists: whether the United States, whose relative lead in terms of military power is still unprecedented in world history, will succeed in the medium and longer term in maintaining its leadership position. In this context there has been a lot of interest in something called 'soft power', a form of legitimacy generated by the dominant state's association with a universalistic culture, attractive values and a liberal and/or multilateral engagement with other states and with transnational organizations. Soft power is important, the former US Secretary of State Joseph Nye has argued, because it aims to bestow legitimacy upon the external projection of power.

Legitimacy is precisely what is often lacking when powerful states seek to apply force beyond their own borders, and projecting power in an environment where the locals do not accept it is an enterprise fraught with difficulty. This is a lesson every modern generation of humans has had to learn anew. Even the United States, notwithstanding its clear global superiority in 'hard power', has sometimes failed to achieve the objectives it set itself. The historian Arthur Schlesinger recalled that at the height of the Vietnam War, President Lyndon B. Johnson 'found it viscerally inconceivable that what Walt Rostow kept telling him was "the greatest power in the world" could not dispose of a collection of night-riders in black pyjamas'. Even military conquests – the most decisive and conspicuous application of hard power – tend to be undermined over time unless the majority of the conquered population comes to identify with the values of the new rulers. Power remains the arbiter of the international system, but its effective exercise in pursuit of durable solutions may depend, even in highly asymmetrical settings, upon a paradoxical intertwining of coercion and consent. And in securing consent, soft power may be essential.

CONCENTRATION AND DISPERSION

Not all power is governmental, of course. But the emergence and/or decline of governments and later of state executives as the holders of a 'monopoly of legitimate violence' (Max Weber) has been one of the central European stories about power. Power can concentrate in governments, states and bureaucracies, but it can also disperse again. In a classic account of the emergence of feudal society, the French medievalist Georges Duby described how the encompassing structures of the Carolingian Empire broke apart into ever more localized entities centred on the fortifications and military might of castellans, men who controlled castles, horses and weapons. In the process, the meaning of power changed; its exercise became less public, more closely associated with relations of proprietorship. It took on more aggressive and exploitative forms.

But this period of fragmentation was followed, according to some scholars at least, by the rise of new forms of government and by the emergence of the demand for good government in which virtue and power are in alignment and power submits to the authority of justice. Ambrogio Lorenzetti's painted allegory of good government of 1338–9, the most powerful articulation of this ideal, proposes that good government establishes the framework for a civic peace that in turn feeds the prosperity and wellbeing of subjects.

Out of a world in which all power was exercised in the form of lordship, close up and personal, there emerged new forms of government driven by the need to contain the excesses of exploitative and violent forms of local dominion. The insistence on lordly rights gave way to 'the recognition of collective interest', in which government could begin to mean not just coercion and punishment, but also 'office, accountability, competence, social utility'. In England, the century between *c.*1160 and *c.*1250 saw the state become 'arguably more powerful than at any other time in English history'. And these developments paved the way for the 'institutionalized territorial state' of the late Middle Ages (Theodor Mayer) in which the power of the sovereign pertained increasingly to the entire surface of a specific territory, a development supported by the increasingly 'spatial' orientation of later medieval legal discourse.

We need not concern ourselves with the details of these arguments, or with the scholarly controversy over their veracity. More important from our point of view is the underlying logic of the narrative. Power is in flux, it disperses, becomes localized and in doing so changes its character. Then it is refocused on a higher plane. A steady state is never achieved; all relationships are subject in the longer term to renegotiation and social upheavals and wars can always intervene to recalibrate the balance. In England, for example, as Christine Carpenter has suggested, the dynastic civil wars known as the Wars of the Roses (1455–85) produced a structural shift in the provincial relationship between gentries and nobilities that refocused authority on the monarchical state and prepared the ground for the era of muscular Tudor kingship that followed.

LEGITIMACY

These changes were accompanied by a deepening interest in the contrast between legitimate and illegitimate forms of power. Those who ruled illegitimately were called 'tyrants'; in the discourse of medieval clerical moralists, they served as 'antitypes to the good ruler' (though John of Salisbury confused matters by positing that the tyrant could be God's way of punishing sinful subjects). The idea of legitimate human power posed difficulties in a universe in which all power came from God. 'Who does not know,' Pope Gregory VII wrote to Bishop Hermann of Metz, 'that kings and princes derive their power from men ignorant of God who aspired to lord over their fellow men by pride, plunder, treachery, murder and lastly by every kind of crime, at the instigation of the devil, the prince of this world?' Coming from a pope at the height of his own power struggle with a German emperor, this was a partisan argument, to be sure. But it touched on a deep vein of medieval thought on the problem of sovereignty, a tradition that reached back to Augustine. Thomas Aquinas conceded that relations of dominion were a natural social fact, given the proclivities of human beings, but he, too, like many of the most influential clerical authorities, believed that it was an institution rooted in sin. Even as the structures of princely and governmental power were rationalized and consolidated in the eleventh and twelfth centuries, Philippe Buc has argued, the biblical commentaries of northern France saw a revived emphasis on the negative aspects of *potestas* and *dominatio*.

The distinction between coercive force and the authority bestowed by right remained one of the animating problems of early modern political discourse. 'Princes oft want power, they have [...] right oft without might,' wrote the Puritan divine Thomas Gataker in 1620. 'And tyrannous Usurpers have power more than is meete; they have [...] might without right.' The very expectation that power should have to 'legitimize' itself implies, as David Sabean has observed, that it is in some sense always arbitrary, that its exercise requires justification or masking.

It is striking that the two most influential early modern students of the problem of secular power, Machiavelli and Hobbes, largely sidestepped (or reframed) the issue of legitimacy, the former by narrowing the rationale of princely power to the pursuit of glory and the 'maintenance of one's state' by whatever means appeared expedient, and the latter by justifying sovereignty in functional terms as the best possible safeguard for public order and the protection of life and property. Whether or not the Leviathan of Thomas Hobbes, who resembles, in his immensity, the monster implanted in Nebuchadnezzar's mind by Daniel – whether or not this vast 'artificial person' is kind or not, whether or not he conforms to common moral standards, is irrelevant to his function as the guarantor of public order. In this way, the rationale for the exercise of sovereign power was separated – emancipated, one could say – from questions about the personal godliness or virtue of the prince.

ASCENDANCY OF THE STATE

'Absolutism' was a concept that helped historians to characterize the transition from the highly mediated and personal forms of power that prevailed in the medieval world to the supposedly centralized and concentrated power of modern states. It was thought that modern centralized states emerged – on the European continent at least – from a long struggle for power between princely executives and provincial elites. Forced to meet the growing costs and burdens of warfare with other states, they swept all before them in the quest for new revenues – the collision of powers thus favoured the concentration of power, and vice versa. Seventeenth- and eighteenth-century princely governments shut down the organs of corporate representation (Estates, Cortes, Diets), replaced locally run and financed militias with standing armies, disabled supraterritorial jurisdictions and imposed new taxes and territorial law codes. Princely executives grew larger: in 1715, Louis XIV had ten times as many *officiers* as Francis I (1515–47) to rule a population that was only slightly larger. In the process, the diverse provinces of 'composite monarchies' were drawn gradually into a closer and more homogeneous association.

Contemporary political theory offered eloquent support for the aggrandizement of princely executives. For the jurist Pufendorf, the most influential German reader of Hobbes, the legitimacy of states derived from the need to forestall disorder through the concentration of authority. But since it was impossible in peace or war to conduct the affairs of a state without incurring expenses, the sovereign had the right to 'force individual citizens to contribute so much of their own goods as the assumption of these expenses is deemed to require'. Here was a powerful rationale for the extension of state authority. Against the *libertas* of the Estates, Pufendorf asserted the *necessitas* of the state.

But how far did the process of consolidation go? Even in the later eighteenth century, most historians would now concede, the powers of monarchical states were still quite limited. Estates may have ceased to convene in territory-wide assemblies, but the nobilities, organized along corporate lines, still ruled the roost in the provinces. Central executives grew, to be sure, but they remained small, all the same. In 1715, the central administrative departments of the French state counted no more than 1,000 men, and a population of just under 20 million were supervised by a corps of only 2,000 police officers. Kings still needed the support and knowhow of provincial elites, not to mention their patronage networks.

If Peter the Great of Russia attacked and undermined the privileges of the Russian nobility, Catherine the Great reversed the polarities of the state-building process, choosing instead to reinforce the nobilities as pillars of the autocracy. Something broadly analogous happened in Prussia between the reigns of the Great Elector and King Frederick II. Even after successive generations of Hohenzollern monarchs had eroded the foundation of provincial noble power, the political life of the Kingdom of Prussia was still marked by residual corporate networks of aristocratic governance, what Wolfgang Neugebauer has called 'corporate latency'.

An uncertainty thus remains about how exactly power was distributed, given that relations of power so often masked relations of interdependency. The problem penetrated to the heart of royal executives, for even the most powerful monarch depended upon those who advised him – indeed his dependency deepened as the workings of the expanding state became more complex. This issue caught the attention of Carl Schmitt, one of the subtlest twentieth-century writers on the workings of political power.

The concentration of power through processes of state-building – absolutist or otherwise – is not a uniquely European preoccupation. In China, one scholar has suggested, the state structure endured through the centuries because successive generations of rulers succeeded in forging an alliance with the landed warrior nobility of the regions. But the relationship between the imperial centre and the periphery changed markedly over time. The Chinese state exercised limited political control over the non-Han peoples on the empire's southern periphery. Under the Ming dynasty (1368–1644), imperial power was mediated through a system of 'native chiefs' to whom control of the non-Han areas was franchised out. But the Yongzheng emperor, who came to the throne in 1722, resolved to do away with the chiefdoms. 'His vision of the state as a centralized entity,' as Madeline Zelin has written, 'was offended by the imposition of native chiefs between himself and some of the people.'

In Japan, too, we can tell a story of alternating concentration and diffusion that in its general outlines closely resembles the European narrative. The early eighth century saw the establishment of a 'centralized polity' that displaced the independent clan chiefdoms that had previously dominated the Japanese islands. The diverse local ancestor cults of the chiefdoms were replaced by a territorial protocol of worship focused on the semi-divine status of the Yamato monarchy. New law codes of 705 and 757 affirmed that authority derived solely from the 'Heavenly Sovereign' in Kyoto. In the thirteenth and fourteenth centuries, however, powerful regional chiefs repeatedly challenged the authority of the court and its military government, the shogunate. By the end of the fifteenth century, rebellions and inter-clan warfare had destroyed the authority of the centralized polity – the court was an 'empty shell'.

Only in 1603 was Japan reunified under Shogun Ieyasu of the House of Tokugawa, who established the foundations for 'a new and vastly more powerful kind of government than had existed in the past'. Under the Tokugawa shogunate, the Edo administration built up a formidable bureaucracy encompassing 17,000 officials; this was the first regime in Japanese history to 'draw and maintain clear physical boundaries for itself'.

The Tokugawa shogunate ruled through provincial potentates known as 'daimyo,' who gradually acquired increasing independence. Here again, we can discern the familiar dialectic: the daimyos started out as the beneficiaries of the Tokugawa supremacy and the instruments of Tokugawa authority in the regions. But with time they began to suck power out of the centre and accrue it to themselves. As the daimyo became more independent, these regional magnates began treating their territories as 'autonomous principalities'. The early Tokugawa shoguns had kept the daimyo under a tight grip, but by the later seventeenth century, the daimyo had begun to behave like little shoguns, issuing their own legal codes and local currencies, imposing taxes and establishing new administrative systems, while assiduously maintaining the fiction of loyalty to the shogunate. Some scholars have argued, paradoxically, that it was precisely these growing limitations to shogunal rule that explain the longevity of the Tokugawa dynasty. The pendulum swung back towards 'concentration' with the Meiji Restoration (1868), a bloodless coup against the Tokugawa system that aimed to reverse the process of devolution and extend central authority over the 280 independent daimyo domains. The appeal to legitimacy was secured through the claim that the new regime would re-establish the centrality and authority (though not the political power) of the 'Heavenly Sovereign' (emperor). As so often in European history, a transfer of power shrouded itself in the mantle of continuity with an ancient tradition.

The paradigm of state power as the projection onto a bounded territory of a more or less homogenous field of authority cannot be universalized. It has been observed of Mexico, for example, that the state's capacity to wield power varied with the landscape: hills and mountains were associated with 'wildness, violence and political freedom', while the plains carried connotations of 'docility, pacification and susceptibility to repression'. In the states of South East Asia, historians have noted a steep gradient of decreasing power and control from the centre to the periphery of the territory; borders were relatively insignificant, the polity was concentrated in the court or capital city. For the eighteenth- and nineteenth-century United States, the

'Frontier Thesis' was premised on the assumption that state power was not sharply delineated in space, but rather petered out by degrees as the density of white settlement declined.

Above all, the 'great but incomplete drama' of African state formation, as one historian has called it, reveals a pattern quite different from the European. Across most of the African continent, low population densities posed an insuperable obstacle to the concentration of power in large state executives. Only in 1975 did Africa reach population densities comparable with those of Europe around 1500; in 1900 Africa accounted for 18 per cent of the world's surface but only 5–7 per cent of its population. These conditions hindered state-building processes in various ways. Firstly, it was prohibitively expensive to impose control over large areas. This was the case, for example, for the nineteenth-century Ibo in what is today Nigeria, who were organized in a highly decentred manner because, on the one hand, the extension of authority over a large region would have incurred grievous costs, and, on the other hand, no other polity in a neighbouring region possessed the means to impose their authority on the Ibo. For these, as for many other Africans, it was not at all clear that the state was a desirable or necessary institution. Secondly, climate and geography combined to ensure that land as such was rarely a highly valued commodity – the struggle over access to specific demesnes that was so characteristic of Europe and Japan was much less important here. Finally, in the absence of well-policed political boundaries, any groups upon which an incipient centralized polity wished to impose its will could vote with their feet by means of 'protest migrations'. In many parts of Africa, Jeffrey Herbst has pointed out, 'people have traditionally manifested their discontent with the existing political community by migrating where they can live unhindered by their former rulers'.

One of the exceptions that proves the rule was Ethiopia, an area of relatively high population density. The era of 'Ethiopian absolutism' (1855–1913), Tsegaye Tegenu has suggested, witnessed 'the rise of a centralized state power' that displaced older and more dispersed forms of authority. Here, as in many parts of Europe, it was the growing scale, frequency and organization of military campaigns that strained traditional systems of resource management and propelled the emergence first of a centralized regional power and later of a centralized state.

Buganda is another case in point. Situated in the resource-rich and densely populated Great Lakes region, Buganda developed from around the turn of the nineteenth century into a powerful state, in which the intensive exploitation of local resources was integrated with the control of regional trade, buttressed by the military power of the state. But if Buganda was powerful, it was not necessarily centralized. Recent studies have suggested that, although the court of the *kabaka* determined the level of taxation and oversaw the use of draft labour on infrastructural projects, it depended on powerful local clan heads and *ssaza* chiefs to implement these policies; commerce, though crucial to the state's prosperity, operated largely outside the control of the central authorities. Here, as in early Tokugawa Japan, the centre was powerful only to the extent that it successfully co-opted the local holders of power over people and resources. And in Buganda, as in Tokugawa Japan, the *batongole* (military chiefs) created by the *kabakas* to reinforce their power subsequently mutated into political rivals capable of mounting a concerted challenge to the central authority.

HYPERCONCENTRATION

In 1934, a Jewish doctor living in Nazi Germany had a startling dream. He dreamt that he was lying peacefully on the sofa in his apartment reading a book about the sixteenth-century artist Matthias Grünewald when all of a sudden the walls of his room and apartment disappeared. Appalled, he looked around to see that the walls of all the other apartments within view of his building had also disappeared. Hardly had he taken this in, but a metallic voice was heard bellowing into the streets through a loudspeaker: 'in accordance with the decree of the seventeenth of the month on the prevention of walls . . .' The dream ended there, because the doctor woke up.

This small fragment, drawn from the most private of all the domains of human existence, conveys something of what it meant to experience the power of a terrorist state that claimed the right to see and know everything about the individuals under its sway. In his dystopian fable *1984*, George Orwell evoked the same nightmarish spectre of the all-seeing state in eerily similar terms. Seated in a detention cell filled with terrified 'suspects', Winston Smith covers his face with his hands. At once, a harsh voice is heard yelling from the telescreen on the wall: 'Smith! 6079 Smith W! Uncover your face! No faces covered in the cells!'

The rise of political regimes with the ambition to shape and control the totality of the life of the citizenry was one of the most remarkable features of the twentieth century. For the fascist, Benito Mussolini wrote in 1932, everything was 'within the state' and 'nothing human or intellectual' existed outside the state. In this respect, he declared, fascism was 'totalitarian' and the fascist state, as the 'summation and unity of all values' interpreted, developed and dominated the entirety of life. Liberal critics of the Italian regime were quick to see the family resemblance between the Mussolini system and the communist regime in Russia. 'One can distinguish between Russia and Italy only in one single respect,' wrote the Catholic political activist Luigi Sturzo in 1926, 'namely that Bolshevism is a communist dictatorship, or a fascism from the left; whereas fascism is a conservative dictatorship, or a communism from the right.'

Observing the new European regimes – Stalinist, Fascist and National Socialist – from across the Atlantic, American political scientists recognized a qualitatively new form of politics, a new 'basic model' of dictatorship in which an extremist party dominated by an all-powerful leader seized control in the name of an all-embracing ideology and replaced the existing parliamentary system with a reign of terror, merging party and state and bringing all means of communication under the 'total control of the regime'. In the 1950s, the US émigré scholars Carl Joachim Friedrich and Zbigniew Brzezinski developed a powerful elaboration of this analysis. Their 'totalitarian' model emphasized the generic structural features that allowed such regimes to achieve an extreme concentration of power, including the deployment of terror, the imposition of an ideology focused on mobilizing the population against real or imagined enemies, control of all aspects of the economy and the exclusive control of communications.

The result was an awe-inspiring concentration of power in one man, or, in the case of post-Stalin communism in the Eastern Bloc, in a vast gerontocracy of political guardians known as 'the communist party'. These regimes exploited all the instruments of administrative and technological modernity, while at the same time excising the power-diffusing armature of *political* modernity – legislatures, pluralist mass communications, and the liberty of expression and association.

Even of these dystopian worlds, however, there are interesting questions to ask about where power resided, and the extent to which its exercise depended upon patterns of consent or acquiescence. Italy, it is now widely conceded, was totalitarian by aspiration only; the Catholic Church, which was never absorbed or fully co-opted by the regime, remained an immensely influential presence: when the government opened its blockbusting Mostra della Rivoluzione Fascista in 1932–3, the papacy responded by declaring an *Anno Santo* for 1933–4 that attracted more visitors to Rome than the exhibition had done.

There was still a semi-autonomous Italian monarchy and state structure (including the state police force, whose officers were sent to arrest Mussolini after his deposition by the Fascist Grand Council – a situation unthinkable in Nazi Germany). The fascists, as Richard Bosworth has shown, unfolded a public culture of leader worship and vainglorious nationalist pomp, but despite their best efforts, they never succeeded in remoulding the beliefs, memories, expectations or loyalties of most of their subjects. The fascist movement was diffuse in both thought and structure. Powerful local bosses (known as *Ras*, a term borrowed, interestingly enough, from the regional chieftaincies of Ethiopia) ran the big cities, and local party agencies became intertwined – as the tax agents and *intendants* of would-be absolutist polities had done before them – with a nationwide thicket of local patronage networks that predated the advent of the regime and would survive its demise.

Fascism, perhaps, is a soft target. The Nazi regime was clearly far more lethal, both in its domestic and external projections of power. But even here questions have been asked about whether the regime derived its power over the German population more from coercion (including the threat of violence) or from the consent or acquiescence of citizens. Some historians have stressed the role played by terrorist violence, especially in the early consolidation of the regime. The torture, beating and murder of communists, prominent social democrats and other inconvenient persons by the SA during the first six months of 1933 made it clear that this was a regime prepared to project its power using the most brutal means imaginable. On the other hand, as Robert Gellately has noted, the organs of domestic political policing (Gestapo) were numerically small and beyond the ken of most Germans. Tip-offs and denunciations from the public were crucial to its day-to-day operation. For the bulk of the population, Gellately argues, the terroristic dimension of Hitler's Germany was 'socially constructed by what was passed along by word of mouth, by what they read of it in the press or heard on the radio'. Terrorist measures took place, but they were 'selective and focused'; Hitler never set out to 'confront large segments of his social world and to break them to his will, as Stalin did'. It follows that consent or at least acquiescence stabilized the regime, rather than the direct application of coercive power. A substantial portion of the German public, Gellately suggests, accepted the new regime because they liked what it was saying and doing.

Even Stalinism, which in terms of its domestic lethality outperformed the other 'totalitarian' states, is susceptible to a degree of nuance in the matter of regime power. When the regime proceeded with mind-numbing violence to terrorize the kulaks who supposedly stood in the way of the socialization of agriculture, huge brigades of urban volunteers, many of them factory workers from peasant families, streamed out into the countryside to assist in 'dekulakization'. Recent studies of the Stalinist terror have drawn attention to the selectivity of regime violence and the complex synergies between state-sponsored coercion and voluntarist pressures within the population. In some areas, denunciations from the public helped to focus terrorist reprisals against specific groups of party and police personnel. This does not in any sense diminish the breathtaking power of the Stalinist regime over its subjects; it is merely a reminder that even in ultra-coercive systems, the currents of power flow in more complex patterns than a simple, top-down model will allow.

In the ground-zero environment of the Nazi concentration camp, where armed guards could beat, maim and kill defenceless inmates with impunity, the balancing of coercion with consent is clearly out of place. But even here, as the memoirs of survivors suggest, there were complex hierarchies and power differentials – between 'criminals' and 'politicals', between Kapos and ordinary prisoners, between inmates with valuable skills and those with none. Even in those ultra-circumscribed systems – concentration camps, the gulag, slavery – where captive humans were reduced to the *nuda vita* of a rightless existence, gradations of power stealthily insinuated themselves.

Nothing, it would seem, about the shared condition of subordination prevents subalterns from dominating or brutalizing other subalterns. In the eighteenth-century Caribbean, slaves newly arriving from Africa were taunted as 'savages' by island-born black slaves, in a process of 'micro-differentiation in which members of oppressed groups strove to carve out what spaces of dignity they might within the framework of white domination'.

In social systems where slaves were employed in large numbers and a variety of functions, huge power differentials emerged. A striking example is Ibadan, a highly militarized state in nineteenth-century Yorubaland (in today's Nigeria). Founded in the 1820s, this republic required immense reserves of labour and military manpower, far exceeding what the warrior lineages of the region could supply. The need was met through the use of large numbers of slaves. Highly coercible and exploitable, not to mention cheap to maintain, slaves served as soldiers in the private armies of war chiefs, as farmworkers on the domains of warriors, as traders, porters, craftsmen and household servants. With time, however, status differences deepened within the slave population. Some slaves took on administrative roles within the compounds of powerful war chiefs, others became diplomats or toll collectors, and these privileged slaves were themselves able to acquire property, including slaves, over whom they exercised power in their own right. Indeed, the slave-holding slaves were known for their ruthlessness towards their human chattels, who frequently complained of beatings, underfeeding, excessive labour and rape. In this setting, we may see more clearly the meaning of Michel Foucault's observation that the individual is both 'an effect of power' and 'the element of its articulation': 'The individual which power has constituted is at the same time its vehicle.'

POWER IN PLURALIST SOCIETIES

In 1969, after the election of Richard Nixon to the White House, President Lyndon B. Johnson gave his successor the following warning:

> Before you get to be president, you think you can do anything. You think you're the most powerful leader since God. But when you get in that tall chair, as you're gonna find out, Mr President, you can't count on people. You'll find your hands tied and people cussin' at you. The office is kinda like the little country boy found the hoochie-koochie show at the carnival, once he'd paid his dime and got inside the tent: 'It ain't exactly as it was advertised.'

How is political power configured in a pluralist, democratic society? Do the representative bodies, federal structures, interest groups and constitutional checks of a large national democracy mute and diffuse the power of the leader? Or does the popular consent manifested in electoral success permit an awe-inspiring concentration of power in the hands of one man or woman? It has been a feature of democratic societies, with their multicameral legislatures and strong judiciaries, that power is continuously renegotiated; it gathers and disperses, or migrates from one node in the system to another.

No office better illustrates the fluidity of power and the difficulty of specifying its locations and quantity in democratic political systems than the presidency of the United States of America. When the British essayist and political journalist Walter Bagehot looked across the Atlantic in 1866, he saw a system of 'Presidential Government' so overwhelming that it threatened to weaken the legislative power. Yet, when the constitutional lawyer and future president Woodrow Wilson published a major treatise on the same political system nearly twenty years later, he called it 'Congressional Government'.

The difference was not a function of divergent theoretical perspectives (Wilson was a warm admirer of Bagehot), but of changing historical circumstance. Bagehot had written during the American Civil War, when President Abraham Lincoln conjured out of the constitutional title 'commander-in-chief' the power to impose a blockade, raise a volunteer army, expand the regular military and naval forces, sweep aside civil liberties, impose conscription and issue the two Executive Orders known as the 'Emancipation Proclamation'.

By the time Wilson published his *Congressional Government*, on the other hand, America had passed through the era of reconstruction and the legislature was now dominant. Indeed, the president was no better placed to shape legislation, Wilson suggested in 1898, than 'any other influential person who might choose to send to Congress a letter of information and advice'. And yet, when he revisited the problem ten years later in a further major study, Wilson took a different line: Americans, he wrote, now viewed the president as the 'unifying force in our complex system'. This appraisal bore the imprint of the activist presidency of Theodore Roosevelt (in office 1901–9), under which the president not only exercised his constitutional right to make legislative proposals to Congress but also used the unique prestige of his office to rally public support for them. Above all, it was America's expanding role in the early-twentieth-century world that revealed new potentialities in the office, since the president's control of foreign policy appeared virtually absolute. 'Our President,' Wilson wrote, 'must henceforth be one of the great powers of the world, whether he act greatly and wisely or not.'

One might thus speak of 'cycles' in the relationship between the presidency and the legislature, in which periods of presidential dominance have alternated with periods of congressional resurgence. There was a reassertion of congressional power after Watergate, for example, when the scandals surrounding President Nixon tarnished the standing of the office and produced a mood of determination to thwart suspect initiatives from the White House through deployment of the 'legislative veto', a statutory provision that permits one or both houses of Congress to disapprove or stall an action of the executive branch.

But these oscillations have occurred against the background of a steady growth in the power of the presidential office. War has had much to do with this consolidation of authority, just as it did in the absolutist states of seventeenth- and eighteenth-century Europe. The 'Imperial Presidency' (Arthur M. Schlesinger) of the twentieth century witnessed a dramatic growth in the war-making powers of the presidency and a corresponding shift in the constitutional balance between Congress and the president. President Harry Truman intervened on his own initiative in the Korean civil war, ordering troops into hostilities without asking either for a declaration of war or for a congressional resolution of support; during the Cuban Missile Crisis, President John F. Kennedy deliberated in 'royal seclusion' with his three closest advisers rather than with the formally responsible Executive Committee and even authorized his brother Robert to make negotiations with the Soviet Union that were not cleared with Congress.

These and other such interventions might appear to reinforce the view that there are two quite distinct presidencies, one focused on the domestic scene and the other on foreign affairs. But in the domestic arena, too, there has been a steady aggrandizement of the office. Even President Gerald Ford, a relatively modest president in the post-Watergate mode, made use of his presidential veto on no fewer than sixty-nine occasions during his period in office; on fewer than one-fifth of those was the veto overruled. As for the legislative veto wielded by Congress, it was struck down by a Supreme Court ruling in 1983. The use of the presidential veto remains an area of contention between the legislative and the executive branches. Some political commentators argued, for example, that the deployment or reactivation of various veto powers by President George Bush Sr over quite minor issues represented an attempt to 'exert prerogative government' by stealth, even in areas bearing no relation to national security.

That presidents lead within the modern American system seems clear; *how* they lead and where the power to lead comes from is still a matter of debate. A classical analysis of the post-war office-holders by the political scientist Richard E. Neustadt argued that, notwithstanding the plenitude of formal powers vested in them, presidents obtain results not by issuing orders, but by persuading other actors in the system to support and share their objectives. 'Presidential *power*,' he wrote, 'is the power to persuade.' Others have argued that the persuasiveness of the man in the White House (i.e. his capacity to achieve outcomes in Congress and secure favourable adjudications from the judiciary) is in fact a function of other variables, such as his electoral success, strategic alignments in both houses of the legislature, the relative strength of opposition and his performance in opinion polls. Whichever view we favour, it comes down to the same thing: power and consent are endlessly intertwined – at least in the domestic exercise of presidential authority.

The presidency is doubtless a highly distinctive institution, created as part of a unique attempt to build a new kind of political order. But power exhibits the same slipperiness and ambiguity in all modern democracies. After a period of wartime concentration and growth, the powers of the British government were challenged from the 1950s to the 1980s by a judiciary increasingly willing to scrutinize and even overturn government initiatives and by a House of Commons that was growing new teeth in the form of the Select Committee System and Parliamentary Commissioners charged with the investigation of 'maladministration'. Under Margaret Thatcher and again under Tony Blair, the system passed through phases of 'presidentialization' marked by high levels of prime-ministerial activism and declining deference to Parliament. And yet at the same time the sovereign powers of the British executive were diluted 'from without' by the incorporation under Tony Blair of the European Convention on Human Rights and the EU social chapter into UK law. These changes, some would argue, diluted the powers of the executive, while bolstering those of the judiciary. Challenges to executive secrecy under the Freedom of Information Act are a further development with the potential to loosen one of the traditional struts of executive power.

In France, too, the hybrid nature of the Fifth Republic, in which elements of presidential and parliamentary government coexist, permits power to concentrate and disperse in different locations, depending on political relations between the president and the prime minister. The power of the French president, David Bell has suggested, depends not upon his formal prerogatives, but upon his skill in 'making the presidency the point of reference in French politics'; in this sense the Fifth Republic presidency is a feat of 'political levitation'. In Germany, the authority of the president of the Federal Republic has tended since 1949 to recede before the growing power of the chancellor, but this was the outcome of historical contingency (above all the unhoped-for stability of party and parliamentary life after 1949), not of constitutional planning. It is a feature of all these systems that the relationships between state executives and the other power centres in modern pluralist states – judiciaries, bureaucracies, legislatures, lobby groups, the media – are in constant flux.

Nowhere, perhaps, is the determination of power relations more contested than in the multistate environment of the European Union. 'Intergovernmentalist' accounts emphasize the control exercised by the member state over the process of integration; power, by this reading, is exercised primarily by the member states, but is dispersed between them. By contrast, 'neo-functionalist' analysts of the EU stress the role of supranational institutions, especially the European Commission and, in more recent times, the European Parliament. 'Institutionalist' and 'network' approaches emphasize the limited potential for the concentration of power in such a complex system; power, they argue, can be exercised only when large coalitions involving actors of different kinds (member states, supranational institutions, societal alliances or 'advocacy coalitions') flow together in support of specific objectives. Power relations are thus played out in the context of a 'multi-level game' involving many different kinds of state and private actor and structured around informal, network-like relationships.

The oscillation in the balance of power between competing agencies is not confined to the sphere of government; it replicates itself across all the domains of economic, social and political life in capitalist countries. A study by Sally H. Clarke of the relationship between consumers and big corporations in the automobile sector in the twentieth-century United States has shown that, while there were certainly attempts by the 'big three' automakers (Chrysler, General Motors and Ford) to manipulate consumers, and efforts by consumer groups to confront them, the evolution of the auto market was not driven by this stand-off alone, but by the intervention of a plethora of state and non-state actors – the courts, the Justice Department, insurance underwriters, state research entities, motor vehicle administrations, the Federal Reserve Board and many others. All of these possessed sufficient leverage to contribute to shaping the outcome; none had the power to shape it alone.

This fractal iteration of power relationships suggests a wider fragmentation and decentring of power in modern democratic societies, whose consequences are difficult to think through. In a lyrical, often perverse diagnosis of late capitalism published in 1980 under the title *A Thousand Plateaus: Capitalism and Schizophrenia*, the French post-Marxist critics Gilles Deleuze and Félix Guattari fixed their eyes on the United States and saw there a new kind of social order in which power did not flow from a single centre and was not anchored in a single core structure. In place of arboreal tropes that opposed centre and periphery, roots and branches, Deleuze and Guattari imagined the 'thousand plateaus' of capitalist society, a world of 'multiplicities, lines, strata and segmentarities, lines of flight and intensities'. They metaphorized the post-modern social order as a 'rhizome', a capillary network in which every point was connected to every other point, an array in which 'power centres' were 'diffuse, dispersed, geared down, miniaturized, perpetually displaced'.

This is a quite extraordinary book. I used to think it was unreadable. Then I realized that my mistake was to try to read it. Don't *read* this book in the conventional manner. Observe it through gauze. Sing or chant it. Skim its chapters in random order. If you approach it expecting the linear development of a single argument via a chain of empirically supported claims, it is bound to end in tears. This is a book whose chapter titles include: '10,000 BC: A Geology of Morals'. Page 47 contains a wonderful exhortation to the reader: 'Admire the tortoise'. A paragraph on the same page opens with the guileless announcement: 'We are a little lost now.' But if you spend some time with this book, without trying to 'read' it, you may be enriched by it.

A related train of thought can be traced – in a less exalted register – in Francis Fukuyama's Hegelian reflection on the meaning of the European revolutions of 1989. In *The End of History and the Last Man*, Fukuyama speculated that the passing of authoritarian communism might herald the definitive triumph of liberal capitalism over its various antecedents, alternatives and adversaries. By this reading, the future was a prosperous suburb in which sharp power differentials had all but vanished, and with them the revolutionary energies that had hitherto driven history on its course.

THE POWER IN US

Power shapes what we have and know of history. This is why the palace of Sans Souci in northern Haiti, completed in 1813 to serve as the residence for Haiti's first and only king, Henry I, is today a ruin, while its namesake in Potsdam, the charming summer residence Frederick II of Prussia built in the 1740s, shines as if it were built yesterday. Even after the abdication of the last Hohenzollern king, power remained close to the Prussian Sans Souci. Frederick's summer lodging was administered as a state palace under the Weimar Republic and later under the communist government of the German Democratic Republic. The foundation that currently looks after it is administered under a state charter and generously financed from public funds. But power swiftly abandoned the huge edifice of the first and only Haitian king. Its first resident, King Henry, formerly enslaved and a hero of the revolution that forced France to acknowledge Haitian independence in 1804, committed suicide on 8 October 1820 when he learned that republican forces were approaching from the south. His son Jacques-Victor, Prince Royal of Haiti, was bayoneted to death in the palace ten days later. There was no succession. The republican government that ruled thereafter from Port-au-Prince took no interest in the upkeep of this memento of Haiti's ill-fated monarchy. Disfigured in the early years by civil war and neglect, the palace was partly destroyed in the earthquake of 1842 that wiped out nearby Cap-Haïtien. Today it remains a wreck, despite its status (since 1982) as a Unesco World Heritage Site. Whether it is inscribed in stone or on paper, historical narrative, as Michel-Rolph Trouillot has observed, 'involves the uneven contribution of competing groups and individuals who have unequal access to the means for such production'.

Historians register and accommodate this asymmetry in different ways. Some are attracted to the spectacle of power and the social locations where it is exercised – cabinets, antechambers, military headquarters, ministries and boardrooms. They admire the skilful use of power, they baptize it in approving rhetoric. Others work against the gradient of power, 'from the bottom up' – this was the aspiration of much social history in the 1960s and 70s, which placed at the centre those individuals and groups who had previously figured as the anonymous objects of policies devised by the powerful. In some such narratives, it is power that is anonymized, the textured portraits of leaders make way for faceless elites and ruling classes. But some historians who focus on subaltern actors find, on the contrary, that power pools around the object of contemplation: the more they know of their protagonists, the more power – at least over their own destinies and immediate environments – these appear to wield. They find wit, strategy, determination, autonomy and resistance among peasant women, Soviet steelworkers, forest-dwellers, slaves, prostitutes. Writing in this mode may come to seem a retrospective act of empowerment, or perhaps it is just that narratives require protagonists, who in turn demand agency and with it a small share of power.

The reasons for making such narrative choices doubtless lie – leaving aside the trends that push historical writing this way and that – within the realm of what Judith Butler called the 'psychic life of power'. We are accustomed to thinking of power as something that presses in on us from outside. But what if we ourselves are actually 'initiated through a primary submission to power' – the power, for example, of our parents? If, Butler suggests, we understand power as a force in our own formation as *subjects*, 'then power is not simply what we oppose, but what we depend on for our existence and what we harbour and preserve in the beings we are'.

In *The Trial*, his dark parable on the mysteries of power, Franz Kafka reflected on the impossibility of grasping power at its source, of rendering its foundations visible. The quest of the forlorn protagonist, 'K', for authoritative clarification of the progress of the 'case' proceeding against him leads down the endless corridors of administrative buildings into broom closets, basements and a rooftop shed full of dusty tools, but never into the central chamber where destinies are decided. Indeed, it remains unclear whether such a chamber exists, and whether, if it does, there is anyone inside it. We could read this as a lucubration on the impersonal power of modern bureaucracy, but Deleuze and Guattari's essay *Kafka: Toward a Minor Literature* offered a more interesting reading. They found in this novel something more visceral and fundamental: Kafka's intuition, unsparingly explored in his *Letter to my Father*, that the power of his own overbearing father was merely the deferred expression of the father's own subordination to *his* father. The one who wielded power had first been obliged to submit to it. The 'line of flight' that stretched back from father to father to father was a long corridor plunged in deepening shadow, at the end of which there could be no definitive reckoning with power.

The Jews and the End of Time

This is the text of a keynote I presented at the Oxford Seminar in Advanced Jewish Studies for a conference called Jews, Liberalism, Anti-Semitism: The Dialectics of Inclusion (1780–1950).

Nearly thirty years ago, I arrived in Berlin, where I intended to study for a doctorate at the Free University. Things didn't quite turn out as planned. The professor I had intended to work with suddenly disappeared. The question arose as to whether my lowly Australian honours degree was an adequate preparation for the rigours of German doctoral research. (After an epic exchange of correspondence between the Examinations Office and the Dean of Humanities at the Free University on the one hand and the Permanent Conference of the Ministers of Culture in Bonn on the other, this question was answered in the negative, but by then I had received an offer from Cambridge.) None of the tenured professors on the faculty seemed interested in supervising or even meeting me. The seminars I audited were hugely oversubscribed. During dull moments, I amused myself by reading the scrawls of graffiti on the walls: 'Fire and Flames for this state', 'Destroy what destroys you', 'Police = SA/SS'. Lectures were frequently interrupted by heckling, student strikes, demonstrations and, on one occasion, by the bombing of one professor's BMW in the car park next to the Friedrich Meinecke Institute. It was a suitably apocalyptic environment in which to start the train of thought that would ultimately lead to the paper I am presenting this evening.

After a few months wandering about looking in vain for a supervisor, I was adopted by the kindest, the most left-wing and the least institutionally secure figure on the Dahlem professorial landscape at that time: Wolfgang Wippermann. Wolfgang and I agreed that I would work on the Pietist mission to the Jews that had operated from Halle in the eighteenth century.

In 1728, a theologian by the name of Johann Heinrich Callenberg founded an Institutum Judaicum, a professional missionary institute that would evangelize among the Jews until its closure in the 1790s. The Institutum was highly unusual. Its missionaries, mostly unemployed young theologians, who were plentiful at the time, were trained specifically for work among the Jews. They received superficial instruction on the Hebrew Bible and on the rabbinical exegetical traditions. They learned Yiddish at the Halle University Yiddish Seminar, the first ever to be established. They used a special missionary dictionary edited by Callenberg specifically to meet the needs of working missionaries. The dictionary was supposed to help working missionaries circumvent potentially awkward situations. Callenberg translated the key phrase 'convert to Christianity', for example, with the phrase 'to gather oneself under the wings of the *Schechina*' (i.e. the holy presence of God), hoping thereby to avoid the derogatory connotations of 'meschummad', the Yiddish Hebraism for 'apostate', whose root was the Hebrew verb 'to be destroyed'. Fortunately for me, the Institutum also produced a rich archive and a remarkable periodical bulletin of its activities, in which the diaries and letters of missionaries were juxtaposed with homilies, letters from pious supporters of the mission, edifying conversion narratives and long lists of donors and their donations.

From the beginning, the missionaries trained there were taught to see the Jews not simply as a religious but also as a social group sharing certain common features and formative experiences. In this respect, the Institutum reflected the social ethics of Pietism. The Pietists – reformers within late seventeenth- and early eighteenth-century German Lutheranism – were interested in social amelioration. When the Institutum Judaicum was founded to evangelize the Jews, it operated from the premises of the Franckesche Stiftungen, a complex of enterprises comprising an orphanage, several highly successful schools, a range of small manufactories, an extremely lively publishing house and a thriving pharmaceuticals business that exported its products as far afield as Russia and the Ottoman Empire. Pietist social ethics embraced work as a sacred calling with the power to facilitate spiritual regeneration. In the Halle orphanage, religious instruction was coupled with training in a range of crafts. Idleness was seen as an existential threat. Old-style charity was disparaged: the poor must be encouraged to help themselves through work.

The Institutum reflected this distinctive social ethics. Its director, Johann Heinrich Callenberg, took the view that the objectives of a proper *Judenmission* must extend beyond mere instruction in Christian doctrine. It must aim to secure a permanent change in the life and behaviour of converts. The Institutum thus became known for its unusually rigorous handling of applicants for baptism. It became the norm to supplement the doctrinal instruction of catechumens with advice on how to find gainful employment, so that the converting Jews 'might be liberated in this way from the misery of a life of directionless wandering'. In other words, Callenberg's converts were to be rescued not only from the error of their religion, but from a way of life which corresponded to the reality of many itinerant small traders, and which had come to be seen as intrinsically Jewish.

What drove these efforts? Why did anyone think it worth their while to take part in such work, or to support it financially, as thousands of donors appeared happy to do? It was not as if the mission among the Jews could boast of success in numerical terms. They made the most of their few converts, but the missionaries themselves acknowledged, as one nineteenth-century missionary put it, that the mission to Israel was 'a harvest of tears'. To put it into twenty-first-century UK academic terms, they scored low on 'impact'. So what was driving it all?

The answer lay in the hope that in facilitating the conversion of the Jews, the mission was expediting the furtherance of a divine plan for the future completion of Christianity's history in the world. The *locus classicus* was a passage by Philipp Jakob Spener, one of the founding fathers of German Pietism – a movement for reform within Lutheranism. It comes from a short treatise with the title *Pia Desideria Or: Heartfelt Longing for a God-Willed Improvement of the True Evangelical Church*:

> If we look at Holy Scripture [Philipp Jakob Spener wrote in 1671], we need not doubt that God has promised a better state of the Church on Earth. We have, above all, the heartfelt prophecy of St Paul and the

mystery revealed to him (Romans, XI: 25, 26), of how Israel shall become blessed after the fullness of the heathens shall be gone in, so that a great part, if not all, of the hitherto stubborn Jews shall be converted to the Lord.

These words take us straight to the heart of the subject matter of this lecture: the strangely intimate relationship between the Jews and the end of days. What struck me about this passage when I first encountered it was its convoluted logic. The promise of *Christian* improvement was folded into a mystery – even Paul acknowledged that it was a mystery – concerning the future salvation of 'a great part' of the Jews.

Spener wrote *Pia Desideria* while he was a senior Church official in Frankfurt. The book was originally published as the preface to his edition of a text by the spiritualist Johann Arndt. Its chief concern was the prophesied future of the Christian Church on earth and the scriptural foundations for the anticipation of 'better times'. Yet, although the essay did not concern itself with the Jews as such, they were repeatedly adduced as evidence for Spener's argument about the present and future of the Christian Church on earth. Spener characterized the continuing 'failure' of the Jews to convert not as a function of their stubbornness or perversity but as a consequence of the evils afflicting contemporary Christianity. From the Jewish viewpoint, he suggested, it must surely be impossible to believe that the Christians really held Christ for a true God, since they were so patently uninterested in following his commands. This naturally strengthened them in their unbelief. It was no wonder if the Jews concluded from the immorality of most Christians that Jesus must have been an evil person. What was distinctive about Spener's approach was the connection he drew in his writings between the conversion problem and the issue of Church reform. The persistence of the Jews in their Jewishness was something caused by Christian misbehaviour. A curiously circular causality was thus established: the parlous state of the Christian churches was the cause of Jewish unbelief; while, at the same time, the promised restoration of the Jews was the only guarantee that the Christian churches would ever find a way out of their current malaise.

Precisely from this causal nexus arose the missionary imperative that would later animate Halle Pietism. To Spener, it seemed that

Christendom was morally responsible for the fate of the Jews. The failure of Christians to rise to this challenge, he warned, would incur a 'great punishment' for our spiritual 'negligence'. The evangelization of Jews was thus an essential Christian task. At various points in his theological works and pastoral correspondence, Spener offered guidelines on how this could best be achieved. He argued, for example, that very specialized conversionary texts would be necessary if the Jews were to be introduced to Christian truth. He suggested that preachers who planned to approach Jews with missionary intent prepare themselves thoroughly by reading authors such as Johann Christoph Wagenseil, who was known for a primer of Jew conversion, though also for a tendentious compendium of alleged Jewish errors and blasphemies bearing the intimidating title *Tela Ignea Satanae* (*Fiery Darts of Satan*, 1681). Spener acknowledged an obligation on the part of all Christians to bear witness to their faith through their just and gentle conduct in dealing with Jews, but he stressed that specialized knowledge would be necessary for the actual work of conversion. The universities should be encouraged to offer more training in oriental languages.

Spener placed the mission to Israel close to the centre of the protestant relationship with God. The mission was urgent because God's honour was at stake. It was a matter of making amends for the history of human ingratitude in the face of God's grace and favour. In this way, Spener made the conversion of the Jews the keystone in the arch of revealed Christian truth. 'If God's word falls', he wrote, 'the whole true and correct religion falls simultaneously. If the latter falls, no-one can achieve grace.'

At least as striking as Spener's integration of prophecy with a practical programme of Church reform was his attentiveness to the sociological dimension of the conversion problematic. If it were to be successful, he argued, any Christian approach to the Jews would have to be sensitive to the social and economic predicament of the Jewish minority. It was not sufficient merely to expose Jews to the word of God. Instead, one should consider ways of eliminating the societal obstacles to a mass conversion of the Jews:

> If the Jews could be brought as a whole to a different way of life from
> that of trading and peddling which feeds them nowadays [Spener wrote

in the early 1680s], I would be in favour of such a step. For this way of life requires that the mind be preoccupied with constant worries, so that they can hardly afford the leisure of scrutinizing themselves.

Since work both influenced and reflected the spiritual disposition of an individual, it followed that the work done by Jews would play a crucial role in plotting the transition from a Jewish to a Christian social and religious identity. Even after baptism, Spener urged, converts must be directed towards 'an active Christianity and industrious work'. Truly reborn individuals would be recognizable by their radically altered social and occupational behaviour, and they would constitute a model for Christians of the transfiguring power of true faith – there again is that circular logic: a more emollient, intelligent and conciliatory Christian approach will cause authentic conversions, which in turn will bring Christians back under the sway of a true and heartfelt Christianity.

The public response to *Pia Desideria* was mixed. Hostile orthodox Lutherans objected that this was a new and arbitrary doctrine. If there were many orthodox who took this view, that may have been because Martin Luther himself had been sceptical about the eschatological claims made in and for Paul's Letter to the Romans:

> This text [Luther wrote in his *Lectures on Romans*] is the basis of the common opinion that, at the end of the world, the Jews will return to the faith. However, it is so obscure that, unless one is willing to accept the judgement of the fathers who expound the apostle in this way, no one can, so it would seem, obtain a clear conviction from this text.

Luther had a point. The Pauline text was riddled with ambiguities and confusions. Who were the 'part of Israel' that would be redeemed? And who would not be redeemed? When Paul spoke of the Jews as the olive branch that had been broken from the original tree, did he mean to emphasize the break, or the continuing integrity of the Jewish covenant with God? Did the redemption of the Jews spoken of by Paul lie in the future or the past? The early treatises on this text all struggled with these questions. Origen denigrated contemporary Jewish observance but affirmed the ultimate salvation of the Jews. John Chrysostom was more sceptical. The olive tree parable in Romans, he argued, merely underscored the rejection of Israel and the adoption of the gentiles, rather than assuring the Jews a future place in God's plan. Ambrosiaster argued that those Jews who had understood Christ and rejected him out of perversity would be damned, while those who had stayed away from Christianity out of loyal attachment to their own laws would be saved. Augustine contradicted himself on this question: he insisted on occasion that the faithless remnants of Jewry would never experience salvation, and yet spoke in other passages of the ultimate salvation of the Jewish people, ostensibly as a whole. In any case, he argued, the persistence of a Jewish presence in the Christian world remained indispensable because in future when false gods were overthrown, it would be 'proved from their books that this was prophesied long ago'.

What is striking about this tradition is its failure to arrive at a consensual reading. The link between the Jews and the eschaton was for the most uncontested, but on the question of the precise meaning of this link, we find complexity, ambivalence and irresolution. In short, what Jeremy Cohen called the 'eschatological Jew' became a tool for thinking about what was known and what was not known about the end time, a way of navigating the terrain of uncertainty around God's intentions for the world he had created.

Rather than putting this question to rest, the Protestant Reformation opened it anew. As Martin Friedrich showed in a vast survey of the seventeenth-century German literature on Jew-conversion, Lutheran orthodox theologians throughout the first half of the century were in almost unanimous agreement that a mass conversion of the Jews had indeed been prophesied in Holy Scripture, Luther's epistemological scepticism notwithstanding. Only from the 1650s did the adherence to the doctrine of a prophesied conversion come to be associated with the extremism of the radical chiliastic fringe. The orthodox consensus on the question of a still outstanding mass conversion fell victim to an increasingly vehement verbal battle between orthodox Lutherans and millenarian spiritualists.

In Britain too, seventeenth-century Puritan Bible commentaries often focused on the idea that a mass Jewish conversion was promised at the end of times. It would be followed by an avenging Hebrew army sweeping into Palestine and defeating the Ottoman Empire.

This became a common eschatological premise; the Church historian Richard Cogley has described it as the Judeo-centric strand of Puritan millenarianism. The Puritans who espoused such ideas were not extremists or freaks – they were moderates lodged firmly within the mainstream Church. As in Germany, there were some who pressed too hard for most of their contemporaries. Thomas Brightman, a Puritan of Presbyterian sympathies and a Fellow at Queen's College Cambridge, wove out of his readings of Revelation, The Song of Songs and the Book of Daniel a remarkable eschatological vision. Yes, it was true that 'the ancient Jewes' had 'killed the *Lord of Life* and embrued their hand with the blood of the apostles', but 'what blessing would ensue when they shall come into favour again with God'. Their conversion would wash away the stain of the crucifixion. And blessings would flow forth to all mankind from a restored Jerusalem. To bring home to his readers the drama of this transformation, Brightman drew on the biblical story of Rachel and Leah. God's joy in saving the Gentiles would be much greater, Brightman argued, 'when he shall take the Jewes into his especiall love and acquaintance againe, who were the first that he made love unto'. What was distinctive about this vision was that the Jews remained a separate group after their salvation, a group superior to the Gentiles. In short, the Jews remained Jews, even after their salvation. To avoid any possible misunderstanding, Brightman hastened to reassure his readers that he had not 'turned Jewe'. He was only reporting what the Bible said.

Brightman's works were widely read in England and in Germany. He was among those philo-semitic interpreters of Scripture whose arguments laid the theological ground for the resettlement of the Jews in England in 1655. Among those who took up his ideas to controversial effect was the lawyer and politician Sir Henry Finch, whose anonymously published book of 1621 was entitled *The World's Great Restauration, or, the Calling of the Jewes*:

> Such shall be the brightnes [*sic*] of the new Jerusalem, the Church of the Jewes wonne to Christ, that the nations of those that are to be saved shall walke in her light; and the kings of the earth shall bring their glory and honour in unto her ... There shall be in them a sovereignty over other Nations: whom their arme and power shall master ...

Other passages described monarchs licking the dust before Jewish kings.

This was going a tad too far for most. Finch was imprisoned and the book was bitterly attacked by the High Commission at Westminster. William Laud, who would become Archbishop of Canterbury in 1633, used one of his sermons before the king to attack Finch's book: 'So it is not now sufficient that the Jews shall be converted to the faith of Christ . . . ?', he enquired, rhetorically. 'They must also wield power over Christian kings?' There was a word of reassurance for King James, sitting in his audience: 'As for the kings of the Gentiles, that they shall serve this king of Jerusalem, you need not believe that till you see it.' The larger point is simply that the 'eschatological Jew' was still at work here, illuminating imagined futures, leading scholars and controversialists across treacherous terrain.

So far, so good – maybe. But wasn't there something a bit dangerous in this proximity between the Jews and the end of days? We have seen already that the ground around the 'eschatological Jew' was anything but firm. Paul himself spoke coyly of a 'mystery' and left the details to the speculations of his readers, who, in turn, found it difficult to achieve agreement on what exactly his prophecy meant. So there was from the start a hermeneutical shakiness in the bond between the Jews and the eschaton. More importantly, there was a potentially unstable emotional logic in this Jewish virtual future, especially in the form in which it was expounded by Philipp Jakob Spener. We saw already the circular causation invoked in his *Pia Desideria*: the Christians will help the Jews to convert so that the Jews can inspire Christians to a truer faith and convert the remaining non-believers. The emotion that lent plausibility to this circularity was *hope*, the heartfelt longing of well-disposed, true and evangelical Christians. But hope contains within itself the possibility of disappointment.

I have already spoken of the difficulty the missionaries faced in stacking up converts. Converts were important because they embodied something to which Pietists and other evangelical Christians were deeply attached: the rebirth of the purely nominal believer into true religious commitment. But the converts won by the mission were rarely of the kind the missionaries and their sponsors longed for. The Jews who approached the missionaries tended to come from among the poorest class of itinerant Jews. To be accepted for baptism brought at least the promise of accommodation and food for as long as the catechetical instruction lasted and perhaps even the hope of small baptismal presents in cash from pious sponsors. No wonder there were converts who allowed themselves to be baptized repeatedly at different locations, mimicking on each occasion for the edification of generous Christians the journey through doubt and desperation to enlightenment and rebirth. In some cases, it turned out that the converts in question were not Jews at all and never had been, but were, rather, indigent Christians masquerading as truth-seeking Jews.

Precisely because the success of the mission was so meagre, Callenberg and his missionaries continued to insist that the ultimate objective of their efforts was not the conversion of individuals at all, but the mass restoration prophesied in Scripture and in Paul's Letter to the Romans in particular. The signs that such a restoration was imminent were plentiful enough, or so they claimed. The Jewish people were supposedly in a state of fermentation and inner crisis that would soon render them ripe for the truth of the gospel. And the mission was that little piece of leavening that, once mixed with the unrisen dough of Judaism, would slowly work a great transformation in the whole. But this confidence in signs presaging wonders was vulnerable to disenchantment as the wonders kept not happening.

There was nothing new about this dialectic. The tension between hope and doubt had always beset the Christian relationship with the Jews. The Augustinian thesis, that the Jews had been kept in store by God in order to serve a salvational purpose and were thus deserving of the tolerance and protection of Christian authorities, came under pressure in the Middle Ages, when the mendicant orders mounted an assault on precisely this entitlement by arguing that the Jews of their own time had distanced themselves so far from the beliefs and way of life of their biblical predecessors that they were in effect no longer Jews at all.

We find the same dialectic in the writings of Martin Luther. In his early pamphlet *That Jesus Christ was Born a Jew*, written in 1523, Luther urged reformed Christians to adopt a friendlier and more conciliatory approach to the Jews, on the assumption that the promulgation of the true gospel and its liberation from the grip of the Catholic

Church would trigger a mass conversion. But when, after twenty years, there were still no signs of any such conversion, Luther produced bitter polemics, declaring that the Jews were no longer Jews at all, but merely idolatrous worshippers of the Talmud, and demanding the destruction of synagogues and Jewish sacred writings. In a landmark biography of Luther, the Oxford historian Lyndal Roper has suggested that the vitriol of the later anti-Jewish writings was a function of the close kinship between Luther's own ideas and Judaism. After all, he was relatively uninterested in the afterlife; his religiosity placed Scripture and the exegesis of Hebrew texts at centre stage; and his 'remarkably positive attitude to the body placed him very close to the Jewish emphasis on fertility rather than virginity'. But this kinship could easily flip into visceral loathing, Roper argues, because Luther insisted that the Christians had themselves become the chosen people and had displaced the Jews, meaning that securing Lutheranism's providential role in history would require the marginalization, discrediting and possibly even removal of the Jews.

Thomas Kaufmann's *Luther's Jews* offers a similar observation: Luther's hatred of the Jews was connected to his love for the Mosaic Bible and for the Hebrew language. He always carried a Hebrew psalter with him on his travels. His own copy of the Old Testament was an Italian edition of 1494, whose previous owner had been a Jew. He took himself extremely seriously as a Hebrew exegete. But the more he immersed himself in the Jewish Bible, the less he felt able to understand the refusal, as he saw it, of the Jews to follow him out of their own supposedly obsolete religion. Rather than nourishing a sense of attachment or respect, this ambivalent intimacy merely intensified Luther's desire to usurp and occupy the privileged position of the Jews, and with it their place in the salvational order. Luther wanted what the Jews had.

When Luther wrote in *On the Jews and Their Lies* (1543) that 'We foolish Gentiles, who were once not God's people, are now God's people', he was referring to a passage from Hosea cited in Paul's Letter to the Romans: 'Those who were not my people I will call my people and her who was not beloved I shall call beloved.' The patristic fathers had failed to agree on the meaning of this passage, as on everything else in Romans. But whereas the fourth-century scholar

Theodore of Mopsuestia viewed it as a reference to the future restoration of the Jews, Origen argued that it referred to the replacement of the Jews by the Gentiles in God's affections. Luther naturally preferred Origen's supersessionist reading to Theodore's more generous interpretation.

Even in the missionary diaries of the Institutum Judaicum we find, alongside many passages invoking the hope of a mass restoration, expressions of rage and rejection. Stefan Schulz, for example, the best known among the missionaries of the institute and certainly the most choleric figure to enter its employment, was prone to tirades against the recalcitrant Jews. On one occasion he received a visit from a young scholar from Poland travelling with letters of introduction from several Polish rabbis. Praising the young man, one of these letters observed that 'there were angels on his head'. 'It appeared,' wrote Schulz, 'that these Jewish angels were in fact lice, which one could see scurrying about on his head, for all the travelling Jews are lice-ridden.' There followed a furious diatribe against the contemporary Jews, whose scriptural traditions and way of life had nothing in common with the biblical Jewry of ancient Israel. Here again was that curious ambition to be the custodian and gatekeeper of a supposedly authentic Jewish tradition. To make matters worse, Schulz went on, the Jews of the present day were not even descendants of the ancient Jews. Their real ancestors were the offspring of mixed marriages between Jewish girls and Roman soldiers. They thus had no legitimate claim to the name of Israel.

The Institutum Judaicum did not survive the Enlightenment. In the era of Moses Mendelssohn, it became increasingly difficult both to sustain confidence in the objectives of the mission and to persuade donors to support its activities. The old Pietist networks withered away and the cash flow dried up. When the missionary Martin Litzke, the last director of the institute, travelled to Berlin in 1788 to visit the great Mendelssohn in his home – a tourist fixture for intellectuals visiting the city – he had, needless to say, no intention of instructing him, let alone trying to convert him: 'I would have to entertain a very deluded view of myself and of my own small knowledge if I were to claim that I went there with the intention of instructing him in Christian doctrine. This time my objective was not to enter into a religious dialogue with this learned Jew, but only to get to know him as a person.' A creditable acknowledgement of the status of that remarkable man, but hardly the basis for a committed missionary effort. By 1790 the money had run out and the mission was shut down. Its remaining capital was transferred to the Francke Foundations in Halle.

In the nineteenth century, in the midst of that new wave of evangelical and revivalist foundations known as the Awakening, the mission to Israel picked up again, this time in the Prussian capital, Berlin. But whereas the Halle mission had operated at some distance from government, sustaining itself through its own Pietist networks, the neo-Pietist Berlin Society for the Promotion of Christianity among the Jews, founded in 1822, enjoyed a place at the heart of the state. Its chairs and board members included generals, court chaplains and evangelical noblemen close to the crown prince, the future Frederick William IV. Once again missionaries trudged off across Brandenburg, Pomerania, Silesia, East Prussia and onwards to the Jewish communities of Central Europe with trunks full of missionary texts, including some, such as the famous 'Light at Evening', that dated back to the old Institutum.

The work of the new mission resonated with the priorities of the state itself. One of the striking features of Prussian Jewish policy after 1815 was a new emphasis on religion as the key to the question of Jewish status. King Frederick William III introduced a royal bounty for Jewish converts – as long as they entered the name of the sovereign in the church baptismal records as their nominal 'godfather'. A concerted effort was made to prevent women who were planning to marry Jewish partners from converting to Judaism, although the legal basis for such action was fragile. Christian clergymen were forbidden to attend Jewish festivities (such as weddings and bar mitzvahs) and Jews were forbidden to adopt Christian first names, so as not to blur the socio-legal boundaries between the two communities. The Prussian state had become a missionary institute.

What was the thinking behind this shift? It seems that Frederick William III gradually moved away from the functionalist conception of religion he had imbibed from the enlightened tutors of his youth towards a belief that the state might exist to pursue ends defined by religion. 'However strong the claim to tolerance may become,' he observed in 1821, 'a borderline must be drawn wherever this implies a step backwards on the road to the redemption of mankind.' By the 1840s, the term 'Christian state' was in wide use. The most articulate and influential exponent of this idea was the conservative ideologue Friedrich Julius Stahl, himself a convert from Judaism, a long-serving director of the Berlin mission. In *The Christian State* (1847), Stahl argued that to emancipate the Jews would amount to denying that the state itself had any Christian content. The Christian character of the state was 'the cardinal question of our time', Stahl wrote.

In a characteristically Hegelian formulation, Stahl concluded that 'the state is a revelation of the ethical spirit of the nation' . The Christian state would therefore seek to regulate public affairs in a way which expressed the 'spirit of a Christian people'. But there was more to it than that. Christianity, Stahl argued, was not merely the 'norm and foundation' of the Christian state, but also its 'purpose'. Ultimately, this latter claim only really made sense when it was embedded in an eschatological timescape. As a young man, Stahl had attended the conventicles and prayer meetings of neo-Pietists, and his political thought reflected the Christian activist assumptions of the awakened. He could not accept the (traditional Lutheran) view that the earthly realm and the kingdom of God were two distinct and separate spheres. If the idea of God were not an absurdity, then the world must strive to attain its ideal condition. In this scenario, the state could and should play a redemptive role.

The oscillation between missionary enthusiasm and disenchantment persisted. With the accomplishment of Jewish emancipation – at least in a formal and legal sense – in the 1860s, the missions – there were now several missionary hubs operating in the German states – struggled to justify themselves. The Jews encountered by the eighteenth-century missionaries had been poor itinerants gathered before the walls of towns that they were not permitted or could not afford to enter. The missionaries never failed to point up the poverty and vulnerability of their interlocutors as the outward signs of a people rejected by God. But these conditions no longer prevailed in the last decades of the nineteenth century. Missionaries struggled to gain entrance to synagogues, and arguing with completely secularized or religiously sceptical hyper-assimilated Jews raised problems they were ill-equipped to handle. Far from heralding the collapse of Judaism, the emergence of Jewish Reform appeared to have revitalized Jewish confessional commitments and partially stemmed the flow of converts to Christianity that had so preoccupied the rabbis of the late eighteenth and early nineteenth centuries. Evangelical Christians responded to these changes with tirades against the sterility of the new 'hollowed-out Judaism', to borrow a phrase used by the newspaper *Evangelische Kirchenzeitung*. Hollowed-out Judaism, an anonymous writer in that journal argued, was the negation of all that was lively, authentic and fresh. Left to their own devices, these empty Jews would, like rats or caterpillars, consume everything in the world that was still green and fruitful.

The appeal of eschatological promise remained overpowering. But its logic was harder and harder to square with a world that appeared to be secularizing at breakneck speed. The confusion and anger of the missionaries is captured in Johannes de le Roi's three-volume history of the Protestant mission to Israel. De le Roi, though he called himself a 'friend of Israel' and eschewed antisemitism because of its elevation of race over the grace of Christ, was prone to extraordinary outbursts of vitriol against the Jews. 'In their rushing haste,' he wrote, 'the Jews will stampede us into a thousand things; they will goad us from sentence to sentence; from catch-cry to catch-cry, from one dissolution of the bonds connecting the nation with Christ to the next . . .'

The rapid acceleration of all domains of life had long been identified as a signal of the impending eschaton. What was new was, first, the idea that the Jews were driving this process and, second, the withering of confidence in the promise that it would culminate in a redemptive form of closure. De le Roi himself made the link to eschatology explicit. Ignoring Paul's promise in Romans (if that's what it was), he referred to the Revelation of John: 'The New Testament,' he wrote, 'speaks of a final alliance that the all-destroying Lord of the World will form with the sovereign spirit of lies and seduction. Let us ask ourselves what that means and let us do so with eyes that enquire after the true objectives of the powers contending in our present.'

Here was an ominous inversion of Spener's eschatological reasoning. To be sure, for de le Roi the Jews were still responsible for the end of days. But in refusing to acquiesce in their self-dissolution through baptism, and in allying themselves with secular culture in a world that no longer seemed to be advancing towards redemption, they threatened to unpick the logic of salvational history. They would bring about the end of days, but only in a secular sense. Against this background it is easy to see how Spener's prophetic Pauline formula: '*Das Heil kommt von den Juden*' – the Jews are our salvation – could be turned on its head and rebooted as Treitschke's slogan, much cited by the Nazis: '*die Juden sind unser Unglück*' – the Jews are our misfortune. And indeed, antisemitic discourses more generally were marked by a cosmic field of vision and a mood of apocalyptic expectation that bore the imprint of eschatology. Antisemites warned that the consequence of leaving the Jews unchecked would be the total destruction and erasure of the Christian-German way of life. Everything – literally – was at stake in the struggle against the Jews, whose ultimate victory would extinguish the future.

It is thus no accident that in January 1939 when Hitler announced to the German Reichstag his intention to use an American entry into the war as a pretext for the annihilation of European Jewry he called himself a 'prophet':

> I have often been a prophet in my life and was generally laughed at. During my struggle for power, the Jews primarily received with laughter my prophecies that I would someday assume the leadership of the state and thereby of the entire *Volk* and then among many other things achieve a solution of the Jewish Question. [...] Today I will be a prophet again ...

Articulating his threat through prophecy framed the future as something ordained and inherited. And that was characteristic of a man who did not work in an incremental manner, weighing up options and probabilities, but oriented himself towards end-states, vanishing points at which all the demands of the present could be presumed to have resolved themselves. Whereas prediction represents the projection into the future of a non-cyclical, historical time in which numerous possible risks and gains have to be weighed up, prophecy, as Reinhart Koselleck observed, draws no fundamental distinction between past, present and future; it anticipates an end that is already given; it is posited upon the projection of millennial time into a foreordained future.

This observation might appear to lend weight to Richard Steigmann-Gall's claim, in a powerful book pointedly entitled *The Holy Reich*, that Nazism was in its essence still a Christian, or Protestant movement. But Hitler's eschaton was not a Christian one. It did not imagine the intervention of a divine being at the end of time. It was a decontextualized, secularized fragment of Christian temporality that could resurface in the language of Hitler precisely because it was no longer recognizably confessional in content. Secularization in this setting did not mean the wholesale removal of religious-derived content, but rather the reorienting of transcendent eschatology to this world. And at the heart of this reorientation was a logic of supersession, the replacement of one eschaton by another. Why else, Alon Confino has asked, were the sacred texts of the Jews – and the Hebrew Bible in particular – burned and defiled in so many German towns during the assault on the synagogues on 9 November 1938, just as they had been in the Middle Ages? 'There is nothing,' Confino has written, 'in racial ideology itself that can explain the symbolic meaning of destroying the Bible.'

Since long before the formation of the Hitler government in 1933, there had been efforts from across the theological spectrum to sever the New Testament from its anchorage in the Hebrew Bible. The 'neo-Marcionites' of the 1920s – named for the second-century Christian preacher Marcion of Sinope, who denied that the God of mercy revealed in the Christian gospels had anything to do with the vengeful God of the Old Testament – argued that, to borrow the formulation of Adolf von Harnack, to preserve the Old Testament as a canonical document in Protestantism was to acquiesce in a 'religious and ecclesiastical crippling'. And these efforts to shed the Jewish ballast of the Christian Bible intensified after the destruction of the synagogues in November 1938. In May 1939, an Institute for the Study and Eradication of Jewish Influence on German Church Life opened in – of all places – Wartburg castle, where Martin Luther had translated the New Testament into German. As Susannah Heschel has shown, the institute became a focal point for the German Christian movement in Protestant theology.

'The memory of the Jews as the possessor of origins,' Alon Confino has written, 'was a basis for the fantasy that made [their] persecution and extermination . . . possible.' This is a valuable insight, but it needs further refinement. Because the place of the Jews in Protestant eschatology situated the Jews not just at the beginning of redemption's story, but also, as we have seen, at the end. Expunging the Jews from their place in this narrative thus implied not only their erasure from the past, but also, and more importantly, from the future. Two different chains of thought converged here. One was the secularized form of the old eschatology, in which it was promised that the Jews would expedite the completion of Christian history, but whose hermeneutical instability created space for the inversion of millennial hope. The other was its radically supersessionist elaboration, in which the logic of the eschaton, of a future accessible only through prophecy, remained, but the Jewish place in it did not. The old eschatology was still latent in the future visions of the nineteenth-century antisemites, in which Jews busied themselves accelerating processes of decay and severing the links between Christ and the nation, reversing the priority of the New Covenant over the Old. The new eschatology manifested itself in the Nazi vision of a future entirely purged of Jews, in which the redemptive agency of the Jews had been replaced by that of the German *Volk*, whose status as the new Chosen People, as Hartmut Lehmann has shown, had long been a central theme of the Protestant German national movement.

In a future emptied of Jews, the entire history and culture of the Jewish people would belong to a remote past. Nowhere was this idea more clearly articulated than in the efforts of the SS in Prague to establish a Jewish Central Museum, staffed by indentured Jewish experts pulled from the ghettos and brim-full of looted devotional and cultural objects, that would in future recall the vanished religious, social and cultural life of still-to-be-exterminated Jewry in Central Europe. This was perhaps the single most perverse institutional articulation of the Nazi regime's eschatological timescape.

Whether the magnetic field of eschatology is still latent in contemporary antisemitism is something we might reflect on. What always distinguished eschatological modes of argument was their global scope, their orientation towards binary schemata focused on the tension between redemption and perdition and their hermeneutical instability – manifested both in the difficulty of building consensus on

47

the specifics of eschatological scenarios and on a persistent uncertainty about the signs that will herald the approach of the end-times. The specifically Pauline tradition always oscillated in an unsettling way between fantasies of Jewish abandonment and dereliction on the one hand and of Jewish ultra-empowerment and domination on the other. There certainly are still live forms of Christian eschatology, particularly in the United States – as the televised sermons of Christian Zionists and philosemitic Christian fundamentalists testify. But more important and potentially more virulent are the submerged chunks of eschatological narrative, no longer recognizable as religious, that still animate those secular antisemitic discourses in which the Jewish question remains an issue of cosmic significance.

Why Does a Battle Matter?

This keynote talk was written in 2016 for an audience of medievalists who had gathered at Battle Abbey to discuss the historical significance of the Battle of Hastings, an encounter that took place in 1066 between the Norman-French army of William, Duke of Normandy, and an English army under the Anglo-Saxon King Harold Godwinson. William's victory laid the foundations for the Norman conquest of England.

When I sat down recently in the hope of having some thoughts about what I would say this morning, there was a moment of sheer panic as I suddenly remembered that I am no longer a medievalist. I say no longer, because I started adult life as a passionate enthusiast for medieval history. At Sydney University I studied with Professor John Pryor, an expert on medieval warfare, among other things, and an inspirational teacher and mentor. My dream as an undergraduate historian was to become, through sheer intellectual will, the latest luminary of the Annales School (not an ambition of which John Pryor approved). I imagined myself scribbling notes in a corner of the Café Saint-Germain, a kind of cross between Georges Duby and Serge Gainsbourg, drawing thoughtfully on a *Gauloise blonde* as I reshaped the discipline with densely worked manuscripts.

It was not to be. Instead of travelling to Paris, I went to West Berlin, where the pull of modern history became irresistible. There was no German Georges Duby and certainly no German Serge Gainsbourg, and though there were many wonderful cafés, none approached the antique splendour of the Café Saint-Germain.

Forgive these solipsistic ramblings. They do have a purpose: they are intended to shrink your expectations. You are all here as experts to discuss a particular battle, in Battle Abbey, in a market town which, because of that battle, is called Battle. So I'm guessing that it would not be a good idea for me to share with you my wikiknowledge of the Battle of Hastings. What I propose to do instead is to offer some thoughts about the different things people mean and have meant when they say that a battle – any battle – matters, when they claim that it is historically significant. And I want to align some thoughts like beads along a figurative string suspended between two battles located far apart in historical time: the Battle of Issus of 333 BCE and the Battle of Jena of 1806 CE.

Let me begin with a magnificent painting by Albrecht Altdorfer, *Die Alexanderschlacht*, known in English as *The Battle of Issus* (Fig. 2). Its subject is the victory of the young Alexander the Great in 331 BC over the Persian army of King Darius III. Issus was an ancient town in southeast Asia Minor near modern-day Iskenderun, Turkey.

Without the text on the tablet suspended in the sky and the inscriptions on the banners, we could not possibly identify the subject. The suspended plaque reads in Latin:

> Alexander the Great defeating the last Darius, after 100,000 infantry-men and more than 10,000 cavalrymen had been killed among the ranks of the Persians. While King Darius was able to flee with no more than 1,000 horsemen, his mother, wife, and children were taken prisoner.

In almost every respect, this image appears to us strikingly anachronistic. The battle in fact took place in what is today Turkey, yet on this painting it is shown in the rocky environment of the Alps with Germanic-looking cities in the background. The soldiers' armour and the fortified town in the distance are unmistakably of the sixteenth century. And what were those ladies decked out in the dress of an early sixteenth-century German court doing on an ancient battlefield in Asia Minor? Altdorfer shows no interest whatsoever in highlighting the historicity of the Battle of Issus. He could have included the date of the battle among the data recorded on the heavenly plaque, but he did not.

We know that he did take pains to research the battle by reading

Figure 2. Painted layers of history: *The Battle of Alexander at Issus* by
Albrecht Altdorfer (1529) (*Alte Pinothek, Munich*)

the classical ancient accounts of it (the inscription on the plaque hints at that), but he did little to incorporate what he found out into what we can see. That the Persian army was up to twice the size of the Macedonian army is not clear, for example, and the relative positioning of the soldiers as reported by ancient sources has been disregarded. You can see this more clearly if you compare the events unfolding in Altdorfer's panorama with a battle-plan reconstructed by twentieth-century military historians (Fig. 3). The battle-plan reconstructed by the military historians is less beautiful than Altdorfer's fanciful maelstrom, but almost certainly more accurate.

The artist's interest in what we would call 'historical truth' was thus sporadic, subject to the aesthetic demands of his composition. Indeed, the whole picture is less suggestive – to us, at least – of ancient warfare than of contemporary depictions of the unsuccessful Turkish siege of Vienna, which took place in 1529, the very year this picture

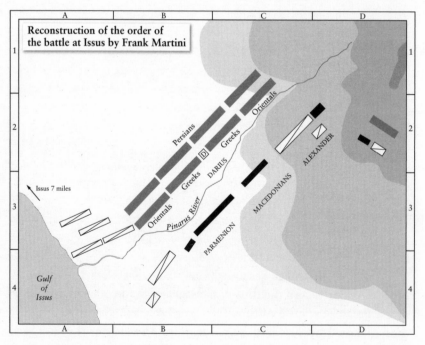

Figure 3. Reconstruction of the order of battle at Issus by Frank Martini (*United States Military Academy Department of History*)

was painted. A contemporary engraving from 1529 by Bartholomäus Beham (Fig. 4) depicts the siege in a way that strongly resembles Altdorfer's handling of his materials. Common features include the elevated vantage point and the chaotic swirling of opposed forces in an ant-like swarm across a busy landscape.

The siege of 1529 was the first attempt by the Ottoman Empire, led by Suleiman the Magnificent, to capture the city of Vienna. When it took place, the Ottoman Empire was at the zenith of its power. The entrenchments around Vienna represented the maximum extent of Ottoman expansion in Central Europe. Military tension and periodic wars would continue for a further century and a half, culminating in the Battle of Vienna of 1683, which marked the start of what proved to be a concerted effort by the European powers to remove, or at least push back, the Ottoman presence.

So what we are seeing in Altdorfer's painting is the overlayering of two events separated from each other in time. How was it possible for Altdorfer to do this? Why was historicity so conspicuously absent from his painting of the Battle of Issus? This was the question that preoccupied the German historian Reinhart Koselleck when he studied this painting in Munich in the 1960s. To sharpen the question, he brought in as a kind of witness the German poet, critic and scholar Friedrich Schlegel. Schlegel, it so happens, viewed the *Alexander-schlacht* in the 1820s and wrote an enthusiastic essay on it, in which he praised it as 'the greatest feat of the age of chivalry' – he was referring to the painting, not the events depicted in it. Koselleck zeroed in on this observation – Schlegel, it seemed, felt that there was an expanse of time between himself and the painting. More than that, he intuited that the painting belonged to a different age – *Zeitalter* – from his own. So it wasn't just a question of the length of time elapsed, as subjectively experienced, but of a break in the fabric of time, a tectonic fault between this time and a previous one.

Something, Koselleck reasoned, must have intervened between the time of Altdorfer and the time of Schlegel, with the paradoxical result that a greater expanse of time seemed to separate Schlegel from Altdorfer than appeared to separate Altdorfer from the deeds of Alexander. Only this could explain why Altdorfer felt so comfortable with what appears to us to be the superimposition of one historical

Figure 4. *The Ottoman Encampment before Vienna* by Bartholomäus
Beham (1529) (*The Picture Art Collection/Alamy*)

epoch over another. Altdorfer's fourth-century BC Persians looked like sixteenth-century Turks, not because he did not know the difference, but because the difference did not matter to him. The *Alexanderschlacht*, in other words, exemplified a premodern, *untemporalized* sense of time and with it the lack of what we would call 'historical consciousness'.

In other words, for Altdorfer, all of the known past was enclosed within a single time-plane, a single temporal envelope. And why was this? Because, for the Christian contemporaries of Altdorfer's painting, the Battle of Issus mattered so much because it signified the transition from one world empire, that of the Persians, to another, that of the Greeks. It was thus an illustration of the unfolding of the divine prophecy outlined in the opening passages of the Book of Daniel, in which the future of the world was foretold as a sequence of four hegemonies, the Babylonian, the Persian, the Greek and the Roman. Now it may seem to us that the age of the Romans had long passed when Altdorfer painted the *Alexanderschlacht*, but to the artist's contemporaries this was not so obvious. It was widely believed that the Holy Roman Empire – still going strong in sixteenth-century Europe – was the continuation of the old Roman Empire; according to this view, the world was still in the age of the fourth monarchy. But how long would the Holy Roman Empire last? The Reformation was in full swing, sowing division among its member states; the Turks were at the gates of Vienna. Perhaps the end of the fourth monarchy – and thus of the world – was at hand. Viewed from this perspective, the Battle of Issus became a moment of anticipation, an analogy: a similar battle would presage the fall of the Holy Roman Empire. So powerful was this analogy that it could bend time, pleating it in the way we see in that picture, where sixteenth-century Turks battle an ancient Greek hero.

We might discern in this pleating of time the manifestation of something fundamental about the temporality of Christian prophecy – namely its recursive and cyclical character. If you look, for example, at how Christian theologians in this era conceptualized the relationship between the 'old' and the 'new' testaments, you find that analogy, not history, is the dominant interpretative device. The almost-sacrifice of Isaac by his father, Abraham, anticipates the sacrifice of Christ; the tree from which Eve picked the apple that spelled doom for Adam and

Eve becomes the gallows-tree of Golgotha – everything anticipates and stands for something else, the future is ultimately just a return to the past. In this sense, time is enclosed at one end, turned in on itself. And this finiteness of time was something Altdorfer and his contemporaries – both Protestant and Catholic – took very seriously indeed. Martin Luther (like Altdorfer himself) saw the turmoil unleashed by religious reform, the peasant wars of 1525 and the arrival of the Turks at the gates of Europe as signs of an ominous acceleration that betokened the imminence of the Final Judgement. God was about to bring to an end the story that he himself had foretold.

Of course, since the sixteenth century, much has happened to loosen the hold of prophetic time on the European imagination. For one thing, the end of days kept on not happening. And Europeans responded to this by postponing it; there was a tendency for each postponement to defer the end by an ever greater time. Melanchthon, for example, turned away from his belief in an imminent end and began to speculate that the final epoch would begin to wane from around the year 2000 – a view whose plausibility is holding up quite well right now. The sixteenth-century French jurist and political theorist Jean Bodin speculated that the world would last for a further 50,000 years or more. For Bodin, it followed that human history belonged to the domain not of prophecy but of probability – it had no foreordained end, or none, at least, the knowledge of which would help us to make sense of its course.

A second and more important innovation was the collapse of the idea that the age of the Romans was still unfolding. The German political theorist and sometime historian Samuel Pufendorf mounted a devastating critique of the idea of the *translatio imperii* (the notion that the Holy Roman Empire of the German Nation was a continuation of the original not-so-holy Roman Empire); in its place he put the idea of the competition of states and empires in endless variations, positing that the interests of states were in constant flux, that they were unbound by 'traditions' in their relations with each other and that the outcome of the conflicts between them was inherently unpredictable. By this means he, along with other contemporary scholars, wrested the history of Europe free of biblical prophecy.

In the process, the Battle of Issus, along with many other battles,

sank back into a remote history. Issus forfeited its anticipatory resonance to become an event among events. The battle mattered not
because it bore witness to the potency of prophecy, but because history, understood now as a sequence of contingent events, would have
been different if the battle had come to a different conclusion, or had
not happened at all. This disenchanted understanding of battles and
their place in history bears the mark of a secular modernity that imagines history – to borrow Peter Fritzsche's phrase – as 'a continual
iteration of the new', the continuous generation of new states of affairs.

And this restructuring of time has a further implication that has
often been remarked upon. Once we began to see history as the record
of an unceasing, tumultuous change with no boundaries and no foreordained destination, the appeal of arguments from the authority of
past example began to wane. The Ciceronian trope *historia magistra
vitae* – history is the schoolmistress of life – began to exhaust its plausibility. The past slipped away, leaving us 'stranded in the present'
(Fritzsche's phrase). The threshold between the present and the past
came to seem an ontological abyss. Hegel articulated the resulting
sense of disconnection when he commented that history teaches us
only one thing, namely that we can learn nothing from history.

Since you have been thinking about a battle at this conference, it is
worth dwelling for a moment on an important exception to this rule:
there are some who see in the battles of the past lessons for present
and future, namely the soldiers who teach and study in military acad-
emies. The historical analysis of battles is a central strand of the
education provided at most American military institutions. The Battle
of Cannae, for example, a major confrontation of the Second Punic
War, fought in the summer of 216 BC in Apulia, is routinely mined for
exemplars of the classical topoi of warfare: encirclement, surprise,
concentration. In this respect, the soldiers proceed like the scholars of
the Middle Ages and the Renaissance, in that they discern in battles
archetypal situations whose relevance to present and future remains
undiminished. At the same time, however, they do recognize in the
history of battles processes of change and progress over time.

When I was preparing my thoughts for this essay I spent some time
online reading a bunch of Pentagon Working Papers, just to see how
they handle the historical dimension of warfare. It was a fascinating

and slightly disorienting experience. In one study, for example, the author uses a sketchy outline of the events of three large battles – the Napoleonic Battle of Ulm in 1805, the German attack on France in 1940 and Operation Desert Storm, also known as the First Iraq War, in 1991, to develop a kind of historical master narrative. Through the study of these way stations, the author argues, we can observe the successive phases of a single process: a dramatic acceleration of battle and a transformative integration of its operative, tactical and strategic elements. Napoleon, he suggests, asserted at the Battle of Ulm a control of the battlespace that was remarkably deep by the standard of his time, but did not achieve the coordination in real time of all domains of battlefield activity. The Germans did better on both fronts in 1940, but only in Desert Storm was true integration realized, thanks to the deployment of 'deep strike delivery systems' that permitted 'a global, three-dimensional annihilatory blow against the enemy, in which all zones of the battlespace were surveyed and attacked simultaneously and with equal intensity'. What is interesting about such studies, apart from the unconcealed joyfulness with which they celebrate the successful projection of annihilatory force and the guileless enthusiasm with which the present is embraced as the telos of all human striving, is the sense that battles themselves belong to a long history – a history *composed* of battles – that in turn is animated by long-term processes of change and perhaps even of progress.

But for those of us who are not military historians in the old sense, battles really only make sense as an object of study when they are embedded in something larger called 'history'. One of the signature features of modernity, and this is another of Koselleck's theses, was an expansion in the meaning of the word 'history', which mutated from a term referring to specific stories or a literary genre (Thucydides, Geoffrey of Monmouth, etc.) into a non-count noun denoting an all-encompassing process of change coextensive with the flow of time itself. In the nineteenth century, Ernst Troeltsch observed, the verb 'to become' became the active ingredient of nineteenth-century German historical consciousness:

> ... the continuous becoming of historical things [...] cannot be imagined purely causally as an array of discrete individual actions; rather

the individual actions are melted together by a unity-of-becoming that flows through them, dissolves them into each other and thereby makes them continuous, [a unity-of-becoming] that is very difficult to describe in logical terms, but the seeing and the sensing of which is the essence of historical awareness.

The capacity to see specific actions and events not as singularities, but as dissolved in the flow of becoming, Troeltsch argued, was the signal faculty, the 'recognizing organ' of history.

Once battles were embedded in this larger terrain of flux and flow, new criteria emerged by which to measure their importance. In a classic treatise on *The Fifteen Decisive Battles of the World*, published in 1851, Edward Shepherd Creasy conceded that in an age of high European civilization in which warfare was increasingly abhorred as barbaric, the study of battles 'merely because they were battles, merely because so many myriads of troops were arrayed in them, and so many hundreds or thousands of human beings stabbed, hewed, or shot each other to death during them, would argue strange weakness or depravity of mind'. Why, then, should we attend to them? The sheer scale of carnage was hardly an argument, because there were battles whose importance was out of all proportion to the numbers of fallen – Creasy cited the example of Joan of Arc's raising the siege of Orleans, which involved few casualties but supposedly changed the course of history. And, conversely, there were other battles (mainly non-European ones) whose immense human cost did not suffice to establish their historical importance. Even if he truly believed, Creasy wrote, 'in the largest number which Eastern historians state to have been slaughtered in any of the numerous conflicts between Asiatic rulers, [this would not] make me regard the engagement in which they fell as one of paramount importance to mankind'. Why this indifference to the mass extermination of Asiatics? Because, if battles had a claim on our attention, then this could only be 'by reason of [their] practical influence on our own social and political condition'.

It thus made sense that the Battle of Hastings should be included among the fifteen almost entirely European battles that had shaped the course of history. In his account of this battle Creasy pooh-poohed those 'writers of the previous century', for whom the victory of the

Normans at Hastings achieved 'little more than the substitution of one royal family for another on the throne of this country, and to the garbling and changing of some of our laws through the "cunning of the Norman lawyers"'. On the contrary, Creasy insisted, the battle had transformed the fortunes of England. After all, 'England owes her liberties to her having been conquered by the Normans'; Saxon institutions were no more than the 'primitive cradle' of English liberties; 'it was the Conquest that infused into them a new virtue'. In the millennial marriage that followed, the Saxons softened the harshness of their Norman lords, while the Normans 'fired the duller Saxon mass with a new spirit of animation and power', 'high-mettling the blood of British veins'.

Creasey's authorities for these claims, interestingly enough, were two *French* historians, the eighteenth-century private scholar Paul de Rapin, author of a fourteen-volume *Histoire d'Angleterre*, and the nineteenth-century Saint-Simonian Augustin Thierry, author of *Histoire de la Conquête de l'Angleterre par les Normands*. Though it must be added that Creasy's is a very odd reading of Thierry, who was in fact an enthusiast for the theory of 'Anglo-Saxon liberty' and viewed Robin Hood, for example, as the heroic personification of the Anglo-Saxon resistance.

Creasy's handy multi-battle format was widely imitated. Malleson's *Decisive Battles of India* (1883), Whitton's *Decisive Battles of Modern Times* (1923), Liddell Hart's *Decisive Wars of History* (1929) and J. F. C. Fuller's *Decisive Battles of the Western World and Their Influence upon History* (1954–6), Paul K. Davis's *100 Decisive Battles: From Ancient Times to the Present* (1999) and Jonathon Riley's *Decisive Battles: From Yorktown to Operation Desert Storm* (2010) are just a few of the better-known titles – this is hardly an exhaustive list. Not all of these works are marked by the upbeat, gung-ho whiggery of Creasy. Jonathon Riley, himself a serving general, condemned Creasy's tendency to frame battles as encounters between virtue and vice and observed that the Victorian author's focus on what 'helped to make us what we are' inevitably viewed the military encounters of the past through the lens of a posterity that was unknown to, and unintended by, the actors taking part in them.

Paul K. Davis cites three criteria for supposing that a battle might be 'decisive'. The first is that 'the outcome of the battle brought about a major political or social change'. This is the rubric under which Hastings qualifies: for 'the Norman invasion of England completely altered', he notes, 'the future of the British Isles, determining the heritage of its people and the nature of its political and social systems. The resulting society then went on to have major impacts on events in Europe and, ultimately, the world' (here, it must be said, we seem almost to be in the world of Creasy). Davis's second condition is a counterfactual inversion of the first: 'had the outcome of the battle been reversed, major political and social changes would have ensued'. And the third criterion relates to the place of the specific battle in the history of battles: namely, 'the introduction of a major change in warfare'. He cites the example of the Battle of Adrianople of 378 CE, because the victory of the Goths there broke the dominance of infantry in warfare, and of the Roman infantry in particular, introducing the cavalry as 'the dominant weapon for the succeeding thousand years'. It doesn't seem a case can be made for Hastings on these latter grounds, though I leave it to the experts to adjudicate that question.

In any case the very category 'decisiveness' – once you strip away the whiggery – implies that the situations through which the course of history is plotted are open-ended, that the resolution is not foreordained. Everything depends upon the issue of the encounter, which is uncertain at the outset. This must be the case, for if it were not, the prospective loser would presumably shrink from the fight and leave it to another day. Sophisticated studies in the New Military History tradition usually stress how finely the outcome was balanced as the conflict opened. In his magisterial analysis of the Austro-Prussian War of 1866, Geoffrey Wawro conceded that the Prussian infantry were equipped with the superior Dreyer needle gun, a breech-loading rifle. But he also noted the superiority of the Austrian artillery, which at that time was probably the best in Europe. Sir Michael Howard's wonderful history of the Franco-Prussian War of 1870 stressed the importance of blunders and omissions, but for which things might have taken a different course. And yet there is an interpretative tension in such highly textured sociocultural analyses of modern battles, because the fuller the account they offer us of the social and cultural forces at work in the armies involved in any specific conflict, the more determined the outcome must seem to become.

To put it a different way: if we think of a battle simply as a roll of the dice in which everything depends on the proverbial luck of the day, then we have little incentive to think hard about the social, political and cultural path dependencies that constrained some actions and encouraged or facilitated others. If, on the other hand, we think of the battle merely as one point in a process of societal standardization, administration, deliberation and force concentration that is not random but deeply determined by the character of a specific culture or society, then we will tend to see less randomness in the outcome. The moment of battle will appear less like a force shaping history and more like an optical device that can tell us something about what those forces are.

A diagnostic approach to the study of battles has been a feature of modern war-waging cultures, though it must be said that it is defeats that tend to receive this treatment, rather than victories. Failure is a far better teacher than success. A case in point is the Battle of Jena fought on 14 October 1806 on the plateau west of the River Saale between the forces of Napoleon I of France and Frederick William III of Prussia. Jena seemed decisive at the time, because, along with another defeat at nearby Auerstädt, it led to the truncation of Prussia, which retained only its four core provinces, the imposition of a French occupation and a massive indemnity and political subjugation to Napoleon's France. But in the longer term, these consequences were relativized. Victory in the War of the Sixth Coalition (1813–14) brought Prussia back into possession of most of its lost lands, cancelled out the indemnity by means of a counter-indemnity imposed on defeated France and restored Prussia's position as a European power.

But Jena was also significant for another reason: the shattering defeat of one of Europe's proudest armies, an army whose pride in itself rested on the extraordinary reputation of Frederick the Great in the previous century, prompted a profound process of self-examination and reform. And this was possible because the army and its failure were viewed diagnostically, as a window onto everything that had gone wrong in Prussia's political culture since the death of the legendary Frederick, not just in the sphere of military organization, but in the management of all resources, human, financial, moral and agrarian.

Just to give a sense of the shock effect of the battle itself, let me draw on passages from the memoirs of one young Prussian who fought in it. On the morning of the battle, twenty-six-year-old Lieutenant Johann von Borcke was posted with an army corps of 22,000 men under the command of General Ernst Wilhelm Friedrich von Rüchel to the west of the city of Jena. The approach to the battlefield took the corps through the little village of Kapellendorf, where they encountered streets clogged with cannon, carriages, wounded men and dead horses. Emerging from the village, the corps came up onto a line of low hills, where the men had their first sight of the field of battle. To their horror, only 'weak lines and remnants' of the principal Prussian corps could still be seen resisting French attack. Moving forward to prepare for an attack, Borcke's men found themselves in a hail of balls fired by French riflemen who were so well positioned and so skilfully concealed that the shot seemed to fly in from nowhere. 'To be shot at in this way,' Borcke later recalled, 'without seeing the enemy, made a dreadful impression upon our soldiers, for they were not used to that style of fighting, lost faith in their weapons and immediately sensed the enemy's superiority.'

Flustered by the ferocity of the fire, commanders and troops alike became anxious to press ahead to a resolution. An attack was launched against French units drawn up near the village of Vierzehnheiligen. But as the Prussians advanced, the enemy artillery and rifle fire became steadily more intense. Against this, the corps had only a few regimental cannon, which soon broke down and had to be abandoned. The order 'Left shoulder forward!' was shouted down the line and the advancing Prussian columns veered to the right, twisting the angle of attack. They were deploying the oblique marching order which had been the terror of Prussia's enemies in the era of Frederick. There had been a time when merely to see this manoeuvre executed with precision by thousands of Prussian troops had been enough to break the will of the opponent. But on this occasion, it appeared to have no effect on the enemy, who continued to subject the Prussian lines to intense fire. The Prussian battalions began to drift apart and the French, bringing up more and more cannon to the front (another unorthodox move), cut ever larger holes in the advancing columns. Borcke and his fellow officers galloped back and forth, trying in vain to repair the broken lines.

Without awaiting orders, the men of Borcke's corps began to fire at will in the direction of the French. Some, having expended their ammunition, ran with fixed bayonets at the enemy positions, only to be cut down by cartridge shot or 'friendly fire'. Terror and chaos took hold, reinforced by the arrival of the French cavalry, who hoed into the surging mass of Prussians, slashing with their sabres at every head or arm that came within reach. Borcke found himself drawn along irresistibly with the masses fleeing the field westwards along the road to Weimar. 'I had saved nothing,' Borcke wrote, 'but my worthless life. My mental anguish was extreme; physically I was in a state of complete exhaustion and I was being dragged along among thousands in the most horrific chaos . . .'

The battle of Jena was over. The Prussians had been defeated by a better-managed force of about the same size (there were 53,000 Prussians and 54,000 French deployed). Even worse was the news from Auerstädt a few miles to the north, where on the same day a Prussian army numbering some 50,000 men under the command of the Duke of Brunswick was routed by a French force half that size under Marshal Davout. Over the following fortnight, the French broke up a smaller Prussian force near Halle and occupied the cities of Halberstadt and Berlin. Further victories and capitulations followed. The Prussian army had not merely been defeated; it had been ruined. In the words of one officer who was at Jena: 'The carefully assembled and apparently unshakable military structure was suddenly shattered to its foundations.'

All regimes are tarnished by defeat – this is one of history's few rules. There have been many worse defeats than the Prussian disasters of 1806–7, but for a political culture so centred on military prowess the defeats at Jena and Auerstädt and the surrenders that followed were definitive nonetheless. They signified a failure at the centre of the system. The king himself was a commanding officer (though not an especially talented one) who had been in regimental service since childhood and made it his business to be seen riding about in uniform before his advancing regiments. The adult princes of the royal family were all well-known commanders. The officer corps was the agrarian ruling class in uniform. The defeat at Jena inscribed a question mark over the political order of old Prussia.

Gathering a new generation of reforming officials around him, the Prussian king focused on extracting lessons from Jena and its aftermath. Together, they launched a salvo of government edicts that transformed the structure of the Prussian political executive, deregulated the economy, redrew the ground rules of rural society and reformulated the relationship between the state and civil society. Defeat could engender societal reform because the disaster at Jena was read diagnostically, as the expression of deeply entrenched systemic dysfunctions.

The case for military reform was especially obvious. It was clear that an army that had so manifestly failed must be overhauled, and it made sense to adopt some of the measures that seemed to account for the success of Napoleon's forces – the use of open-order deployments, the enhanced and more flexible deployment of riflemen, more versatility in the use of artillery, and so on. But the overhaul went deeper than that: the reformers recognized that men who went to battle out of fear of their officers, rather than out of zeal for their cause, would make less effective soldiers. Correcting this deficit would mean treating soldiers as citizens – an approach with far-reaching implications for military discipline and potentially for society as a whole. Whether it was actually the case that the Prussian troops of the *ancien régime* had lacked motivation and élan is in fact doubtful. It was rather that the reformers internalized the ideology of revolutionary warfare promulgated by their enemy.

The reformers also had wider objectives. They aimed to overcome the caste-like exclusiveness of the officer corps. Aristocracy must make way for meritocracy. In a document known as the 'Declaration of Ortelsburg', a statement composed by Frederick William on 12 December 1806 while he was still fleeing the French, the king began to draw his own conclusions. In future, he wrote, any fighting man who performed with distinction should be promoted into the officer corps, regardless of whether he was a private, a warrant officer or a prince. The army, it was argued, must become the repository of a virtuous patriotism, which in turn would infuse it with the élan and commitment that had been so manifestly lacking in 1806. The objective was, in the words of Scharnhorst, one of the leading reformers, 'to raise and inspire the spirit of the army, to bring the army and the nation into a more intimate union . . .'

The perceived need to mobilize patriotic commitments – and to raise productivity – throughout all strata of Prussian society produced a raft of parallel reform processes: the removal of the remaining vestiges of servile agrarian tenures ('feudalism'), the emancipation of the Jews, the expansion of tertiary education and improvement of training for teachers in elementary schools, the creation of new consultative assemblies, municipal self-government; anything, in short, that would raise the productivity and cohesion of Prussian society.

The significance of the Battle of Jena, then, lies not in its military consequences, but in the fact that a political elite capable of collective reflection and deliberation read in the entrails of defeat a judgement on a supposedly failing society. Whether the defeat was really the *consequence* of these features of Prussian society is another question; what matters is that the defeat was interpreted as such, licensing an all-encompassing audit of social, political and economic institutions. Read in this manner, the Prussian defeat at the Battle of Jena seemed revelatory rather than decisive. Indeed, it appeared inevitable, since it was the manifestation of inferiorities that went to the heart not just of the Prussian army, but of the society whose structure and character were reflected in it. The sense of openness and historical contingency that had emboldened the king to try his luck against Napoleon was forgotten. What had once seemed merely possible appeared, in retrospect, inevitable.

Whether the Battle of Hastings might lend itself to this kind of reading, I leave it to others to decide. The Anglo-Saxon polity was perhaps too swiftly overcome by the invader to begin construing the defeat as a political failure. Its temperament and intellectual equipment may have militated against the interpretation of battles as tests of the social structure. The idea of the 'decisive battle' is itself an invention of the nineteenth century and specifically a legacy of the nineteenth-century readings of the Napoleonic Wars (Jomini, Clausewitz, Mahan, for example). What is interesting today about the epoch of decisive battles is that it seems to be over, at least as regards the larger geopolitical context.

Since the end of the Cold War, regional conflicts apart, the world system has been disciplined principally by the projection of American power through a sequence of asymmetrical conflicts in which 'battles' are merely local flashpoints in a theatre of conflict onto which an over-whelming preponderance of force is applied. While I was thinking about my talk, I happened to bump into Air Commodore Mike Hart, Director of Military Intelligence at the MoD, on the night train from London to Cambridge. Our conversation on the modern battle became an email exchange, in which he made the following comment:

> I've been involved in all of the operations the UK has mounted since 1990 except Sierra Leone, and we didn't plan for a decisive battle in any of them (which is not the same thing as saying we didn't plan to defeat the enemy at whatever level we could). We tend to think and plan in terms of campaigns, whether against conventional, hybrid or asymmetric opponents. The idea of a decisive battle against (say) the Afghan Taliban, is frankly ludicrous, though the cumulative effect of many tactical engagements (small battles) over time could be decisive.

And these insights also appear to be borne out by the struggle against the so-called Islamic State. Few strategists today would claim that the defeat of the physical caliphate will bring about the eradication of ISIL as an organization or an idea. As an organization, it will survive defeat by morphing back into a Sunni insurgency. As an idea, it is already off and running in cyberspace and among diaspora communities.

The phenomenon of the battle in which highly organized state actors are engaged has made way for a decentred form of ambient violence in which non-state actors skirmish with each other or with unarmed civilians, cyber attacks disrupt economies or elections and missile-bearing drones cruise over insurgent suburbs. The resulting deterritorialization of violence in regions marked by decomposing states makes the kind of 'decision' Clausewitz associated with battle difficult to achieve or even to imagine. The age of battles may be over, even if the age of warfare is not.

Learning from Bismarck?

This essay grew out of my puzzlement in 2019 at the unexpected elective affinity between Dominic Cummings, architect of the Brexit campaign and special adviser to Prime Minister Boris Johnson, and the Prussian statesman Otto von Bismarck.

In the autumn of 1862, the Kingdom of Prussia was paralysed by a constitutional crisis. King William I and his military advisers wanted to expand and improve the army. The liberal-dominated Prussian parliament refused to approve the necessary funds. The problem was not the issue of military expansion as such. There was widespread support for that across the liberal majority. Rather it was the question of the army's constitutional status and of who had the right to determine policy vis-à-vis the military. The liberal view was that the parliament's control of the military budget also implied a degree of co-determination in military matters. In the eyes of the crown, by contrast, the army was an organization bound in personal loyalty to the monarch that must be shielded entirely from the scrutiny of civilian deputies. Now, after two successive dissolutions of parliament, the two sides were in deadlock and the king was said to be contemplating abdication.

This is the crisis Otto von Bismarck was brought into office to resolve. His appointment to the Minister-Presidency of Prussia was a measure of last resort. In 1862, the forty-seven-year old Bismarck appeared a somewhat dubious figure. His perfervid scheming on the fringes of the reactionary right during the 1848 revolutions had earned him the reputation of an extremist, someone, in the words of the king's older brother and predecessor, Frederick William IV, 'to be used only when the bayonet rules without limit'. In reaching for Bismarck, William I and his entourage were taking a risk.

The risk paid off. Bismarck opened play with an attempt to conciliate: he concocted a modified military programme that would enlarge the army and secure government control in key areas, while at the same time meeting some of the main liberal demands. This gambit might well have worked, but it was blocked by the reactionary head of the king's military cabinet, who persuaded the king to withhold his support from Bismarck's compromise.

Bismarck immediately saw that the rules of the game had changed. The key to remaining in office was no longer to secure a deal between parliament and crown, but rather to eliminate all rivals for the king's confidence. He altered his policy accordingly. The idea of a compromise was abandoned. Bismarck switched to a policy of open confrontation. The military reforms were bulldozed through, over the bitter protests of the liberals. Taxes were collected without parliamentary approval. The parliament was baited into ineffectual and self-undermining expressions of outrage. All this sufficed to convince the king of his new minister's skill and dependability. Bismarck soon overshadowed all the other competitors for influence over the monarch. It was the beginning of a career at the summit of German politics that would last until Bismarck was forced into retirement twenty-eight years and two kings later.

One contemporary British political figure who claims to have learned from Bismarck's manoeuvring in 1862 is a certain Dominic Cummings, chief special adviser to Prime Minister Boris Johnson and former special adviser to Michael Gove, currently Minister of the Cabinet Office of the United Kingdom. During the political struggle of 2019, when the British government found itself paralysed by a parliament unwilling to sanction any of its proposals for departure from the European Union, Dominic Cummings, who spent the summer of that year 'gaming' the British crisis, found himself returning again and again to the question: what would Otto von Bismarck do in the situation currently faced by the British government?

We know this, because Cummings's sprawling and fantastically self-revealing blog (still live at the moment of writing) is punctuated with thoughts about Bismarck. For Cummings, who studied history at Exeter College, Oxford, Bismarck is the sacred monster of tactical politics, the genius statesman whose political moves repeatedly surprised and wrong-footed friends and enemies alike, at home as abroad. The nineteenth-century Prussian statesman may appear an improbable model for political strategizing in the era of Twitter and Cambridge Analytica, but it is one of Cummings's core convictions that what may seem, as he puts it, to be 'very esoteric' sources can turn out to be 'extraordinarily practical', i.e. 'give you models for creating super-productive processes'.

The differences between 1862 and 2019 are obvious, but the parallels are thought-provoking. At the heart of the 1862 crisis was the dualism of the Prussian constitution, an unresolved tension between the crown and the legislature that was typical of the German constitutions of that era, a deliberately avoided decision about how power should be shared between the military monarchy and the civilian parliament. It was the resulting gap in the constitution's logic that Bismarck sought to exploit in 1862. Contemporary Britain does not suffer from a constitutional dualism of this kind (the English Civil War shut down most of the dualism between crown and parliament and what remained was largely tidied away by the 'Glorious Revolution' of 1688 and then comprehensively eliminated under the Hanoverians). But the referendum of 2016 had opened up a dualism of a different kind, between representative and direct forms of democracy. The problem was not the use of a referendum as such, because many stable and mature democracies use this tool, supplementing the operations of representative democracy with the recourse to the citizen's initiative. Rather it lay in the fact that the 2016 referendum was understood by the government and the pro-Brexit lobby as a once-and-for-all articulation of the 'will of the people'. It admitted of no compromise and, most importantly, it could not be repeated, as is common in states with mixed systems such as Switzerland, where there is no taboo against calling a referendum on the same subject in successive years.

This created a problem that the British constitutional structure was unable to resolve, namely that, whereas the choice offered by the referendum was binary, the choices facing the UK as the Brexit debate gathered momentum were anything but. There was no binary cleavage between one camp and another but a plurality of faultlines that cross-cut each other, producing a pattern of fine cracks like the fractures on the surface of old paintings. And these chaotic interactions were reflected in the bewildering parliamentary constellations of 2019. Even if one agreed that the referendum was binding (there was controversy on this point), the assumption remained that its implementation must be subject to parliamentary approval. The stand-off between a parliament unable or unwilling to generate a majority in support of any option and a Boris Johnson government determined to 'get Brexit done' as quickly as possible produced political paralysis. It was in this context of constitutional malfunction that Dominic Cummings looked back to Otto von Bismarck.

Two governments in pursuit of important business were minded to push a recalcitrant parliament aside, at least temporarily. The baiting of MPs and civil servants and the threatened recourse to prorogation and early elections were common themes. Bismarck invoked the theory of the 'constitutional gap', according to which the executive was entitled – and indeed obliged – to continue governing, even if parliament refused to collaborate in supposedly crucial tasks. A broadly similar case was made for the British government's course by the British prime minister. Cummings's solution was to propose the prorogation of parliament in September 2019, manoeuvre the executive through the resulting gap and 'get Brexit done' during the interim, on the grounds that government business cannot come entirely to a halt, just because parliament is not in session. This particular gambit failed after a legal challenge. A solution was then found in the dissolution of the two-year-old parliament and the calling of elections in December 2019.

Both crises remind us of how difficult it can be for parliaments to handle a hostile executive: large, unwieldy and committed to complex procedures, elected chambers can appear hopelessly slow-footed in stand-offs with politicians willing to break or bend the rules. And among the most potent weapons the executive wields is the power under certain circumstances to dissolve parliament. Whereas emergency legislation and appeals to national security are subject (in law-abiding democracies) to parliamentary and judicial revision, the dissolution of parliament kills off one parliament and creates another.

Once dissolved, an inconvenient parliament will never return. Bismarck deployed this measure during the Prussian constitutional crisis, but without success because each successive parliament contained ever larger liberal, dissenting majorities. Boris Johnson's use of the same technique in December 2019 – on the advice of Cummings – was much more successful: it replaced the 'awkward squad' of the Brexit referendum years with a more compliant body of MPs dominated by pro-Brexit Conservatives.

When governments goad parliaments, insult judges and civil servants and go in search of adventurous executive solutions to complex problems, the focus of interest naturally shifts from the deliberative world of advisory committees, public inquiries and legislative process to the cut and thrust of what used to be called 'high politics'. And once that happens, attention focuses on questions of tactics and technique. Imagine that someone had persuaded the retired Otto von Bismarck to distil his wisdom and experience into one of those bullet-pointed, shiny-covered, corporate strategy handbooks they sell in such vast numbers at American airports. Let's suppose it bears the title *Leadership: The Bismarck Way*. If we boil that imaginary bestseller down, it might reduce to five salient points (we could call them 'Otto's mottos').

Axiom 1: *Seek to Provoke*. Most politicians in modern democracies prefer consensus to conflict. Bipartisan bridge-building is, or used until recently to be, seen as a higher order achievement in environments where partisan antagonisms can easily have a disruptive effect. Bismarck operated differently. From the very beginning, he understood that the outrage and conflict stirred by provocative gestures were more clarifying and more enabling to the skilful politician than the deceiving peace of ostensible harmony. According to a thinly disguised pen portrait by his American friend John Motley, the eighteen-year-old Bismarck found his way into the most exclusive student fraternity at the University of Göttingen not by ingratiating himself with its members, but by 'insulting them all publicly and in the grossest possible manner' and using the resulting duels as opportunities to wound them so grievously that eventually, 'desiring to secure the services of so valorous a combatant', they welcomed him into their ranks.

Bismarck did exactly the same thing again in 1847, when he made his sensational maiden speech – the first political speech he had ever given before the United Diet in Berlin. Bismarck had aligned himself with the aristocratic 'ultras' of this assembly and used his speech to mount a gratuitous assault on the liberal memory of the campaign against Napoleon in 1813 as a 'people's war for liberty'. It was a shot aimed at the historical heart of the liberal ideology and it stirred the benches opposite into a froth of outrage. The stenographic records of the session note the following moment: 'murmuring and loud shouting interrupts the speaker; he draws the *Spenersche* newspaper from his pocket and reads it until the Marshall has restored order. He then continues ...' Had Bismarck merely contributed intelligently to a debate on local government reform, he would never have achieved the notoriety that secured him access to court circles during and after the revolutions. Throughout his career, Bismarck deliberately courted controversy, exploiting the way it pressured friends and enemies into showing their true colours.

Axiom 2: *Mature the Chaos*. Critics of *The Bismarck Way* might complain that this is really just an extension of Axiom 1, but it was a hallmark of Bismarck's political style that he resisted the temptation prematurely to resolve political conflicts and crises. It wasn't just a question of encouraging them in the first place, but of letting the resulting turmoil evolve to the point where plausible options began to surface. For example: Bismarck allowed the awkwardness generated by the Austro-Prussian parallel occupations of Holstein and Schleswig after the Danish War of 1864 gradually to escalate to the point where it provided him with an opportunity to seek an open and clarifying conflict with Austria. He did the same with the crisis over the Hohenzollern candidacy for the Spanish throne in 1870, allowing the tone of relations between France and Prussia to deteriorate until the French government was foolish enough to risk a declaration of war. In the later 1870s and 80s, he applied the same approach to the tensions fermenting on the Balkan Peninsula. His policy on the 'Eastern Question' was not designed to evacuate conflict from the European states system, but rather to deflect it to the periphery, where it would disturb the system in ways that would not threaten Germany and might well even enhance its security. Bismarck was never in control of events and he knew that, but he understood that situations of instability have their own evolutionary dynamic. Given time, they may well provide you with the tools you need to achieve your objectives.

Axiom 3: *Act Unpredictably*. Bismarck operated outside the ideological prescriptions of any single interest. He hailed from the boondocks of Pomerania, from that flat expanse of rural estates where the noble landowner was a king in his own little world. But though he counted many 'old conservatives' among his friends, he never adopted their nostalgic, corporatist politics – his attitude to the milieu of his own class was marked by a sense of ironic distance. Nor, on the other hand, was he or could he be a liberal. And though he revered the monarchical state as an executive with the capacity for autonomous action, he was often frustrated by the slowness of the civil servants, the 'pen-pushers' of the fourth estate.

The result of all these non-alignments was a remarkable freedom from ideological constraint, an ability to spring from one camp to the other, wrong-footing his opponents or exploiting the differences between them. Scarcely had he humiliated the liberals in the constitutional crisis, but he was offering them a parliamentary indemnity, much to the chagrin of his conservative allies. He collaborated with the forces of liberalism against the conservatives (in the 1870s) and vice versa (in the 1880s); he brandished the democratic franchise as a weapon against elitist liberalism, and menaced the social democrats with the armature of an embryonic welfare state; he punctured the pretensions of the nationalists by seeming to take charge of the nationalist cause.

Bismarck was not a man of principle; he was the man of detachment from principle, the man who disconnected himself from the political commitment of an older generation to mix politics in new combinations. His career is punctuated by the astonished gasps of those who, having enlisted Bismarck for their cause one day, found him bombarding them from an enemy position on the next. The protean nature of his politics infuriated his allies and his enemies, who were sometimes the same people, but at least it kept them guessing. It was one of the keys to his success.

Axiom 4: *Recruit the Boss*. Bismarck could risk these dangerous manoeuvres because he was not an elected leader. He had no party and, for the most part, no parliamentary majority. He was not a tribune of the people, but a royal appointee. He recognized from very early on that in an only partly parliamentarized monarchical system, the king remained the taproot of all real political authority. While Bismarck used up successive waves of political friends, extracting the value from them before moving on into new combinations, the Prussian monarch remained the fixed star at the centre of his system.

For twenty-six years, Bismarck micromanaged his relationship with Wilhelm I, King of Prussia and, from 1871, German Kaiser. His interactions with that bewhiskered patriarch are a study in long-term co-dependency. Bismarck pressed, wooed, bullied and cajoled the Kaiser into agreement on most issues of importance. Wilhelm had not wanted the war with Austria in 1866 (in later years Bismarck jested that the most difficult challenge of his career had been getting the king into Habsburg Bohemia; the second most difficult had been getting him out again). The Kaiser disliked the liberal flavour of German politics in the decade after 1871 and he disapproved of Bismarck's campaign against the Catholics. When direct confrontations did occur, Bismarck could unleash the full force of his personality, pressing his arguments home with tears, rages and letters of resignation – all refused by the monarch, of course, who found it impossible to imagine how he would manage without his Bismarck. It was these scenes, which Wilhelm I found almost intolerable, that moved him to make the observation: 'It is difficult being the Kaiser under this Chancellor.' This was an exhausting way to run a relationship, but it worked for twenty-six years.

Axiom 5: *Target Multiple Goals in Breadth and in Depth*. Pedants will object that this axiom is really just a further elaboration of Axiom 3. But a closer look at Bismarck in action will suffice to parry their barbs, because, whereas 'mixing it up' is about promiscuously combining styles and alignments, axiom 5 is focused on the formulation of objectives. It is about always having a plan B up your sleeve. There has always been controversy, for example, over the question of whether Bismarck planned the 'war of unification' that broke out with France in 1870. The answer, as so often with Bismarck, is neither yes nor no. A war was on Bismarck's option list, but he had no intention of starting one. ('To start a preventive war,' he once quipped, 'is like committing suicide in order to avoid dying.') A diplomatic humiliation of Paris would have been acceptable too. Menaces from Paris without a declaration of war might also have been useful, since they would have reminded the still independent southern German states of their precarious security situation and the need for a closer alliance with Prussia. But there were also moments when Bismarck envisaged a longer-term, entirely war-free evolution into some kind of German union. Only if you have multiple targets in view can you profit from conditions of instability that may throw up more than one option. This applies both to the axis in breadth (war with France? / diplomatic humiliation? / closer union with the South?) and to the temporal axis in depth (union now through war? / union in the next few years under conditions of external tension and threat? / conflictless union at some later juncture?).

To be sure, Bismarck did pursue certain stable key objectives. The most important was to strengthen the position of Prussia within Europe and thereby maintain the independence of the monarchy he served. Initially, this meant supporting the king in the quest for military reform. Then it meant asserting the executive's freedom of movement vis-à-vis the legislature. The next step was to challenge Austrian pre-eminence in Germany, and then to unite the states of northern Germany under Prussian control. Historians still argue over when exactly Bismarck conceived a plan to unify all of the German states but there was clearly a point before or during the French war when the maximization of Prussian security merged with the unification of the German states under the captaincy of Berlin. It was not the ultimate goals that were remarkable, it was the dynamism of the framework in which he formulated and sought to pursue them. In almost every major enterprise of his career, Bismarck entered the fray with a relatively open mind, not only as regarded methods and affiliations, but also the prioritization and timing of objectives.

So much for *The Bismarck Way* – may it become the next runaway corporate strategy bestseller. It should help that, by a happy accident, these axioms – *Seek to Provoke, Mature the Chaos, Act Unpredictably, Recruit the Boss, Target Multiple Goals* – line up to produce a handy and eminently marketable acronym: SMART.

Like all such books, this one will doubtless end up making success look much easier to achieve than it actually is. Not all the ingredients of Bismarck's pre-eminence can be boiled down for general use; some were artefacts of his historical and cultural context. None of our five axioms would have done him the slightest bit of good if he had not been the scion of an ancient lineage, comfortable in the company of the noblemen who comprised the ruling class of his kingdom. Bismarck's extravagant manoeuvres in the space between the Prussian military monarchy, the parliament, the federal states of the Reich and German civil society would have been impossible in a system less centred on the monarchical executive. Moreover, the Prussian statesman's tactical brilliance was effective only because it was yoked to something more mysterious: political instinct, an uncanny ability to see around the next corner, a knack of recognizing opportunities where others saw only threats.

There is a further and more important point on which *The Bismarck Way* will presumably be entirely silent, namely that all this success was purchased at horrendous personal cost. Politics ate up everything else that there was inside Bismarck. In a literal sense, it became his consuming passion. It fed on and ultimately destroyed most of his friendships (a remarkable exception was his warm and enduring attachment to his friend from Göttingen days, the American historian and diplomat John Motley, who loved Bismarck and, of course, posed absolutely no threat to him). By the 1870s, Bismarck could only tolerate the company of those who were willing to allow their individualities to be swallowed entirely into the Bismarckian enterprise. An example is the likeable and intelligent Christoph Tiedemann, who entered Bismarck's employ as his personal assistant in 1875 and left again in 1880 in much poorer health after being worked to distraction for five years. Increasingly, it was people in this kind of position who got to see the real Bismarck.

And what they saw was often horrific. The unrelenting struggle to dominate his opponents, the obsessive-compulsive need to see the entire political system function in conformity with his own priorities, and the sheer frustration at how slowly things actually changed, even when one pushed as hard as one could, unleashed torrents of grief and rage that often brought the chancellor to the brink of physical and mental collapse. Bismarck spent more and more of his time in a state of boiling anger (perhaps this happens to all of us, but it was

77

especially acute in Bismarck's case). Even on the occasion of the proclamation of the Empire in the Hall of Mirrors at Versailles on 18
January 1871, the symbolic highpoint of his career thus far, Bismarck
was in a stinker of a mood because of earlier arguments with the new
Kaiser about the exact wording of his imperial title.

The wit and verve of the memoirs, which are one of the great
nineteenth-century literary works in German, thus belied a personality
that was always flying off the handle – over the Kaiser's preference for
a certain ambassador, or the Federal Council's refusal to ratify the
appointment of a postal official, or the alleged errors in the stenographic record of one of his speeches, or the suspected intrigues of the
Kaiser's wife, Empress Augusta, or any one of an endless sequence of
real or imagined vexations. He got into such a rage, he told his brother,
'over those who keep knocking at my door and annoying me with
questions and bills that I could bite the table'. All these political frustra-
tions were somatized in one of the nineteenth century's most grandiose
cases of hypochondria. They manifested themselves in itches, fevers,
headaches, chronic fatigue, dizziness, sleeplessness, vomiting, paralysis,
'blood stoppage', congestion, stomach cramps and 'irritated nerves'. Of
the 1,275 days between 14 May 1875 and November 1878, Bismarck
spent no fewer than 772 either on his estates or at spas.

It is Bismarck's ability to keep changing the game that fascinates
Dominic Cummings who, as a non-member of the British Conservative Party (and indeed of any party), enjoys a similar freedom from
conventional constraints. In this respect, the British special adviser
resembles those Germans who, as Max Weber observed in 1917,
admired the Prussian politician not for the 'grandeur of his subtle,
sovereign mind, but exclusively for the element of violence and cunning in his statesmanship, the real or imagined brutality in his
methods'. Cummings has often returned to that transitional moment
when Bismarck began breaking the rules. On the day the 'fateful telegram' arrived summoning Bismarck to the prime ministership of
Prussia, Cummings wrote in a blog essay of 2014, 'a profound nonlinearity hit world politics'.

Nonlinearity may be scary and even dangerous, but it is also cre-
ative and exciting, especially for Cummings, whose blog essays fizz

with amoral speculations in which recondite branches of knowledge and counterfactual scenario-designs intertwine with each other to produce unexpected 'hybrid solutions' rich in suggestions for the present. In a job advertisement posted on his blog at the beginning of January 2020, Cummings declared that Downing Street were looking to hire a new generation of 'unusual' people, 'misfits with odd skills', 'true wild cards, artists, people who never went to university and fought their way out of an appalling hell hole' and 'weirdos from William Gibson novels'. The aim was to shake up established thinking and procedures in government and prepare the ground for what another government adviser has called 'seismic changes' to the civil service. The advent of such thinking at the apex of politics is not a uniquely British phenomenon. In some ways, Cummings, who was asked to leave Downing Street in November 2020 after he fell from favour with the Prime Minister's inner circle, resembles the sometime theatre director and senior Putin adviser Vladislav Surkov, composer of geeky dystopian fictions and prophet of 'non-linear warfare'. It remains to be seen what impact this thinking will have on the character of political life in Britain, but one thing is already clear: the scenarios of institutional disruption imagined by the new generation of special advisers are intended to augment, not undermine, the power and independence of the political executive.

A new cohort of aggressive, commanding personalities has emerged at the apex of many of the world's political structures. The deliberate engineering of crises, the use of provocation to galvanize the political support base, intense round-the-clock media management and the personalization of political authority have become unexpected signatures of governance in the early twenty-first century. Those who deploy such techniques usually lack Bismarck's intelligence and foresight. They know how to disrupt institutions but not how to build them. They know how to start and stoke culture wars, but not how to end them. The presence on the world stage of such uninhibited personalities has already done much to reduce the transparency and predictability of the world system. In this febrile climate, it may be useful to reflect both on the advantages and on the risks that come with the tactically mobile template of modern political leadership pioneered by Otto von Bismarck.

From Prussia with Love:
Zealotry, Liberalism and the Public
Sphere in 1830s Königsberg

For Jonathan Steinberg

Contention over the role played in public life by religious doctrines, associations, performances, customs, values and symbols is one of the central themes of European modernity. This was the issue at the heart of the Culture Wars of the late nineteenth and early twentieth centuries, conflicts that shaped the political cultures of the European states. Recent controversies over cartoons and veils have shown that disputes about the relationship between religion and the public sphere retain the power to perturb.

The relationship between the two is also problematic in a narrower semantic sense. The concept of the 'public sphere' as Jürgen Habermas so influentially defined it, originally possessed, at its core, a secular or post-religious character. In the critical, dialogical, rational, bourgeois and liberal public sphere theorized by Habermas, it almost seemed as if religion were the remnant of a traditional and in essence already obsolete social order. The exclusion of religion from the public sphere, imagined in its turn as the fruit of processes of societal and economic modernization, appeared to be licensed by the sources themselves. After all, it was a defining feature of those bodies that were taken to constitute the emergent public sphere – eighteenth-century reading clubs, masonic lodges and patriotic, musical or scientific societies – that religion, at least in principle, was barred from entry, on the grounds that it would divide members against each other and thus endanger sociability.[1] And these biases within the sources were amplified by an ideal-typical schema in which the public sphere was defined in terms of its function as a 'space of reason-giving', while religion figured as inherently irrational and authoritarian.[2]

Since the appearance of Habermas's *The Structural Transformation of the Public Sphere*, numerous historical studies have in fact insisted on drawing attention to the place of religion in the evolution of European public life. These have not merely explored the many ways in which religion was present in public life, but have also demonstrated its constitutive role in the development of the public sphere. Confessional networks didn't merely shape public life in individual states, they also played a crucial role in prestructuring the emergent transnational or global public sphere. Whether they embraced 'modernity' or not, the great religious corporations were deeply entangled in processes of modernization.[3]

Pointing to these connections does not mean turning one's back on Habermas's concept, but rather expanding it, while at the same time uncoupling it from the 'anti-religious' normative assumptions that underwrote the original investigation.[4] It is a mark of the power of Habermas's concept that it has the potential to survive this operation largely intact. He has himself reacted to historical and sociological critiques by arguing for the formulation of what he calls a 'postsecular stance' founded on an acknowledgement of the continuing global vitality of religion, and of an awareness both of the limits of the normative arguments advanced by supposedly 'free-standing' intellectuals and of the distinctive value of religious traditions as resources capable of generating meaning and identity.[5]

This essay focuses on an episode in which it seemed – at least to many of those involved – that reason and religious zealotry were in bitter contention. It is inspired by two features of Jonathan Steinberg's work that have influenced my own writing since I completed my doctorate under his supervision. The first is a feeling for how circumscribed but emblematic transactions and episodes can illuminate larger problems. The second is a sensitivity to the place of personality, psychological textures and subjective perception in the dramas and conflicts that interest historians. Jonathan, whose own unique self is now being consumed by Alzheimer's disease, saw in personality one of the drivers of history. When circumstances placed specific personalities in the proximity of power, he argued, they became forces that could shape the lives of others.

The essay explores the public controversy around the activities of a religious group – denounced as a 'sect' by its opponents – in the city of Königsberg during the 1830s. This was the era of Governor Theodor von Schön (1773–1856), a renowned reformer and luminary of pre-1848 liberalism in Prussia and a clear-eyed philosophical rationalist. In the late 1830s, scandalous developments in the turbulent religious life of the East Prussian capital confronted the governor and his reason with unexpected challenges. Then, as in some places today, religious zealotry appeared in the eyes of a liberal elite to threaten the cohesion and equanimity of public space. The resulting struggle against a growing urban religious movement laid bare the limits of liberal tolerance. The escalation of rhetoric around claims to 'reason' and the mobilization of public opinion – both in its printed and in its less mediated forms – make this an interesting case study, not just for thinking historically about the boundaries of the 'liberal public sphere', but also for reflecting on the conditions in which the idea of a secular and rational public sphere acquired its normative power. Finally, the intertwining of theological, ecclesiastical and political conflict with gendered discourses of sexual scandal opens up interesting questions about the place of gender in secular–religious conflict decades before the era of the European Culture Wars.

First a few words on the broader context. In religion as in politics, the decades between 1815 and 1840 were an era of differentiation, fragmentation and conflict. Across Prussia, revivalist movements mobilized the faithful in ways that unsettled the chemistry of the official religious communities. Voluntary Christian societies sprang up dedicated to the distribution of charity, the housing and 'betterment' of 'fallen women', the moral improvement of prisoners, the care of orphans, the printing and distribution of bibles, the provision of subsistence labour for paupers and vagrants, the conversion of Jews and heathens. The Protestant missions, institutes and pious societies of the post-war era represented a diverse social constituency. Wealthy individuals from the social (and often the political) elite loomed large among the founding fathers, mainly because they alone had the capital to acquire premises and equipment and the influence to secure privileges from the authorities. There was also a far-flung network of supporters in the lesser towns and villages of the Prussian provinces, in which artisans formed the overwhelming majority. They organized themselves in auxiliary societies that met for prayer, Bible-reading, discussion and the collection of donations for Christian purposes. This may not have been the sceptical, critical, contentious, bourgeois public sphere idealized by Jürgen Habermas, but it did represent an impressive self-organizing impulse capable of feeding into proto-political networks and affiliations. It was part of that broader unfolding of voluntary energies that transformed nineteenth-century middle-and lower-middle-class society.

At the same time as these energies welled up from below, the state intervened more aggressively in the confessional life of the kingdom than at any time since the reign of the Great Elector. On 27 September 1817, Frederick William III announced his intention to merge the Lutheran and Calvinist confessions into a single Prussian 'evangelical-Christian church', later known as the Church of the Prussian Union. The king himself was the chief architect of this new ecclesiastical entity. He designed the new United liturgy, cobbling together texts from German, Swedish, Anglican and Huguenot prayer books. He issued regulations for the decoration of altars, the use of candles, vestments and crucifixes. The king invested immense energy and hope in the Union. The aim was to absorb and discipline the energy given off by revivals and to stabilize the ecclesiastical fabric of Protestantism in the face of the greatly enlarged Catholic minority in the post-war Prussian state. One finds at the heart of the Unionist project an obsessive concern with uniformity that is recognizably post-Napoleonic: the simplification and homogenization of vestments at the altar as on the field of battle, liturgical conformity in place of the plurality of local practices that had been the norm in the previous century, even modular standardized churches designed to be assembled from prefabricated parts and available in different sizes to suit villages and towns.[6]

There was abundant potential here for conflict with the secular authorities. Protestant revivalism in Prussia tended to seek expression outside the confines of the institutional Church. Some awakened Protestants openly disparaged the official confessional structures.[7] In some Prussian rural areas, local populations refused to patronize the services of the official clergy, preferring to congregate in prayer meetings.[8] And alongside these separatist tendencies there flourished in the numerous interstices of religious belief and practice a rich variety of eccentric variations on the norm, in which the tenets of licensed dogma blended seamlessly with folk belief, speculative natural philosophy and pseudo-science. These were the hardy weeds that shot up ceaselessly between the paving stones of official religion. They fed to some extent upon the energies released by the religious revivals. Religious belief could interact with folk magic in ways that the authorities found unsettling. In a context where the practice and institutional structure of official religion were increasingly coming under state control, the boundaries between religious non-conformity and political resistance were likely to become increasingly blurred.

Every departure from the Union rite, every critique of the official Church, every attempt to conserve or reinvigorate the old Lutheran or Calvinist traditions, every potentially sectarian or separatist activity was construed as a dangerous challenge to public authority. The king ordered that long reports be prepared on sectarian activity in his lands. Throughout the 1820s, Altenstein, chief of the new Ministry of Church, Health and Educational Affairs, founded in the same year as the Union Church, kept a close eye on sectarian developments both within and beyond the borders of the kingdom – of particular interest were the Swiss valley sects of Hasli, Grindelwald and Lauterbrunnen, whose adherents were said to pray naked in the belief that clothes were a sign of sin and shame. The ministry assembled lists of sectarian tracts, subsidized the publication of counter-sectarian texts and closely monitored religious groups and associations of all kinds.[9] Frederick William expected the edifying and accessible rituals and symbolic culture of the Prussian Union, whose liturgy he himself designed, to arrest the centrifugal pull of sectarian formations, just as Napoleon had hoped that the Church of the French Concordat founded in 1801 would close the rifts that had opened among French Catholics since the revolution.[10]

In the 1820s and 30s, the minister for church affairs circulated questionnaires to all the districts of the Prussian provinces. Every district government was required to fill in a form setting out an 'overview of the associations conducting extra-ecclesiastical religious rites or hours of devotion'. The questions to be answered included: which associations exist and where?; how large is the number of participants?;

who leads the meetings?; what do they consist of?; and last but certainly not least: in what manner does their influence make itself felt on the lives of the participants and on the orientation of their spirit? The replies from the District of Königsberg in 1822 revealed a range of local activities. In the parish of Altrossgarten there was a 'pious association' led by the gardener Mittrich, 'an honest and blameless man who regularly attends church'. There were '20 Pietists' in Schmelz. Far more numerous, especially in the inspectorate of Labiau to the east of the city, were the 'Maldeniker', whose prayer and song meetings attracted hundreds of adherents. Their leaders were 'men of the lower class who believe themselves inspired', claimed the authority to interpret the Scriptures and 'wander from one congregation to another'. Their meetings consisted of singing, praying, scriptural exegesis and religious discussions. 'The Maldeniker believe that they alone are clever, holy and deserving of salvation. Other people are in their eyes children of the devil.' It was rumoured that their supreme leader 'received his instructions from England', though the respondent added that this claim was as yet 'unverified'. The adherents of this sect were to be recognized by their 'wild glances, the rolling of their eyes and their distorted facial muscles'.[11] The answers of the district governments offer a glimpse of the range of local expressions of piety. They also bear eloquent witness to the fearfulness bordering on paranoia with which the authorities contemplated the religious energies at work in parts of Prussian society during this post-Napoleonic 'age of flux and hiatus'.[12]

During the 1830s, the government intensified its efforts to police religious conformity in response to deepening resistance among the Lutherans to the new Union Church. Its early consolidation had proceeded harmoniously enough, but opposition soon increased, mainly because the Prussian administration gradually extended the scope of the Union to the point where its liturgical regulations became binding for all Protestant public worship across the kingdom. Many objected to this element of compulsion. An 'Old Lutheran' movement formed which demanded the right to secede from the Church of the Prussian Union. The king was enraged and genuinely bewildered by this resistance. He had conceived his Union Church as a broad church in which all Protestant Christians could find a comfortable home – how could anyone object to that? Urged on by their monarch, the Prussian authorities made all the usual mistakes. They presumed, above all, that the Old Lutherans were merely the hapless dupes of malevolent agitators.[13] They bore down heavily on separatist preachers, imposing draconian fines and terms of imprisonment, and quartering troops in areas where congregations refused to see the government's sense. These measures were predictably futile. Repression merely stimulated sympathy for the beleaguered Lutherans, so that the movement steadily spread during the 1830s from its original stamping ground in Silesia into the neighbouring provinces of Posen, Saxony and Brandenburg.[14]

The scandal that shook the city of Königsberg in the later 1830s has to be seen against this background of wildcat religious revival on the one hand and heightened official vigilance on the other. At the heart of the Königsberg struggle was a religious 'sect', or so it was called by its detractors, that had gathered itself around two clergymen in the city, Dr Johann Wilhelm Ebel, preacher at the Altstadt church, situated in a prominent central location with the largest congregation in the city, and Georg Heinrich Diestel, preacher of the Haberberg church. The Altstadt church served a fashionable audience that included many noblewomen from the best families. The Haberberg church, lying in a suburb beyond the Pregel, was frequented by farmers, artisans, clerks and other middling townsfolk. According to the charges levelled against them, Ebel and Diestel had – in contravention of Prussian law – created a sect-like following about their persons and thereby abused the authority of their churchly offices. To make matters worse, the basis of this 'sect' was a doctrine that appeared substantially to diverge from the official teachings of the Church of the Prussian Union. On the basis of this doctrine, cobbled together from biblical teachings and an improvised form of natural philosophy, Ebel was alleged to have indulged in 'impure speculations' and to have encouraged inappropriate sexual behaviour between the men and women of his circle.

Wild rumours of sexual excesses conducted under the cover of ritual solemnities circulated across the city, leading in 1835 to a protracted trial that soon acquired a certain infamy across the German states as the 'Königsberg Religious or *Mucker* Trial', *Mucker* being a term that circulated at the time to denote religious zealots, with connotations of uncleanliness and immorality – one contemporary press report linked the word to a term used by hunters in connection with the mating of hares.[15] Ebel and Diestel were suspended from their respective clerical posts; the trial was transferred to Berlin. On 28 March 1839 the accused were acquitted of the charges relating to sexual impropriety, but found guilty of founding a sect, dismissed from their respective posts and declared unfit to perform any public office. Diestel was sentenced to three months of fortress arrest for contempt of court and Ebel was confined in a public penitentiary, there to remain until he should be in a position to persuade the court that he had arrived at a 'better state of mind'.

As the scandal unfolded, attention focused on a curious figure who might otherwise have fallen into obscurity. Johann Heinrich Schönherr, who had died in Königsberg in 1826, was identified as the influential mentor of Ebel's youth and the true author of the 'doctrine' propagated within his sect. Schönherr had initially been destined for a trade. At the age of seventeen, he decided instead to become a preacher. However, since the boy had never received any formal education and lacked the temperament for systematic analytical thought, he was unable to make any sense of formal theology, or of the fashionable rationalist philosophy of the day, which struck him as dry and empty jargon incapable of satisfying spiritual longings. Forsaking his studies, he went wandering instead, in a manner characteristic of other restless sages of that era, to Greifswald, Rostock and thence to Rinteln on the River Weser.

It was on the banks of the Weser that Schönherr experienced the epiphany that would shape his adult life. He happened to notice plants (waterlilies, perhaps?) lit by the sun, floating on the water's surface. With almost painful intensity, it struck him that these aquatic plants owed their life and vitality to light and water alone – they required (or so it seemed to him) no other nourishment. And this observation led him by degrees to the belief that the entirety of creation was founded on the union of two principles, embodied in two 'primal entities'. These he imagined as two opposed spheres, one of water and thus dark, the other composed of fiery light. These spheres had originally floated or wandered in primordial space, until the moment when at last they collided and merged with each other. Only then did each of the spheres acquire consciousness of its own existence, for it was, Schönherr believed, only through relations of opposition that knowledge of oneself was possible. Light was the vivifying male principle, water its nurturing female counterpart. These two originary beings, the supreme male and the supreme female, bound in eternal and necessary union, explained everything. Schönherr described to his disciples – almost as if he had been there – the long meandering journey of the primal entities through the abysses of space and the glorious moment of their encounter, when the strong luminal arms of the lightsphere penetrated the cool darkness of the watersphere. Schönherr saw in every act of sexual reproduction a reenactment of this originary union.[16]

Schönherr was so convinced of the power of this insight that he attempted to win the allegiance of the philosopher and Königsberg celebrity Immanuel Kant. Having secured a brief interview, he expounded to Kant with passion and candour his system of the two primal entities. Kant replied that if all of this were true, then man ought in theory to be able to subsist by light and water alone, without any other organic nourishment. With disarming naivety Schönherr conceded the point, whereupon Kant advised him to try this method himself, with a view to adopting its success as an advertisement for the truth of his doctrine. Schönherr spent several days trying to live from light and water alone and was soon persuaded by hunger to abandon the attempt.

That Schönherr succeeded in securing an enthusiastic following was in part a function of his eccentric charisma. He had, in the words of the Königsberg theologian Hermann Olshausen, who had at one time known him well,

> an eminent personality, whose resonance was greatly heightened by his costume. [...] His physiognomy was noble, his eyes radiant. [...] A long black beard flowed down as far as the belt, and the hair on the sides of the head was also grown to a great length. A long gown, oriental in style and a broad-brimmed hat completed the image of this unusual man.[17]

Among Schönherr's hobby-horses in the last years of his life was the plan to construct a boat on the River Pregel in accordance with a design that had supposedly come to him in a dream. Schönherr imagined that this mystical ship would be capable of sailing against wind and tide 'without sails, oars or horses'. The thing was eventually built with the charity of friendly merchants and the freely given labour of wharfmen affiliated with his circle, but when it was launched, it sank immediately into the mud near the bank of the river, where it remained until it was broken up.[18]

By 1822, when the Berlin government asked all district authorities to report on unofficial religious activity in their area, Schönherr had acquired a regular following. In its return for that year, the Inspectorate of Königsberg listed 'the sect of Herr Schönherr' as one of the unauthorized gatherings convening in the city. The respondent was unable to state the number of adherents, merely noting that these consisted of 'women and men, among who there are said to be a number of school teachers'. Details on the teachings expounded at these gatherings were not available because these were 'kept secret'.[19]

Schönherr was not the only eccentric sage to acquire a following in the Germany of those tumultuous years. Friedrich Ludwig Jahn, father of the gymnastics movement, was a closely analogous figure. Jahn, too, was an epic wanderer who sported 'Old German' clothes of exotic appearance, designed by himself. His style of life was unconventional – at various points in his wandering phase, he lived in caves. Jahn and Schönherr represented a form of activism in which the project on offer to potential followers was performed by, and embodied in, the person of the charismatic teacher.

For the young aspirant clergyman Johann Wilhelm Ebel, the power of Schönherr's teachings lay both in their cosmic explanatory scope and in the sage's ability to build bridges – as Ebel saw it – between philosophy and faith. Ebel hailed from a clerical household with a mystical bent. Even as an adolescent, he had been drawn to the Book of Psalms, the Song of Solomon, the gospel of John and the Book of Revelation. But the decision to leave his small home town of Passenheim (East Prussia) to study theology at Königsberg in preparation for the ministry plunged him into a world suffused with a sceptical philosophical rationalism. Mockery of religion was the norm among his fellow university students and Ebel found it hard to reconcile the rationalist teachings of his instructors with the warm positive belief he had grown up with at home. Schönherr became the mentor whose encompassing speculations offered a key to the resolution of doubt.

There was something emblematic in this curious alliance between a young theologian and an uneducated sage. The tension between reason and faith, between philosophy and revelation, was one of the central themes of these years. It ran like a red thread through countless clerical and intellectual biographies. For many of those preoccupied by it, this was an issue filled with urgency and pain. Resolving it was not simply a matter of establishing and defending a theoretical standpoint; it was a quest for personal equilibrium founded on a harmony between world and Scripture, between liberty and grace. And Ebel was not unusual in seeking these goods from a marginal and unorthodox source. In the early post-war years, when the spring rain of religious revival and fashionable sentimentality stirred the dull roots of rationalist theology, it was fashionable for the 'Awakened' to frequent mystical seers and visionary nuns, to whose hermitages earnest young Protestants made long pilgrimages.

Whatever Ebel learned from Schönherr, he was himself clearly blessed with quite remarkable charismatic gifts. By the end of the Wars of Liberation, he was famous in Königsberg for the fiery power of his sermons and the power of the prayers with which he began and ended his religious instruction. As a man of the Awakening, he cultivated a style that mixed the rough and the smooth, high eloquence with moments of earthy directness. He was, as one chronicler put it, 'bold, sentimental and original, never scrupling to throw into his most solemn passages a homely phrase, an old saw, a snatch of song, even a touch of comedy, which all but forced his hearers into shouts of mirth'. Good looks helped: the young Ebel wore his hair very long, so that it fell in cascades of dark curls around his neck, parting it down the centre of his head, 'like a lady'.[20] Ebel also possessed a sympathy for and insight into the specific predicaments of women. In 1816, this latter gift helped him to build a friendship that would shape the rest of his life.

Ida, Countess von der Gröben, was the daughter of the governor of East Prussia, Hans Jakob von Auerswald. Theodor von Schön, who would succeed Auerswald as governor of East Prussia when the former retired in 1824, had been married to her sister.* When Ebel met her in 1816, von der Gröben was still in the depths of a protracted depression. Devastated by the shock of her husband's death at the Battle of Lützen during the Wars of Liberation, she had left Königsberg and returned as a widow to her home in Silesia, where she had languished ever since, unable to take any interest in the things or people around her. The effect on the countess of Ebel's arrival bordered on the miraculous. He seemed to have a power over her spirit that roused her energies and rekindled her interest in life. Von der Gröben returned to Königsberg with Ebel in tow, fully restored to the gaiety of her youthful self. This was Ebel's definitive entry into Königsberg high society. He had always been drawn to the most elevated social milieus, but now he was treated like one of the family. The Auerswalds took him under their wing, so did the Kanitzes, the Münchows and other powerful clans. Society ladies flocked to his sermons. His future seemed assured: after all, Governor Auerswald was also *ex officio* the chairman of the Consistorium, the supreme ecclesiastical council in the province, with responsibility for the appointment and promotion of all clergymen. Ebel was appointed archdeacon at the fashionable Altstadt church.

All of this transformed the social location of the Schönherr gospel. While the old sage was still doling out his teachings on water and light to artisans, peddlers and wharfmen on the banks of the Pregel, Ebel was addressing the cream of Königsberg high society. Under the pressure of this divergence in social horizons the pupil and the sage parted company. The adventurous days of the early post-war were over and Schönherr was simply too unkempt and odd to follow Ebel into his new world. Ebel later tried to renew the contact, but Schönherr, embittered by the betrayal, refused ever again to receive him; the old man died in poverty in 1826.

Ebel was now at the apogee of his career, a celebrated figure in the city whose sermons were so popular that they emptied the churches of his rivals. His alliance with Diestel (another Schönherr disciple) at the Haberberg church created an axis that linked the aristocratic and mercantile elites of the city centre with the tradesmen of the Königsberg

* Schön's first wife was Ida's sister, Lydia von Auerswald, who died of typhus in 1807.

suburbs. Yet the success of these years also sowed the seeds of his later troubles. Ebel was widely loathed by many of the clergymen of the city. Professional envy played a role here, but so did genuine distaste at the improvised theosophical (Schönherrian) doctrines he was rumoured to propagate alongside the official teachings of the Union Church and concern at the unconventionality of the relations cultivated among the women and men of his inner circle.

By 1824, when Theodor von Schön came to take up the governor-ship of the Province of Prussia,* rumours about sexual improprieties among the Ebelians were already circulating in the city. It was said that the ecclesiastical authorities were turning a blind eye, partly because a superficial investigation failed to find any evidence that the meetings in question constituted illegal 'conventicles', partly because the groups around Ebel involved some of the most powerful families in the prov-ince and partly because it was expected, as Archbishop Borowski put it in a conversation with the governor, that 'the thing would soon end with an [unwanted] pregnancy'.[21] But the scandal intensified in the mid-1830s, when the group split, producing a faction of renegades eager to discredit Ebel and Diestel. One of these, the theologian Her-mann Olshausen, began to write and preach against Ebel. Family feuds added further pepper to the mix: Count Finkenstein, a former Ebelian, fell foul of the founder's strict discipline and left the group under a cloud. In January 1835, when he learned that his cousin Zelina von Mirbach was being drawn into the preacher's orbit, he wrote to her hinting of practices among the Ebelians that no morally upright man or women could endure. The cult of the two original beings, he warned her, had degenerated into a sordid preoccupation with sexual urges that posed a serious threat to the mental and physical health of any young woman who entered Ebel's orbit.[22] The letter was passed via Zelina's friends to Diestel, who responded with an epistle violently attacking Finkenstein.[23] Finkenstein took the matter to court. The Consistorium launched an investigation. The cat was out of the bag.

We need not dwell in detail on the suits and counter-suits that

* Auerswald had been the governor of East Prussia and Schön governor of West Prus-sia. In 1824, following Auerswald's retirement, the two provinces were merged under the name of Prussia and Schön inherited the Governorship of the new entity.

followed, or on the toxic relationships that embittered the struggle around Ebel from the start. What matters is that the investigation and then the trial of Ebel and Diestel took place in a veritable media storm. It was claimed in the newspapers that Ebel had surrounded himself with naked women in order to put his moral rectitude to the test, that he practised polygamy, that he regarded himself as a new messiah, that he had urged unmarried members of his circle to indulge in 'immoral relations' with each other and that he condoned a form of 'spiritual marriage' with a partner other than one's legal spouse. According to one newspaper account, Ebel had suffered some years before the trial from a 'revolting skin disease'. At that time, he happened to be living near a lake, 'surrounded by many female zealots'. His doctor, a man by the name of Ludwig Sachs, recalled that he had paid a visit to his patient, only to be told that he had gone bathing. But, whereas the section of the bathing beach reserved for men was empty when Sachs approached, the bathing area for women appeared to be occupied:

> Becoming suspicious, he approached the women's section of the lake shore. A half-naked lady approached him and warned him to go no further and not to disturb them, because 'Ebel was being washed by the ladies' and indeed ten or twelve younger and older ladies had already gone into the water and were vying to outdo each other in the irrigation of the saint.[24]

It was even claimed in some quarters – in all seriousness – that men *and* women had attended the conventicles of the 'sect' in a state of complete nakedness, that newcomers regularly received the 'seraphic kiss', and that two young women had fallen ill and died as a consequence of the abnormal levels of sexual excitement stimulated by the group's practices.

The public arousal generated by these allegations was remarkable. The king wrote to Altenstein expressing his indignation at the fact that such a sensitive matter was being so widely discussed in the journals.[25] The populace, Theodor von Schön reported, was 'worked up' by the affair. Students descended on the services attended by Ebelians rowdily demanding seraphic kisses from the ladies as they left church. Lampoons appeared on street corners.[26] The press hounded Ebel unmercifully, and not just in Königsberg.[27] 'The aberrations in religion, the immoralities, the activities insulting to Christian faith [perpetrated by the Ebelians] are such that a chaste pen cannot describe them,' frothed an article in the Leipzig paper *Unser Planet*. The author went on to describe in exquisite detail one of the rites conducted within the circle. A certain gentleman had hoped to ascend from the lower to the higher 'level' of the 'sect'. He was summoned into Ebel's presence.

> And received the instruction to pray kneeling in an antechamber, in order to prepare himself for this important step. After he had kneeled and prayed for some time, the door of a dimly lit adjoining room opened. In the dull glow of a lamp, the Leader of the sect could be seen on a sofa with a beautiful young girl from one of the finest families of the city on his lap. He received the instruction to approach more closely. They asked him whether he possessed the fullness of humility and could prove it. He answered in the affirmative. What the girl sitting on the Leader's lap now did is such, that even the most superficial description of it would amount to a punishable transgression against everything that goes by the name of morality.[28]

Rather in the manner of the now defunct London scandal sheet *News of the World*, which used to close its most lurid stories with the coy formula 'Our man made his excuses and left,' the Leipzig *Planet* tied up the narrative with the assurance that its informant, 'in whose heart the sense of shame was not yet extinguished', shrank from these horrors and fled from the scene, 'like Joseph with Potiphar's wife'.[29]

A journal for clergymen and interested lay people, the *Kritische Prediger-Bibliothek von Dr. Röhr,* was less coy. It reported that the young girl had opened the novice's shirtfront and 'playfully caressed his breasts':

> While he was obliged to endure this, he received the instruction to do the same with the holy girl. After these mutual titillations, known as the 'Seraphic kiss' had taken place for some time, the holy girl made to take things further, but our unworthy young man found this too shameless and ran away.[30]

Whether these claims should be taken seriously as descriptions of what actually happened within the Ebel circle is doubtful. The formulaic character of the allegations, the prominence of hearsay and their theatrical inversion of mid-nineteenth-century bourgeois sexual and social norms should give us pause. Groups alleged to be sects were often accused of sexual excesses – this was one of the central strands of anti-sectarian discourse. Even of the modest auxiliary societies of the Berlin Society for the Promotion of Christianity among the Jews – innocuous small-town gatherings of pious artisans and their wives and daughters – it was claimed by local officials in the 1820s that their prayer meetings had produced an unacceptable level of arousal in the young women present.[31] When he was asked about the activities of the sect known as the 'Maldeniker' in the District of Labiau on the vast lagoon known as the Kurisches Haff, the local superintendent, who had never attended or observed their meetings, reported in 1822 that it was their custom to invite the women to confess in dark chambers, 'from which a few unhappy marriages had arisen, if the spouse was not a member of the sect'. We find similar speculations about sexual misbehaviour in the anti-Catholic discourses of the Culture Wars.[32]

It does seem clear, however, that Ebel and Diestel's notion of a pure Christian life did involve intense self-scrutiny and mutual examination in the domain of sexual behaviour. The male members of the group were invited to confess their most intimate sins, especially sexual ones, sometimes in writing. These confessions were occasionally passed to the women close to Ebel, who functioned as moral inquisitors with responsibility for the rigorous management of male physical desire – an unusual procedure in the context of 1830s northern European Protestantism. It was never Ebel's intention, however, or that of his closest followers, to stir sexual lust for its own sake. Nor on the other hand, did he seek to drive it out or deny its existence (as the exponent of the Schönherr primal entity theory, he could hardly do that). Rather he aimed to manage desire, to subject it to the sovereignty of the will and of faith. For this reason he urged the married men who took him into their confidence with concerns about the quality or moral status of their conjugal relations not to make love to their wives with the lamp extinguished, but rather in the light, because, as Ebel put it: 'the contemplation of nakedness could help to free the fantasy from its images and transform blind lust into conscious affection for the spouse'.[33]

Taken out of context, of course, Ebel's phrase 'the contemplation of nakedness' could be made to sound voyeuristic or even pornographic. The claim made in the press that Ebel and Diestel had offered this and other similar advice to unmarried persons, thereby inciting them to 'immorality', was never proven. Both men strenuously denied it. Diestel also denied that either of the two men had ever encouraged the stimulation of sexual urges outside the context of procreative coupling between spouses. Diestel insisted that he abhorred, and had never endorsed, the idea of 'artificially over-exciting the body'.[34] And there seems little doubt that, in some cases, witnesses who had fallen out with Ebel maliciously misrepresented his advice. One of the witnesses for the prosecution, the physician Professor Dr Ludwig Sachs, whose testimony contained some of the most sensational claims of immorality, turned out to be an estranged former adherent of Ebel, whose long written confessions of his own rather garish sexual misdemeanours, which had circulated among the ladies close to Ebel, raised questions about his probity as a witness against his former confessors. During the trial, the advocate representing the accused called in statements from women who had been the patients of Dr Sachs; they reported that he had a propensity to press unwanted intimacies upon the women in his care. A certain Fräulein Sophie Louise von Billerbeck, who knew Sachs as her family doctor, recalled how, when she was sixteen or seventeen, shortly after the death of her father, Sachs had cornered her in a doorway 'and kissed her in such a manner that he had pressed her head right back and stuck his tongue as far as he possibly could into her mouth'. Other patients too recalled unexpectedly finding Sachs's tongue in their mouths, and one described an occasion on which he had asked 'whether she would like to see him completely undressed and totally naked? which offer, however, she rejected'.[35]

Another alienated former disciple who testifed against the pair was Count Fink von Finkenstein. Finkenstein told the court that Ebel had expressed to him the desire to be present while he was making love with his wife. Asked to comment on this allegation, Diestel produced an earlier letter from Finkenstein's wife, Charlotte, in which she had reported that it was her husband (i.e. Finkenstein himself) who had proposed this as a means of helping him to make love to her: 'it could help me most [Finkenstein was reported to have said], if I imagine that a third person, who I know has sanctified himself in the Lord, were present as well and I can very easily think of such a person, before whose eyes we could make love.'[36] Why Finkenstein felt that he would find it easier to engage in sexual congress with his wife if Ebel were standing to one side looking on is anyone's guess. What these allegations above all revealed, Diestel suggested in his own deposition to the consistory, was the vulnerability of the clergyman charged with pastoral responsibility for an endangered marriage. When marriages broke apart, releasing formerly private resentments, the pastor who had attempted to guide both partners could find himself in an exceptionally exposed position.[37] Ebel himself conceded in a letter to the Ministry of Church Affairs that he had been 'libelled for years by people who formerly enjoyed my pastoral care', but added that this was merely the consequence of the rigour with which he monitored the morality of the individuals who submitted to his supervision.[38]

In any case, the charge that Ebel and Diestel had committed crimes against sexual morality was rejected as unproven by the Berlin Criminal Senate, so that the formal prosecution confined itself to charges relating to the illegal foundation of a sect. This was the offence of which the two men were subsequently found guilty by the Criminal Court, after a trial of two years' duration, in March 1839. Two years later, even this charge was overturned by the Supreme Court. The case relating to the foundation of an illegal sect had always been weak: Ebel and Diestel had called themselves Lutherans or Christians; they had never directly challenged the authority of the Union Church or of its doctrines. Moreover, they both denied having adopted or promulgated the thoughts of Schönherr in the form of a 'doctrine' or 'system'. It was a mistake, Ebel insisted, to view Schönherr's foray into natural philosophy as a 'doctrine, it is actually only a key for solving the riddles of nature and for illuminating the truths contained in the Bible'.[39]

It was not illegal for a pastor to offer marital advice, even on sexual matters. Nor was it illegal to propagate views that did not directly conform with the official teachings of the Church, so long as these were expressed as private opinions and not passed off as Union doctrine. The old king, Frederick William III, had died in 1840, along with Minister Altenstein. Frederick William IV was much friendlier to evangelical and pietist forms of spirituality than his father had been and so was the new minister of church affairs, Eichhorn, who replaced the dyed-in-the-wool rationalist Altenstein. The disciplining urge that had driven the campaign against nonconformist religion waned and the two men were released, though the convictions against them were never quashed.

So what was all the fuss about? Why did the case against Ebel and Diestel stimulate such excitement? And what principles, if any, were at stake? To this last question, the liberal press gave an unequivocal answer. It was about the struggle between reason and fanaticism, between rationalism and the darkness of sectarian obscurantism. One contemporary publicist spoke in suggestive terms of the 'despoiling of reason, that crown of universality'. Here was a neat means of filing away the troubles in Königsberg. Whatever Ebel and Diestel were saying in private to their closest associates, one thing was clear: their spirituality was out of sympathy with the theological rationalism that still prevailed at the University of Königsberg and among many of the clergymen of the city. At a time when the government had stepped up its vigilance against separatists and sectarians of all types, the eccentric flavour of their teachings might even seen politically suspect, especially if it appeared to challenge the legitimacy of the Union Church, viewed by its supporters as the rational solution to the plurality of religious subcultures that had flourished in turn-of-the-century Prussia.

In the struggle between light and darkness, the governor of Prussia, Theodor von Schön, viewed himself as a champion of the light. Like many of his contemporaries, he described the Ebelians as 'darklings'. In a letter to the minister of church affairs, he described the religious enthusiasm cultivated by the Ebelians as a form of '*Pietisterey*'. Its teachings were laughable: how could one take seriously a doctrine claiming that at the beginning of time 'two enormous eggs or balls are supposed to have swum around in vacuo [. . .] from whose intimate union the world and everything that is in the world originated'?[40] He was horrified when he discovered that his kinswoman Ida von der Gröben had joined the Ebel group. Having failed to persuade her to separate herself from him, he shut her out of his social circle. When the Russian tsarina, a daughter of the Prussian king and a childhood intimate of Ida von der Gröben, visited Königsberg in 1829 and asked after her old friend, she was told by Schön: 'Nobody gets to see her these days – she belongs to a sect.'[41] In 1835, when the conflict around Ebel and Diestel was coming to a head, Ida wrote a letter to her brother-in-law, imploring him to put a halt to the campaign underway against the two clergymen. 'I know you, my dear Schön,' she wrote, 'and [I] know that in you it is not an evil heart, a heart motivated by evil, that has made you err so deeply, but it is also not a good heart, not a heart that generously and selflessly seeks the good.'[42] Schön answered with an expansive gesture of impartiality. He would always be willing, he told his sister-in-law, to extend his hand to her. But having read the first page of her letter, he had ascertained that she was writing to him in the matter concerning Ebel, a matter in which, in view of his high office, he was not permitted to receive correspondence. He had also forbidden Ebel's opponent Count Finkenstein to visit him. His sister-in-law would surely understand that he could neither read nor keep her letter. His position called for maintenance of the strictest neutrality, difficult as this might prove to be.[43]

Whether Schön was really as impartial as he claimed on this occasion to be is doubtful. In the evangelical circles of the city he was viewed as 'an antagonist of Christian belief and striving'. He was deaf to the appeal of positive Christianity and revealed religion. The fact that members – especially women – of the city's best families had been drawn to Ebel was particularly vexing. His view of Ebel and his followers derived above all from the letter Finkenstein had sent to his sister, not from the testimony of Ebel, Diestel or those who remained loyal to them. It was from this source that he derived the claim that Ebel had declared sexual coupling among 'sanctified ones' as being without sin and that the Ebelianer saw in sexual intercourse (whether or not it took place between married persons) a holy re-enactment of the encounter between wet and fiery balls that had initiated the creation of the world.[44] When far-fetched reports began to circulate in the Königsberg press, Schön refused to invoke the censorship against them.[45] On the contrary: he encouraged them by insisting, for example, that the witness Professor Dr Sachs be heard in court, despite his chequered history within the circle. He supported the prosecution from behind the scenes.[46] He ordered that the Altstadt church be closed for repairs, and subsequently had the entire structure demolished. And, through his correspondence with Minister Altenstein in Berlin (like Schön, a rationalist of the old school), he helped to create a climate in which the two men were highly likely to be found guilty of at least one of the charges levelled against them. In these letters, Schön conveyed a clear sense of the significance of the conflict unfolding in his city: it was a battle between reason and obscurantism.

There was a certain irony in this situation, because the roots of the Ebel movement, if it was a movement, lay in the aspiration to reconcile the scriptural content and moral teachings of Christianity with human reason.[47] As a child, Ebel had been raised to contemplate the word of Scripture 'with sacred awe'. But at school he had found that faith in the word of the Bible alone did not suffice to ward off the doubts and counter-arguments of his teachers and fellow-pupils. In Schönherr's curious teachings, Ebel saw a means of bringing revealed religion into harmony with a reason founded upon observations from nature. Only a biblical faith reinforced by philosophy would be capable of dismantling the resistance of mainstream Christians to revealed religious truth – a task that appeared especially urgent in Königsberg, renowned both for its association with Kantian philosophy and for the rationalist flavour of its theology and governance. The attraction of Schönherr's writings, Diestel explained, lay precisely in their 'genuinely philosophical' character. Schönherr's thought represented the cutting edge of contemporary philosophical speculation; it was

> the only possible way of communicating the famous *crux philosophorum* [puzzle of the philosophers], the *salto mortale* of philosophy, the transition from the infinite to the finite.[48]

The pamphlet they composed together in 1837 to explain their views bore the telling title *Understanding and Reason in Alliance with God's Revelation*.

This was not the 'reason' preferred by Schön, of course: Ebel's was not a 'religion within the boundaries of reason' in the Kantian sense, but rather a reason within the boundaries of religion. Reason, in his thinking, was not the precondition and legitimate test of belief, but the handmaiden and tool of religious faith. Ida von der Gröben captured this view of the matter when she observed in a letter to the king's younger brother, Prince William of Prussia, that only the 'reasoned understanding of the Bible using the key supplied by the recognition of the two original entities' was capable of restoring nominal Christians of the modern type to a faith in the truth of the Bible.[49] In any case, it is important to note that Ebel did not absorb the Schönherr doctrine wholly into his thinking and teaching. What he did absorb was the notion that creation was not a completed event, but an ongoing process. The idea that the cosmos might owe its existence to a collision between water and light (fire) had a certain resonance in an era fascinated by steam power.

Linked with these ideas were important ancillary psychological and therapeutic impulses. Of these, the most striking in contemporary eyes was the prominence assigned to women – the majority of the senior associates of the Ebel circle were women. Hostile observers described the group as a 'Frauenkirche', macabrely attractive to 'women and effeminate males'.[50] It was notable that women were in a number of prominent cases assigned direct moral authority over men. Coupled with this was a distinctive emphasis on the importance of reciprocity in marriage, the effort to cultivate an open and frank relationship with sexuality (if only to diminish its power over the psyche) and the cultivation of a joyful and unforced form of sociability among the adherents, a sociability that did not exclude very intimate platonic relations between men and women. Only through Ebel's sermons, Ida von der Gröben reported, did she become aware for the first time that Christianity can serve every need, including the needs of the intellect, and that this was 'the religion of awareness and therefore also of joy'. She had learned, moreover, that 'Christians were not servants, but rather children, volunteers, friends of God'. And the preacher – here she touched on the core of Ebel's style as a pastor and teacher – 'was not the lord over the faith of his congregation, but rather the facilitator of their happiness'.[51] Many contemporary testimonies in support of Ebel touch on this notion of happiness. The word 'fun' (Spass) was not yet in use in this sense, but it comes close to capturing what they meant. It was fun to be around Ebel – at least for women like Ida von der Gröben. It was said of several members of the Ebel congregation that his preaching and pastoral advice had awakened them from years of melancholy, rendering them capable of taking pleasure in everyday life. Ebel himself testified in court that he had sought clerical office only because he wanted to help people. He did not say, interestingly enough, that he had hoped to serve God. In other words: the Ebel group was not a frontal attack on reason, but rather an exotic religious effort to find an accommodation with it.

That the clergymen of the Union Church in Königsberg should have reacted so allergically to these events is perhaps unsurprising. With their peculiar cosmogony and the therapeutic oddities of their pastoral method, Ebel and Diestel were out of the ordinary, at a time when there was a premium on rigorous compliance with the liturgical and theological culture of a composite state church that was still struggling to establish itself in many parts of the kingdom. The orthodox theologian Olshausen, a former adherent who subsequently broke with Ebel, had a point when he observed that the theory of the two primal spheres left very little room for God in the narrative of creation – where was God when the two balls were rolling about in the nothingness?[52] Others, like the consistorial councillor Ludwig August Kähler, regretted the element of rancour and division introduced by Ebel and his associates into the religious life of the city.[53] But there were other motives too. Ebel was for a time the most popular preacher in Königsberg. The Altstadt church was so full on Sundays that all of the side-chapels and other adjoining rooms were filled with worshippers – and this at a time when in many of the city's churches only a few faithful congregants or none at all could be seen attending services. His elevated social connections appeared to provide him with a special leverage. Collegial envy reinforced professional indignation.

In retrospect, it is the vehemence of the public attacks on Ebel and Diestel that commands our attention. Their energy reverberates in the polarized printed sources generated by the scandal.[54] Behind the partisanship for 'reason' was concealed an unarticulated and unexamined emotional and psychological investment in the idea of a male-dominated social order. Women – stripped naked, seduced, contaminated, impregnated – played a prominent role in denunciations against the group. A fastidious horror resonated in contemporary commentary: 'This matter is so dreadful, so horrifying,' Schön confided to Minister Altenstein, 'that one can scarcely find the words to express one's disgust.'[55] It was precisely the fact that women from the best families of the city had been encouraged to rethink their marital relationships, that prominent single women had been delighted and satisfied by the relationships they had forged within the circle, that they had vouchsafed to Ebel a trust that they denied their husbands and male kinsmen, that enraged the city's liberal elite. Theodor von Schön's sister-in-law Ida von der Gröben was exactly such a case. For the widowed countess, who had sunk into depression after her husband's death, the encounter with Ebel inaugurated a new life; after Ebel's release from prison in 1841, she moved with him to Ludwigsburg, where she remained until his death in 1861.

That the sleep of reason engenders monsters is proverbial, but this adage is often taken to mean that monsters are born when reason is disempowered. In the context of the *Mucker* trial of 1830s Königsberg, however, one could read these words in another way: namely that the dreams of reason can themselves be monstrous. The grotesques conjured up by the liberal press – choirs of naked women, polygamous unions, kisses so obscene that to describe them would incur legal sanction – were not images of what had transpired around Ebel, but the fantasies of a liberal imagination anchored in the idea of a world composed of compact clan and household units governed by independent and authoritative males. And this returns us to the reflections on the emergent public sphere with which I opened this essay. That the public sphere played a crucial role in the Königsberg troubles is without question. One might even admire the skill with which the city's elite helped to build the negative publicity generated by the scandal and the subsequent trial. But it cannot be said that the publicity around this case exemplifed the 'reason-giving' virtues of the Habermasian public sphere, or that it created a climate in which 'the best argument won'. What we have here is not the triumphant demonstration of the Habermasian ideal type, but one rather dark – if far from definitive – glimpse of the historical conditions in which the idea of an exclusively liberal and rational public sphere was born. In this connection, one might say that the efforts of sociologists and political scientists – including Habermas himself – to find a place for religion in the discourse of the public sphere represent a belated symbolic victory for the *Mucker* of Königsberg and their forlorn demand to be heard by the city authorities.

The history of Prussia has often been seen as an interplay of light and darkness. In the process, complex interactions have sometimes been reduced to confrontations between opposed historical principles: progress and reaction, light and darkness, reason and superstition. But reason could be a strict mistress, a tyrannical one even, when her champions sought in her name to impose on the incorrigible a better way of thinking and living. As a reformer, as an opponent of the Berlin police state and as a Prussian federalist Schön is a sympathetic figure in our eyes. We rightly see in him one of the luminaries of early-nineteenth-century German liberalism. But the light was not always on his side and his opponents were not always immersed in darkness.

The Kaiser and his Biographer

On 16 March 2013, John Röhl, the celebrated British-German biographer of Kaiser Wilhelm II, was awarded the Einhard Prize for European Biography, named for the famous biographer of Charlemagne. The award was conferred in Seligenstadt, where Einhard lived from 830 as a lay abbot and died in 840. Across the span of almost 1,200 years, two imperial biographers shook hands. And there are, it must be said, some similarities between the two. Like John Röhl, Einhard wanted, as he himself put it, to capture not just the 'public', but also the 'domestic life and in no small way the deeds' of his subject. And both Röhl and Einhard have shaped the memory of their respective protagonists in a lasting way. In 1917, the French scholar Louis Halphen wrote of the still dominant influence of the *Vita Caroli Magni*. Even after eleven centuries, he noted, no one would set about studying Charlemagne without first consulting Einhard's *Vita Caroli*.

The same can be said of John Röhl. It is impossible to contemplate Wilhelm II – and indeed the entire era of the German Empire – as a field of historical knowledge without John Röhl. With his monumental studies of the Kaiser, his court, the political and moral life of the imperial entourage – the essence, in short, of what Walther Rathenau called 'Wilhelminism' – he has created a lasting memorial. It is hard to imagine that anyone will ever surpass, or even match, his mastery of the sources or his familiarity with Wilhelm II and his milieu.

But this is the point at which the commonalities between the biographers of the first and last emperor come to an end. Einhard spent part of his life as a courtier. In a mocking reference to his small stature, his friend Theodulphus compared him – friends can always be counted on for this kind of thing – with an ant hastening about everywhere in pursuit of his business. Einhard wrote his *Vita* not just because he wanted – in his own words – to preserve the memory of 'the glorious [. . .] deeds of the excellent and greatest king of his time', but also because he felt personally obliged to the deceased emperor: 'the care' he had enjoyed at court and 'the friendly relations that I entertained with the [emperor] and his children'. All of this, Einhard writes, 'has placed me in his debt'. And this relationship may help to explain why Einhard's depiction of Charlemagne is perhaps a little too smooth and one-sidedly positive. The British medievalist Charles Previté-Orton even accused Einhard of *suppressio veri* (suppression of the truth) in those passages where questionable or ill-conceived decisions by the hero are passed over in silence. The *Vita Caroli* is in this sense not a biography of the modern type, but rather an idealized portrait of his subject, shot through with pretty phrases and rhetorical flourishes cribbed from Roman Antiquity.

John Röhl could scarcely be more different. His three-volume biography of the last German Kaiser is no song of praise, but a work of rigorous reconstruction, bearing all the hallmarks of history as a modern critical discipline, drawing on a profound knowledge of the sources and on decades of archival research. In the pages of his great work we meet the last Kaiser in all his contradictions, impulsiveness and energy, alive and three-dimensional before our eyes. Every false move – and there were many – every marginal jotting, every indiscretion is painstakingly tabulated and interpreted. Whereas Einhard strives to observe 'the greatest possible concision', in order 'not to frighten away those who did not care to learn anything new', John Röhl aims squarely at comprehensiveness. The source material is exhaustively compiled and documented. In his striving for exhaustiveness Röhl demonstrated a stubbornness that verged on bloody-mindedness. He wrote no fewer than seven times to the archives of Potsdam and Merseburg in what was then the German Democratic Republic asking for access to the files. Seven times he was turned away. When the eighth request arrived, they finally caved in. With indefatigable industry, a remarkable nose for new sources and deep commitment, Röhl has illuminated the life of the last German Kaiser from every possible angle.

It has not been a labour of love. In *Young Wilhelm* (the English translation appeared in 1998) readers were introduced to a brash, awkward, pasty-faced youth, slow at his lessons, arrogant, emotionally cold, oversensitive and prone to outbursts of rage. Ear infections, gauche effusions of oedipal love and early sexual adventures were analysed in as much detail as the sources allowed, all with a tone of fastidious disgust, as if Röhl were examining an unsightly and venomous species of amphibian. Nevertheless, the book became a bestseller in Germany and it is easy to see why. Because life is flowing in this volume – the life of individuals but also of the state itself. It is a peculiarity of monarchy as a state form – and surely one source of its fascination – that it places at the apex of the state not an elected president or representative with a limited tenure of office, but a family. Already as a baby, the person who will later be a king is the object of legitimate public interest. His birth, his education, the company he keeps, his physical and mental health, his relationships with his closest relatives, his sexual orientation and behaviour, his betrothal – indeed every facet of his growth into maturity are political facts. In this way, the airy formulae of a constitution acquire concrete, biological form, they are clothed in 'flesh and blood'. No one has penetrated deeper into the thicket of issues that arise from this state of affairs than John Röhl. The result is a capacious, comprehensive work with all the breadth, detail and emotional intensity of a late-nineteenth-century novel. At the centre of the narrative are Wilhelm and his parents – an irascible but ineffectual father and a fussy, intelligent, power-obsessed mother. Around them, Röhl meticulously reconstructs the riven world of the Prussian-German court.

As his protagonist matures into an autonomous political actor, Röhl broadens the context of his narrative to encompass the imperial political structure, dynastic diplomacy and foreign policy in the late Bismarckian era. What emerges from this account is above all the extent to which Wilhelm's early adulthood was shaped by the bitter factional strife at the Hohenzollern court. When Wilhelm II was born in 1859, his grandfather had not yet ascended the Prussian throne. He would do so shortly before Wilhelm's second birthday, in January 1861. Nearly three decades were to pass before the grandfather died, at the age of ninety, in March 1888. From an early age then, Wilhelm was in a position to observe that his father was not the ony person who commanded respect. Above him there was another, greater father, a figure of almost mythical reputation with the gravitas and whiskers of a biblical patriarch. The grandfather was not only the ruler of a kingdom (Prussia) and, from 1871, the founder of an empire, but also the head of his household, a fact with far-reaching implications for the family life of his living descendants. To complicate things further: from the 1860s, Wilhelm's parents, and particularly his mother, formed an oppositional court 'party' that was hostile to the illiberalism of Bismarck and the reigning monarch and provided a focal point for progressive political aspirations. The young Wilhelm thus faced a choice: he could align himself with his parents against his grandfather or he could align himself with Wilhelm I and Bismarck against the court of his father. Encouraged by Bismarck, who deftly exploited the prince's appetite for public recognition, Wilhelm soon established himself as a stalwart supporter of the 'reigning party', a role that involved spying on and conspiring against his own father. It was Germany's misfortune, Röhl notes, that the liberal, anglophile potential embodied in Wilhelm's father, Frederick, and his mother, Vicky, the daughter of Queen Victoria, was never given the chance to realize itself. The book closes on a menacing note with the warning that Wilhelm, once installed on the throne, would prove to be 'the Nemesis of world history'.

Röhl is reticent on the vexed question of exactly how differently Germany's political culture might have evolved had Wilhelm's father, Kaiser Frederick III, not died prematurely of cancer after only ninety-nine days on the throne. But the trope of the 'lost liberal generation' has looked less plausible since the appearance of Frank Lorenz Müller's study of Frederick, *Our Fritz: Emperor Frederick III and the Political Culture of Imperial Germany* (2011), which showed that the crown prince's political vision, though it encompassed a number of liberal commitments, was in fact much more authoritarian than most accounts have allowed. Müller showed that Frederick's understanding of the German monarchy was constitutional, but not necessarily parliamentary. There was, Müller argues, much less blue water between Frederick and Bismarck than has generally been supposed. Indeed, by the mid-1880s, Frederick and Bismarck had come to a close, partly implicit agreement on how Germany would be run after the death of Wilhelm I. In other words: once in power, the 'liberal generation' may have been less liberal than expected.

In volume two, Röhl takes up the story at Wilhelm's accession and we follow an increasingly autocratic thirty-something Kaiser through the nervous 1890s. This is terrain that Röhl knows like the back of his hand and he offers a fine-grained account based on an exhaustive analysis of the documents. The state papers stashed at Bismarck's rural retreat in Friedrichsruh are combed for incriminating imperial marginalia. The highly informative Waldersee diaries are cited from their archival originals, not from the heavily bowdlerized edition published by Heinrich Otto Meisner in the 1920s and still widely used by historians. There is a wealth of detail on the young Kaiser's infatuation with the navy, his hostility to the conservatives, his role as the head of his dynastic house and his interventions in the sphere of cultural policy and the arts. The reader gains a sharp sense of the texture of the Kaiser's life from one year to the next – the court occasions, the public appearances, the journeys by train, car and boat, the trips to England, the endless circuit of diplomatic appointments at home and abroad. There are recherché details of life at court, such as the 'battle with wet towels between the Tsar and his son on one side and Wilhelm and his brother Heinrich on the other' that followed a dinner at the Peterhof in 1888.

A gallery of unlovely portraits crowds Röhl's pages: the brutish and manipulative Herbert von Bismarck (son of Otto), the grossly paranoid and antisemitic Alfred von Waldersee, the fawning and obsequious 'best friend', Philipp von Eulenburg, the unscrupulous intriguer Friedrich von Holstein, the sallow and opinionated princely tutor Hinzpeter and many more. But Röhl reserves his sternest judgements for Wilhelm himself. The preface to this volume opens with a clarion denunciation of the book's subject: 'After many decades of neglect, Kaiser Wilhelm II is at last coming to be recognized internationally as the powerful and pernicious ruler that he actually was, a kind of missing link, as it were, between Bismarck and Hitler ...'

One could hardly ask for a pithier summary of Röhl's two main contentions. The first of these is that the Kaiser was very bad (he was supposedly mad, too, but I will come to that later). We read of the monarch's 'narcissistic coldness' and 'dynastic arrogance', his unhealthy curiosity about the sexual life of other monarchs, his haughty condescension towards the princes of the Balkan states, his antisemitic prejudice and his 'war-like' moods. When Wilhelm undertakes an action or makes a remark, he does so not prudently or kindly, but 'self-righteously', 'spitefully' or 'contemptuously'. As if this were not already bad enough, Wilhelm was also – Röhl's second key claim – very powerful. He was 'almost invincible', his 'pernicious influence' and 'explosive force' transformed German politics; his 'restless and scheming political activity' had 'international consequences', his passion for the navy was 'catastrophic for Germans and the world'.

Even in biography, the most sanctimonious of the historiographical genres, it is unusual to encounter this kind of sustained denigration. The problem has less to do, it seems to me, with the truth value of the characterization than with the way in which the consistent attribution of base motivation can impoverish and distort our understanding of the subject's actions. It leads, firstly, to a drastic narrowing of context. The Kaiser did, to be sure, show an interest in the sexual conquests of other monarchs, but was this so unusual as to raise questions about his 'psycho-sexual constitution'? The diplomatic correspondence of the Wilhelmine Empire, as indeed of most other European states, was full of scandals, sexual and otherwise, and the content of today's daily newspapers does not suggest that adult human beings on the whole are bored by each other's sexual activity. Then there is the temptation to interpret all actions in reductionist terms that accord with the negative evaluation of character. To give just one example: when Wilhelm is frank about his grievances against his English relatives, he is faulted for his tactlessness and self-absorption. But when in 1895 he writes to his grandmother Queen Victoria of the 'ties of esteem and friendship excisting [sic] between our two navies', Röhl denounces the letter as 'bordering on hypocrisy'. Wilhelm, it seems, is damned if he does and damned if he doesn't.

Fortunately, Röhl is so scrupulous in his handling of the sources and so full in his citations – the book includes numerous passages of cited material, some extending over many pages – that the reader is generally free to dissent from the biographer's assessment. Take, for example, the letter in which Wilhelm explained to Queen Victoria his reasons for despatching the controversial 'Kruger Telegram'. In December 1895, a political crisis blew up when a British force in the Cape Colony mounted an illegal raid on the Boer Republic of

Transvaal. On 3 January 1896, after news had reached Berlin that the raid had been defeated, the Kaiser sent a personal message to the president of the republic, Paul Kruger. The 'Kruger Telegram', as it came to be known, wished the president a happy new year and congratulated him on having defended the 'independence of his country against external attack' without 'appealing for the help of friendly powers'. The British newspapers responded to this innocuous communication with a torrent of rage, and Queen Victoria fired off an angry letter rebuking her grandson for his 'outrageous' and 'dreadful' telegram. In reply, Wilhelm composed a mild-mannered epistle to his 'Most beloved Grandmama' defending his decision to despatch the telegram. Why then should Röhl dismiss this text as 'hypocritical' or as 'one of the strangest documents [Wilhelm] ever penned in English'? As Röhl himself has discovered, the Kaiser's letter was cleared with the responsible German politicians; it makes a succinct and inoffensive case for Germany's actions while at the same time gently exposing the inconsistencies in the British reaction. Victoria's observation that the letter was 'lame and illogical' – which Röhl cites approvingly – does not reflect a balanced analysis of the text, but rather the queen's intensely partisan perspective on the Transvaal crisis.

As this example suggests, Röhl interweaves his own commentary with a dense tapestry of contemporary citation. The voices of the chief actors resound through the volume. At some points the clamour can be almost disorienting – Röhl takes us into a house of mirrors in which we perceive each player through the eyes of others. He defends this technique on the grounds that it demonstrates that the book's interpretation is not his alone, but 'also very much that of the people directly involved'. But if sources from close to the Kaiser are used to authorize or even replace an interpretative meta-narrative, there is the risk that we may gain colour and intimacy, but lose analytical distance. This, perhaps, is one of the areas where the imperatives of biography and those of history remain unreconciled.

Did the Kaiser really wield the kind of power attributed to him in this volume? It is worth noting that Röhl has, over the years, mellowed somewhat on this question. He has abandoned 'personal rule' – a key term in his earlier works – in favour of the fuzzier concept 'personal monarchy'. Yet he remains convinced of Wilhelm II's immense power and influence. By the later 1890s, he suggests, both the Reich and the Prussian governments were putty in the Kaiser's hands, 'mere administrative organs' carrying out his 'imperial commands'. As for his freedom of action in the sphere of foreign policy, this was 'infinitely greater', for it was unrestrained by the need to consult parliament. Two things above all sustained the monarch's pre-eminence: the imperial power of appointments that allowed the emperor to select the leading personnel within the Prussian and Reich administrations, and the 'kingship mechanism' by which obsequious courtiers and politicians vied with each other to carry out or anticipate the monarch's will.

Here, as I see it, Röhl overstates the case. Even in the 1890s, the era par excellence of personal rule, the power of the emperor remained subject to formidable constraints. The peculiar indeterminacy of the German constitution permitted the concentration of power in the hands of the sovereign, but also facilitated its dissipation, allowing it to change hands unexpectedly, especially in the context of the pivotal relationship between the Kaiser on the one hand and 'his' chancellor and generals on the other. The Kaiser could use his power of appointment to weaken the government, as he did in the ministerial reshuffle of 1897–8. But he was unable to develop or realize a domestic political programme of his own, or even consistently to impose his will on the executive. The debacle of the Anti-Socialist Bill and the later Canal Bill – both of which were publicly backed by the Kaiser and both of which were thrown out by parliament – revealed the system of concentric constraints that impeded the monarch's exercise of power. Nor did the Kaiser's appointment of 'favourites' to key offices necessarily translate into an aggrandizement of his power. This was partly because imperial placemen, once installed, tended to go their own way – the most striking example is Chancellor Bernhard von Bülow, who came to office with assurances of fealty and love for his imperial master but soon emerged as an arch-manipulator who was quite prepared to sacrifice the reputation of the Kaiser on the altar of his own ambition. But a more fundamental problem was the Kaiser's utter inability to devise or follow through a coherent political programme of his own.

This is where we encounter one of the central tensions in Röhl's view of Wilhelm II. The 'kingship mechanism', borrowed from

Norbert Elias's analysis of the absolutist court of Louis XIV, can only work in a political sense if the monarch's objectives are known to all and can be anticipated by his courtiers. But this was hardly true of Wilhelm II, for, as Röhl himself makes clear, his goals changed drastically from one moment to the next. He picked up ideas, enthused over them, grew bored or discouraged, and dropped them again. He was angry with the tsar one week but infatuated with him the next. He was supportive of Austria but also on occasion keen to appease and win over the Serbs. He was hugely excited by the idea of Zionism in 1898, and even pledged his support for the movement at an extraordinary meeting with Theodor Herzl. But he soon lost interest when it became clear that the Ottoman sultan was hostile to the idea of a Jewish homeland within the compass of his empire.

Indeed, the Kaiser's proneness to short-lived enthusiasms was one of his most widely remarked character traits. He was, Holstein observed, 'unfortunately very impressionable'; his sometime intimate Herbert von Bismarck described him as 'tractable, sensible and easy to win over'. Bismarck the elder famously remarked that the Kaiser was apt to wander off at any moment 'like a balloon'. None of this means that the Kaiser was unimportant. However, it does suggest that his significance lay less in the imposition of an autocratic will than in a chronic failure of leadership.

Was the Kaiser insane? Röhl has long been arguing that he was, and he reiterates the claim in this volume. However, readers familiar with the earlier work will notice that the ground of the argument has shifted. In the 1970s, Röhl speculated that the Kaiser's idiosyncrasies might be linked to a repressed homosexual orientation. In the 1980s, he began to develop the argument that the Kaiser suffered from a 'character neurosis' resulting from brain damage incurred during his birth. The first volume of the biography developed this diagnosis over eighty pages of detailed obstetrical analysis, in which Röhl made a case for the view that Wilhelm was deprived of oxygen during delivery and consequently was born with a 'minimal cerebral dysfunction', a condition that has been linked in recent medical research with hypersensitivity, irritability and lack of concentration and objectivity in adults.

It was this 'organic psychosyndrome', Röhl argues, that predisposed

Wilhelm to a 'secondary neuroticization' brought on by the rigours of his childhood – the esoteric therapies deployed to enliven his paralysed arm, the 'head-stretching machine' used to straighten his neck, the rigours of his tuition regime, and so on. But if the Kaiser's childhood was hard, it was not loveless. Whereas Thomas Kohut argued that Wilhelm's parents failed to provide the kind of emotional support required to foster the maturation of a 'cohesive and well-integrated self', Röhl finds no evidence for the view that Wilhelm's early development was disrupted by a deficiency of parental love. On the contrary, Röhl contends, the emotional tone of the crown prince's household was unusually warm and affectionate by the standards of dynastic households at the time. Röhl also tackles the black legend of the 'Hinzpeter regime'. Georg Ernst Hinzpeter, tutor to Wilhelm and his brother, figures in the best-known older biographies of the Kaiser as a thin-lipped, unsmiling and sadistic figure whose rigorous pedagogical system warped young Wilhelm in his tender years. Röhl demonstrates that there is more myth than reality in this picture; his account reveals a pedagogue of liberal inclinations and progressive instincts, whose relations with the princes were amiable (it is notable that Wilhelm remained closely attached to his tutor in later life).

Between volume one and volume two, Röhl's explanation for Wilhelm's mental abnormality shifted. In the 1990s, Röhl became involved in an interdisciplinary collaboration with two geneticists from University College, London, the highlight of which came when the trio were granted permission to exhume Wilhelm's long-dead sister Charlotte in Thuringia, in order to test her remains for the gene mutation that causes porphyria. Her corpse tested positive and Röhl suggests in the volume under review that Wilhelm may himself have suffered from a form of *porphyria variegata* inherited from his great-great-grandfather George III. Indeed the book closes with a quotation from the diary of Lord Esher, a close friend of Wilhelm's cousin and enemy King Edward VII (though not, it should be noted, a doctor): 'I am sure that the taint of George III is in [the Kaiser's] blood.' It seems that the passing enthusiasms of popular science (sexual psychology in the 1970s, neurology in the 1980s and genetics in the 1990s) have left their mark here. At any rate, the case for each of these diagnoses (or all of them combined) must remain speculative, since there is no direct evidence for repressed homosexuality, cerebral damage or porphyria in Kaiser Wilhelm II. (The Kaiser's sister, who clearly *was* congenitally ill, is another matter.)

In January 1904, King Leopold II of Belgium came to Berlin to attend a birthday dinner for Kaiser Wilhelm II. The two monarchs were seated next to each other and everything was going nicely until the Kaiser suddenly raised the question of a possible future French attack on Germany. In the event of a war between Germany and France, Wilhelm explained, he would naturally expect the Belgians to side with Germany. Warming to his theme, he added that if they were to do this, he, the German Kaiser, would see to it personally that Belgium was rewarded after the conclusion of hostilities with territories annexed from northern France. As for King Leopold himself, if he stood by Germany he could expect to be rewarded with 'the Crown of Old Burgundy'. When the king of the Belgians, unsettled by these speculations, countered that the ministers and parliament of his country were hardly likely to approve of such far-flung plans, Wilhelm became flustered. He could not respect a king, he replied, who felt himself answerable to ministers and to parliament rather than to God alone. 'I will not be trifled with!' he snapped. 'As a soldier, I belong to the school of Frederick the Great, to the school of Napoleon. If Belgium does not go with me, I will be guided solely by strategic considerations.' Leopold is reported to have been so upset by this exchange that, on rising from the table, he put his helmet on backwards.

The career of the last German Kaiser is littered with effusions of this kind. They range from the gross and offensive to the bizarre or merely foolish. This ruler spent most of his waking hours talking, arguing, shouting, speechifying, preaching, predicting, threatening, telegraphing, interviewing and generally unbosoming himself of his latest preoccupations to whomever happened to be within earshot. The Kaiser was like a Tourette's tic at the heart of the German state executive. Even when he made the utmost effort to restrain himself, the indiscretions kept slipping out.

The summit meetings between the German and Russian leaderships at the Baltic port of Paldiski in the summer of 1912 are a case in point. On instructions from the German ambassador in St Petersburg, the Kaiser had been told to avoid tendentious conversation topics and to adopt a 'listening attitude' wherever possible so that the tsar would be able to get a word in edgeways. For the most part Wilhelm succeeded in reining himself in. But then, after the first lunch on board the Russian imperial yacht *Standart*, the Kaiser drew Sergei Sazonov, the Russian foreign minister, aside and spoke to him ('at him' might be a more appropriate locution) for over an hour in detail about his relationship with his parents who, he claimed, had never loved him. Sazonov later recalled this as a shocking illustration of the German emperor's 'marked tendency to overshoot the boundaries of the reserve and dignity that one would expect of someone in such an elevated position'.

On the second day of the visit, during a tour in crippling heat of the ruined fortifications constructed around the port by Peter the Great, William again forgot his instructions and buttonholed the Russian prime minister, Vladimir Kokovtsov, on one his latest hobby horses, the importance of establishing a pan-European oil trust that would be able to compete with American Standard Oil. The conversation, Kokovtsov recalled, 'became extremely animated and went beyond the limits set by court etiquette':

> The sun was scorching. The Tsar did not want to interrupt our conversation, but behind Emperor Wilhelm's back he made signs of impatience to me. The Kaiser, however, continued to answer my arguments with increasing fervour. Finally the Tsar seemed to lose all patience, approached us, and began to listen to our conversation, whereupon Emperor Wilhelm turned to him with the following words (in French): 'Your Chairman of the Council does not sympathize with my ideas, and I do not want to permit him to remain unconvinced. I want you to allow me to prove my point with data collected at Berlin, and when I am ready I should like to have your permission to resume this conversation with him.'

It is worth picturing this scene – the glare of the sunlight on the broken stone of the old fort, Kokovtsov sweltering in his jacket, the Kaiser red-faced, gesticulating as, oblivious to the discomfort of his companions, he unfolds the ramifications of his theme, and behind him the tsar, trying desperately to end the ordeal and get the party out of the sun. No wonder the German Kaiser was a figure of terror on the royal circuit.

Among the company of the royal 'club' that still ruled Europe in the years before 1914 the German Kaiser's inordinate loquacity stood out. Tsar Nicholas II was retiring by nature and George V was painfully shy. Scarcely a peep was heard in public from the elderly Austrian emperor Franz Joseph, a notoriously austere and laconic figure. And the contrast is heightened in retrospect by the fact that virtually everything the Kaiser said, no matter how risible, was recorded and preserved for posterity. One consequence is that the reputation of this monarch has been shaped (as it was for contemporaries) much more by what he said than by what he did.

In the third and final volume of John Röhl's immense biography of Wilhelm II, the Kaiser's voice is the thread that holds the text together. He babbles at us on page after page, bombarding his interlocutors (and the reader) with fantastical geopolitical speculations, crackpot plans, sarcastic asides and off-colour jokes. Reading Wilhelm on every conceivable subject for over 1,200 pages (over 3,000 if you read the three volumes in sequence) is a disorienting experience, to say the least. It is rather like listening for days on end to a dog barking inside a locked car. And the effect is heightened by the fact that volume three is focused more narrowly on the person of the monarch than its predecessors – there are fewer excursions into the life-worlds of the imperial elite and fewer pen portraits of friends and associates.

Even more than the other two volumes, the third is focused on the claim that Wilhelm II possessed immense personal power, and that he wielded this power to catastrophic effect. Right up until 1914, Röhl declares, Wilhelm II 'controlled every fundamental decision on matters of personnel, armaments and foreign policy'. His power in domestic politics may have been undermined by the crises of the Eulenburg scandal of 1907–9 (when the homosexuality of persons close to the emperor was exposed by a liberal smear campaign) and the *Daily Telegraph* Affair of 1908 (when the Kaiser's jejune remarks to a British journalist triggered a media storm across Germany), but in the sphere of foreign policy his 'decision-making power' continued undiminished. In short: this was the man who 'steered' Germany and Europe 'into the vortex of the world war'.

Did the Kaiser really wield this kind of power? How important were his interventions in shaping the course of German foreign policy? The main obstacle to answering these questions is simply that Wilhelm's objectives in this sphere were anything but consistent. Had the Kaiser pursued throughout his reign a clear and coherent political vision or programme, we could easily measure his influence by weighing intentions against outcomes. But Wilhelm's interventions were often impulsive shots from the hip and his objectives were diffuse and constantly shifting. Outraged by a strike among Berlin's tramway workers in 1900, the Kaiser fired off a telegram to the Guards Corps command: 'When the troops move in, I expect at least 500 fatalities.' This brutal effusion conveys something of the monarch's volatility and lack of self-restraint, but it had no consequences, since it does not appear to have occurred to anyone to act upon it. In the late 1890s, William became enthusiastic about the idea of founding a 'New Germany' in the jungles of Brazil and 'impatiently demanded' of the imperial administration that it do everything in its power to stimulate German emigration to Brazil. Nothing happened. In a conversation with Cecil Rhodes in 1899, he declared that he had always planned to acquire Mesopotamia as a German colony (that never happened; the British wound up getting it instead). A year later, he proposed to Chancellor Bülow that China should be partitioned among the great powers. In 1903 he announced that 'Latin America is our goal' and ordered the imperial admiralty staff – which appears to have been drastically underemployed – to prepare invasion plans for Cuba, Puerto Rico and New York. The result was *Operationsplan III*, presented to the Kaiser by the naval staff in March 1903. But the idea got nowhere because, among other things, the army never agreed to supply the necessary troops or logistical support. In 1906 the plan was declared 'obsolete' and filed in the archive.

The Kaiser picked ideas up, became excited about them, got bored and dropped them again. Alliance proposals flowed endlessly from the imperial pen: for an alliance *with* Russia and France *against* Japan and England; or *with* Russia, England and France *against* the United States; or *with* China and the United States *against* Japan and the

Triple Entente; or *with* Japan and the United States *against* the Entente and so on. In 1902 he proposed that Britain should be integrated into Germany's Triple Alliance with Austria–Hungary and Italy. At around the same time, the former general staff chief General Waldersee reported that the idea of a lasting 'reconciliation with France' belonged to 'the Kaiser's many plans for the future'. On the other hand, if France and Britain were to turn against Germany, Wilhelm proposed in a letter to the chancellor in 1905, the Russians should be lured into a German alliance by 'the pleasing prospect of plundering and laying waste to beautiful Gaul'.

These are not especially likeable or admirable interventions, but neither do they suggest a man with a tight grip on the policy-making process. Wilhelm II stood at the central node of the German constitution. He was the point – the *only* point – at which the civilian and military chains of command converged. But he was unable to play the kind of coordinating role that might have compensated for the absence in Germany of unified command structures comparable with the Conseil Supérieur de la Guerre in France or the Committee of Imperial Defence in Britain. And he remained incapable of developing or realizing a political programme of his own.

Did the Kaiser, as Röhl suggests, 'steer' Germany and thereby the world into the war that broke out in 1914? Does the power wielded by 'the mightiest throne on earth' hold 'the key to understanding how the world came to be plunged into the seminal catastrophe of the Great War'? Here, I must confess to being unconvinced by the case Röhl makes. To be sure, he presents a plethora of documents for the reader's inspection. And there is no doubt that Wilhelm's flamboyant, aggressive and careless language makes it easy to set him up as the inveterate warmonger.

Yet even the documents cited by Röhl suggest that Wilhelm continued right until the outbreak of war to vacillate between dovish and hawkish postures, just as he had done before. In February 1913, when a militarized Balkan stand-off between Austria and Russia stirred fears of imminent European war, the Kaiser wrote to his friend Archduke Franz Ferdinand, urging him to take the initiative in de-escalating the crisis. Austrian efforts at 'disarmament', he suggested, would delight the Russian tsar, who was about to celebrate the 300th jubilee of the House of Romanov and 'be welcomed with sheer joy all over the world'. In early and mid-October 1913, on the other hand, as a crisis broke out over the invasion of northern Albania by Serbian troops, he urged Vienna to take a hard line against the Serbs: 'Now or never! It is high time that peace and order were established down there!' And yet, in mid-December 1913, we find him pressing the Austrians to be moderate and flexible in their dealings with Belgrade and to win the Serbs over with money, concessions and officer exchange programmes.

Context, I would argue, is crucial here. When the risk of an Austro-Russian conflict was high, as it seemed to be in February 1913, Wilhelm tried to apply the brakes. In October 1913, by contrast, the risk of a major war was low, since the great powers were united in condemning the Serbian invasion of Albania. At this juncture, Wilhelm was all for taking a hard line against Austria's Balkan neighbour, precisely because the risk of serious consequences appeared so low. By December 1913, however, with tension rising between Berlin and St Petersburg over the future status of the Turkish Straits, Wilhelm once again urged caution. This pattern repeated itself throughout the reign. 'It is a curious thing,' remarked Jules Cambon, the French ambassador in Berlin, in 1912, 'to see how this man, so sudden, so reckless and impulsive in words, is full of caution and patience in action.'

Röhl offers a very different reading of the same episodes. The Kaiser, he argues, had already 'decided' in the winter of 1912 to bring about a European war by one means or another. His subsequent utterances and actions must be construed in this context. When Wilhelm hesitates or urges the case for peace, he is merely 'postponing' to a more convenient date a war that he has already decided upon as a matter of policy. Pressing the Austrians to conciliate Belgrade becomes a mere tactical move to strengthen the ally's position against St Petersburg in preparation for the instigation of a war with Russia. On the other hand, when Wilhelm assures the Austrians of his support for action against Serbia, as in October 1913, Röhl accuses him of providing the 'blank cheque' that will be cashed by Vienna in the summer of the following year.

We have here a seemingly unfalsifiable thesis. But the thesis appears unfalsifiable only if we accept that the prior imperial decision really exists. And yet, with the best will in the world, I can find in Röhl's exceptionally generous citations from the documents no evidence that such a decision occurred. I see a great deal of dangerous talk about threats and future conflicts, speculative scenarios and a worrying blend of paranoia and aggression, but no imperial 'decision for war' eighteen months in advance of the summer crisis of 1914. And it must be said that in insisting on this point, Röhl is virtually alone among scholars of the war's aetiology, even among those who join him in affirming Germany's preponderant responsibility for its outbreak.

Several problems seem to arise here. The first is a tendency to construe disparate utterances as born of a coherent intention, a particularly problematic assumption in the case of this monarch, who was the soul of inconsistency in word and action and remained so until and beyond the summer of 1914. The second is merely empirical: why, if the Kaiser wielded such immense power in peacetime, was he so easily shunted to the sidelines during the July Crisis, when, as even Röhl concedes, German Chancellor Theobald von Bethmann Hollweg took control of German policy? And why did his power collapse so irretrievably after the outbreak of war? Finally, there is the question of context.

For Röhl, 'context' means first and foremost other statements by the Kaiser or by members of his circle. The dynamics of the international setting are barely sketched in, so that Berlin appears as an island of seething aggression in an otherwise peaceable continent peopled by grandfatherly great powers keen to rub along together and keep the peace. But what if we can find analogous posturing and dangerous talk among the pre-war decision-makers of the other powers? If the deputy chief of the French general staff tells the Russian ambassador in December 1912 'that he personally is ready for war and even that he would like a war'; if the semi-official journal of the Russian general staff writes in January 1914 of an impending 'war of extermination' between the Slavs and the Germanic peoples; if the Russian minister of war inserts a leader article in a newspaper in March 1914 declaring that 'Russia is ready for war and France should get ready too', are these utterances evidence of a coherent Franco-Russian 'plan' to instigate war? Of course they are not. Rather they express the wariness and aggression of decision-makers who were willing to accept the risk that by preparing for the worst, they might help to bring the worst about. It is a striking feature of Wilhelm II's most hawkish outbursts that they were coupled not with threats of a war of aggression launched by Germany, but with the (admittedly often deluded) fear of sudden attack by another power: even the appalling birthday conversation with Leopold II in 1904 opened with the imagined scenario of an unprovoked Franco-British assault on Germany's western frontier.

Röhl's epochal work on the Kaiser opened as the chronicle of a life. It closes as an indictment. The author acknowledges as much when he describes the extensive quotations from the sources that make up such a large portion of his text as 'forensic evidence', to be compared with 'fingerprints or DNA evidence in a criminal case'. Whether the sources presented here can carry the full weight of the indictment is, in my view, doubtful. But this does not in the least diminish the magnitude of what Röhl has achieved.

It is worth emphasizing this last point, because as the debate on the outbreak of war in 1914 reopened during the anniversary year, Röhl attacked with great bitterness those (me included) who dissented from his view, accusing them of 'suppressing' key evidence of German war guilt and of wilfully distorting the past in the service of a propagandistic 'revisionism' whose purpose is to exculpate the Germany of 1914, break the spell of 'war guilt' on today's Germany and thereby reinvigorate the ancestral Germanic totems that poisoned the first half of the twentieth century. Such calumnies are wrong and unfair, but they also sell short the significance of what Röhl has done. His reputation does not hang upon his ability to prove (or not) that the First World War was deliberately planned and instigated by Kaiser Wilhelm II and twenty of his German 'paladins'. The unique importance of John Röhl's contribution lies in the scholarly depth and spacious textures of an oeuvre that has done more than any other to illuminate the summit of the imperial German state in the last decades of its existence. All of us who have ventured onto this historiographical terrain are deeply in his debt. This biography of Kaiser Wilhelm II is a meticulous and thought-provoking portrait of a beleaguered elite unsure of its place in a dangerous world, preyed upon by dark visions of catastrophe and prepared to risk everything to secure its future.

Whatever one makes of Röhl's interpretative framework and broader conclusions, his scholarship is profound and beyond reproach. This biography of the last German Kaiser is a monument not only to its mercurial subject, but also to a highly distinctive academic career. John Röhl grew up as a genuine British–German hybrid. His English mother and his German father met each other on the boat from Rostock to Devon. That was in 1938. For reasons that are no longer clear, the couple made the fateful decision to move to Germany in August 1939. Turbulent years followed: sojourns in Forst an der Neisse and Pécs in Hungary, the arrest of his father after the failed attempt on Hitler's life, escape into the American Zone, a brief spell at a Swiss school in the Berner Oberland and finally the move to England, where his mother had secured a post as lecturer in German at the University of Manchester. The little boy who in Germany had always felt himself to be 'English' was now bullied and beaten up in the playground as a 'Nazi'.

As a doctoral student under the relaxed supervision of Sir Harry Hinsley at the University of Cambridge, John Röhl studied the political history of the German Empire after Otto von Bismarck's departure from office. It was no coincidence, he would later concede, that he chose precisely that era in which his two homelands became entangled in conflict with each other. The resulting doctoral thesis became the classic *Germany without Bismarck*, which was one of the first studies of imperial politics to draw on extensive archival research and is still today one of the standard works on the period. In the later studies of Wilhelm II, that composite, German–English personality – the tension that Paul Kennedy called 'the anglo-German antagonism' – remained a central theme.

These early research decisions placed John Röhl at some remove from the partisan conflicts of the German historical profession. In the 1970s, the young scholar got a cold reception from the German historians. The older conservative colleagues resented his negative take on the German Empire. But the new generation of 'critical historians' on the left had no time for him either. They were busy constructing a post-Marxist Weberian paradigm in which history was about the epochal shifting of tectonic social structures; individuals – especially monarchs! – counted for little. Since then, Röhl suggests with a certain understandable *Schadenfreude* in the preface to volume two, the rest of the world has caught up with him. There has been a revival of interest in the workings of courts and each year sees the publication of new scholarly studies of imperial politicians, generals and even the Kaiser himself. It is due in good part to the tireless, passionate and eloquent research of John Röhl that no one would nowadays dare to write a history of the Wilhelmine Empire without taking full account of the eponymous Wilhelm who sat on its throne.

The Life and Death of
Colonel General Blaskowitz

On the morning of 5 February 1948, the day on which his trial was due to begin, Colonel General Johannes Blaskowitz climbed over the security barriers in the military prison at Nuremberg and threw himself down a stairwell. His suicide prompted shock and astonishment. Blaskowitz had little to fear from the tribunal. The prosecution's case against him was weak and his defence counsel had been given to understand that an acquittal was highly likely. It was a characteristically mysterious end to a career spent in the grey zone between courage and obedience.

Today, Johannes Blaskowitz is chiefly known for his official protests against the atrocities committed by German police formations in Poland during the winter of 1939–40. Late in November 1939, scarcely a month after his appointment as commander of the German military units in German-occupied Poland, Blaskowitz submitted a report to Army Supreme Command complaining of the disruptive impact of police unit activity. In the weeks and months that followed, he fired off several further reports with detailed lists of crimes committed against civilians. As a consequence, Blaskowitz forfeited the confidence of the regime's leadership and with it any prospect of further professional advancement. He was relieved of his post in May 1940 and relegated to the command reserve in Dresden. In October 1940, he was appointed commander of the 1st Army stationed in occupied France, where he was responsible for overseeing the training of troops destined to fight in the Soviet Union.

Perhaps the most remarkable thing about Blaskowitz's outspoken early stand against the ascendant SS empire is that it remained an episode. Blaskowitz never joined the resistance, even after he became aware that the atrocities he had protested against were not individual 'excesses' committed by 'psychically disturbed' police personnel, but the logical consequence and expression of the regime's policy. And yet, in 1944, when he took on an active command role in the withdrawal from France, Blaskowitz again made strenuous efforts to ensure that his troops complied with the traditional 'laws of war', in particular by interdicting reprisals against French civilians during operations against the resistance. Blaskowitz's story – reconstructed from archival documents – can help us to explore the ambiguous space between resistance and full compliance in a totalitarian dictatorship.

Johannes Albrecht Blaskowitz was born on 10 July 1883 in Peterswaldau in the district of Wehlau, East Prussia. His father, pastor in nearby Walterkehmen, was known on account of his penitential sermons as the 'thundering conscience' of his congregation. The son was admitted at the age of eleven to the cadet school at Köslin, from which he subsequently transferred to the Central Cadet School in Berlin-Lichterfelde. He was sixteen when he was accepted as ensign into the 18th Infantry Regiment in Osterode, East Prussia. Two years later, the family suffered a tragedy that attracted wide notice in Germany and beyond. Blaskowitz's elder brother, Lieutenant Kurt Blaskowitz, was serving in the garrison at Insterburg, East Prussia, when he fell victim in 1901 to a duel forced upon him by a fellow officer after a drunken altercation. Kurt Blaskowitz was about to be married and the altercation with two artillery officers took place after his bachelor's party. He was summoned to a military 'court of 14th honour' at Insterburg on the day of his wedding, which was postponed so that the duel could be held. Blaskowitz was killed by his opponent's first shot. The case was raised by a member of the Reichstag and was widely noted as an example of the 'antiquated German code of military honour'.[1] After this blow, Blaskowitz senior supported Johannes's military ambitions with redoubled zeal. A letter of 1902 entreating the military authorities not to delay the promotion of his eighteen-year-old son and reminding them of his recent bereavement conveys a sense of the intense paternal emotion invested in Johannes's early career.[2]

During the First World War, Blaskowitz saw action on several fronts. After a spell on the Western Front, he was assigned in the summer of

1915 to the 3rd Jäger Regiment of the Alpine Corps, where he commanded a machine-gun company in the Dolomites and subsequently led the 1st Batallion in the Serbian campaign. Early in 1916, having proved himself as a front officer, he commenced general staff training with the 10th Army Corps in France. It was as a staff officer that he took part during 1916–17 in the battles of Kowel and Riga. When the war came to an end he was serving as a liaison officer with the Austro-Hungarian Imperial and Royal 1st Honvéd Infantry Division.

During the Weimar years, Blaskowitz served in various command roles in Stuttgart, Ulm and (from 1930) Konstanz, where he took over as Commander-in-chief of the Baden Infantry Regiment. The association with Baden dated back to the years before the World War, when he had requested a transfer to the south on health grounds, and thereby acquired Badensian nationality.[3] As the most senior officer possessing local nationality he was also appointed Kommandant of the State of Baden, a post he held until the beginning of 1933. He would later view his years in Konstanz as the happiest of his professional life.

Blaskowitz was popular with the officers and men of the Konstanz regiment, who appreciated the clarity of his character and the informality of his dealings with subordinates. In a memorial essay of 1955, members of the regiment recalled his 'heartfelt warmth', his Christian commitment and his 'combative commitment to unconditional fairness'. 'We [men of the 14th Regiment] felt for and respected him not just as a commanding officer who decided the fate of many, there was more to it than that, we loved him!' A capacity to win not just the respect but also the affection of the men committed to his charge remained one of his most conspicuous attributes. The 'compelling and transformative power' of his speeches at public occasions and his 'mastery of the right word at the right time', a legacy, no doubt, of his preacher father, earned him an excellent reputation among the civilian population of Konstanz, the Baden civil authorities and even the provincial press.[4] For a man whose exotic East Prussian diction must at first have jarred in southern ears, this was no small achievement.

His charisma and personal authority helped Blaskowitz to make a success of his posting (from 1 February 1933) as inspector of the Berlin Weapons Schools, with responsibility for the education and training of aspiring army officers. Blaskowitz was known for the emphasis he placed on fitness and physical education – an area in which, as an outstanding gymnast and horseman, he had always excelled.[5] Blaskowitz oversaw the introduction of reformed ensign training courses and the new Schools of War that would permit the faster and more intensive training of officer aspirants in all weapon types. In Berlin and later (from 1 April 1935) as Commander of Military District II stationed in Stettin, Blaskowitz made an important contribution to the establishment and expansion of the young Wehrmacht. As late as 1 May 1944, an appraisal by his superior officer General Field Marshal Gerd von Rundstedt described him as an 'outstanding trainer of troops'.[6]

Little is known of Blaskowitz's political orientation during the Weimar Republic. Hellmuth Stieff, who would later play a key role in the anti-Hitler resistance, reported to his wife in August 1932 that Blaskowitz believed the parties of the Weimar parliamentary system to be 'Germany's misfortune', because 'their selfish pursuit of their own ends' hindered 'any kind of stable and useful government work'. But this did not imply any admiration for the National Socialists; on the contrary, Blaskowitz saw the rise of the Nazis as symptomatic of the Republic's malaise. 'In the event that they try any stupid moves,' he declared at an exercise for his troops in 1932, 'they will be opposed with force and we will not shrink even from the bloodiest conflict.' In order to propel Germany 'out of misery', he proposed, the government 'would have to be freed from the fetters of parliamentarism so that it could operate independently'. The key prerequisite for such independence was 'the trust of the Reich President and the power of the Reichswehr'.[7]

In short, Blaskowitz was an exponent of that Reichswehr ideology that viewed the army as a kind of foreign body within the Republic, whose loyalty was not to the currently existing political authority, but to the German Reich, understood as an imperishable and transcendent entity. According to a letter from Hans Gies, a former soldier of the 14th Baden Infantry Regiment, Blaskowitz believed so fervently in the principle that the Reichswehr must remain 'above politics', that he refused, even at home in the company of his family, to discuss the political questions of the day. Gies recalled an occasion during Blaskowitz's

Konstanz command in 1932 when the latter's wife, Anneliese, had come to him with questions about Hitler and his party 'because she was not able to speak about these things with her husband'.[8] Blaskowitz shared this commitment to a supposedly transcendent and apolitical state authority and the wish to see the Reichswehr take a more independent role in managing the destiny of the nation with many of his fellow officers. In an essay published in 1928, the sometime Chief of the Reichswehr Command, Colonel General Hans von Seeckt, set out his views on the status of the military within a republican state. He acknowledged that the 'supreme leadership of the state' must control the army, but also insisted that 'the army has the right to demand that its share in the life and being of the state be given full consideration'. The meaning of these rather obfuscating reflections was made somewhat clearer at a later point, when Seeckt observed that the German army was subordinate only to 'the state as a whole' and 'not to separate parts of the state organization'.[9] The root of Blaskowitz's hostility to the NSDAP thus lay above all in the party's demand for political power, a demand whose realization was irreconcilable with the notion that state occupied a place above politics.

The reorientation of the Reichswehr leadership after the March elections of 1933 towards a policy open to an alliance with the Hitler government and an ideological rapprochement with the Nazi movement can also be discerned in Blaskowitz, though here, too, the evidence is fragmentary and indirect. On the occasion of the unveiling of a memorial for the fallen of the World War in March 1935, Blaskowitz delivered a speech in which he depicted Adolf Hitler as God's answer to Germany's moment of need:

> And when the need was greatest, God's help was close at hand. It gave us our Führer, who drew together all of the national forces into one powerful movement and enabled the true community of the people to rise up anew, who yesterday reestablished the military sovereignty of the German people and thereby fulfilled the last will and testament of our dead heroes.[10]

The reference to the 'gathering' of 'national forces' and the resumption (in contravention of the Versailles peace treaty) of universal military service suggest a primarily instrumental and limited approval of the goals of National Socialist domestic and foreign policy, rather than a comprehensive affirmation of the ideology of National Socialism. Blaskowitz's fundamental outlook was and remained that of an avowedly 'unpolitical' conservative. He felt, one contemporary recalled, an instinctive and abiding commitment to 'tradition', he always felt 'connected and bound in duty to that which had naturally emerged and grown'.[11]

When he moved to Stettin in 1935, the fifty-two-year old lieutenant general and military district commander could afford to be satisfied with his progress. In his new post, he was the successor of Fedor von Bock, who would later ascend to the rank of general field marshal. He enjoyed the full confidence of his superiors. However, he was soon to fall from favour with the political leadership. At a military exercise attended by Hitler, Blaskowitz's views on the deployment of tank units were vehemently rejected by the dictator. Instead of seeing that 'the operative deployment of tanks brings impetus to forward movement and thereby assures superiority', Blaskowitz had supposedly characterized the tank as a mere 'heavy weapon of the infantry'.[12] Hitler immediately came to the conclusion that Blaskowitz was unsuited for higher command tasks. But for the moment, it was Blaskowitz's military superiors rather than the regime that determined his prospects of promotion. His ascent through the ranks continued: at the end of 1938, he was appointed Supreme Commander of Army Group 3. He now occupied one of the seven highest command posts of the army.[13] On 15 March 1939, he led the deployment of German troops in the occupation of Bohemia, where he wielded executive authority for a time in the name of the Army Supreme Command. At this point, Blaskowitz's relations with the Nazi regime appear to have been cordial. In a letter of 14 May 1939 signed 'Heil Hitler!', Blaskowitz thanked the officials of the Reich Ministry for Propaganda and Enlightenment who had supported his army command for their 'comradely collaboration' in the fulfilment of his military tasks.[14]

In the Polish campaign, Blaskowitz commanded the 8th Army as the northernmost unit of Army Group South. He was assigned the task of providing offensive flanking cover for the left wing of the 10th Army against Polish units believed to be encamped around Łódź-Kalisz and in Poznań Province. In order to achieve this objective,

Blaskowitz was required to keep pace with the neighbouring army as it passed through the attack zone from Gross Wartenberg via Sieradz on the River Warta and Łódź towards Warsaw, all the while remaining prepared to meet an expected Polish attack from the north. The main task, to break the troop masses of the Polish Cracow Army and thereby clear the path for an advance on Warsaw, was assigned to the 10th Army under Walter von Reichenau. But as the campaign progressed, it was Blaskowitz's 8th Army that gradually became the focal point of military operations.[15]

On 9 September, when Polish units attacking the 8th Army near Łęczyca came close to achieving a breakthrough in the direction of Łódź, Blaskowitz decided to turn his army, which was still making for Warsaw at speed, around to the northwest and mount a counter-attack against the Polish forces threatening his flank. In the Battle of the Bzura that followed – the largest of the Polish campaign – Blaskowitz's 8th army played a central role in achieving a German success. Casualties on the Polish side were 20,000, including three generals; the corresponding German figure was around 8,000. On the other hand, the encirclement and destruction of the Polish forces on the Bzura had delayed the German advance on Warsaw by several days, giving the Polish armies around Warsaw time to improve their defensive preparations. Once again, there was a confrontation with the political leadership. During a visit to the front, Hitler expressed his dissatisfaction with Blaskowitz's handling of operations, but he did not countermand the army's decision to place him in command of the final assault on the Polish capital.

For his contribution to the Polish campaign, Blaskowitz was promoted to colonel general and awarded the Knight's Cross. He was assigned at first to the command of the 2nd Army, which had been earmarked for future action on the Western Front. Blaskowitz later reported that Hitler himself had assured him that he would follow his staff to a western command role.[16] He was already on his way west in a staff car when he was stopped by an officer near Eisenach and told to call his chief, General Felber, who ordered him to return east immediately.[17] On 23 October Blaskowitz's western command was terminated and he was appointed Supreme Commander East, widely known as 'OberOst', a post that placed him in command not only over the troops stationed in Military District I (East Prussia), but also over all German units remaining in conquered Poland. Despite the impressive title, Blaskowitz viewed the reassignment as a career setback. Hitler's attention and the focal point of German military planning had already switched to the west. Not for the last time, Blaskowitz was to be kept at arm's length from the central theatre of events. His sidelining can be attributed to the continuing hostility of the dictator due to Blaskowitz's handling of the Polish campaign, although his candour in communications with his superiors no doubt also played its part. Blaskowitz later recalled a conversation with Hitler that had taken place at the end of the Polish campaign. Hitler asked him how the SS Regiment Leibstandarte, commanded by Sepp Dietrich, one of Hitler's personal favourites, had fought in Poland. Blaskowitz, who had found it difficult to control the impetuous Dietrich, replied that the Leibstandarte was 'an average unit, still inexperienced, warranting no special mention'.[18] A diary entry of 18 November 1939 by Hitler's wing-adjutant Major Engel noted that the dictator's 'long-harboured aversion' to Blaskowitz was starting to manifest itself. Hitler, it seemed, had 'never been confident [in Blaskowitz]. And he had been against entrusting him with the command of an army.'[19]

In accepting his new post, Blaskowitz acquired authority as Supreme Commander East over all German troops stationed in occupied Poland. But he exercised no direct authority over the civilian administrative organs or over the police units and deployment groups (*Einsatzgruppen*) that were increasingly active in the occupied area. Relations between the military commanders and the special police formations in Poland had cooled since the middle of September. With the successful completion of the campaign and the formal cessation of hostilities, it became increasingly clear that the police units were overstepping their formal remit to see to security and order behind the front. A number of commanders expressed their outrage at the brutal measures taken against the Polish population by the police formations without any prior consultation with the military authorities.

Hitler's response to the growing friction between military and police units in Poland was to impose a narrower definition of military executive authority in the occupied zone. On 25 October 1939, two days after Blaskowitz's appointment as Supreme Commander East, the military administration in Poland was formally dissolved. In his Order of the Day for 26 October, the new OberOst announced that the army would henceforth be confined to 'purely soldierly tasks' in the eastern occupied zones – 'it is to be freed from administrative tasks and from those relating to domestic policy'.[20] But this measure did not discourage Blaskowitz from continuing to condemn the activities of the police units in the sharpest terms.

After only three weeks in his new post, he confided in Lieutenant Colonel Helmuth Stieff, a staff officer at Army Supreme Command, urging him to bring the issue to the attention of his military superiors. Blaskowitz and Stieff had known each other since at least the early 1930s. Stieff had shared Blaskowitz's scepticism of party politics and his praetorian understanding of the army's political role. The army alone should be 'carrier of the movement' to restore German integrity and independence, Stieff had written in 1930, and must never subordinate itself to the interests of any one party, not even the National Socialists.[21] Even after the Nazi seizure of power, Stieff remained privately hostile to what he called 'the madness of one-party rule'.[22] Most importantly, Stieff shared Blaskowitz's sense of outrage at the atrocities committed by the police units against the civilian population in occupied Poland. 'The wildest fantasies of atrocity propaganda look pale beside the crimes committed by an organized band of murderers, thieves and plunderers, approved, it seems, at the highest level,' he wrote to his wife in November 1939. 'This extermination of entire family groups with women and children can only be the work of subhuman elements that no longer deserve the name of German. I am ashamed to be a German!'[23]

When Stieff's representations to Army Supreme Command failed to have any effect, Blaskowitz had a formal report prepared for the Supreme Commander of the Army, Walther von Brauchitsch. Signed on 27 November 1939, the report referred to the 'rather disturbed' relationship between the German army and 'the organs of the Security and Order Police'. So far, Blaskowitz pointed out, the police had made 'no visible contribution to the maintenance of order, but [had] merely spread terror in the population'. Since police actions were carried out in the grey uniform of the German military, they represented an 'intolerable burden' for the army. 'Summing up, it can be said that conditions within the occupied area are in urgent need of swift reorganization.' Blaskowitz justified his critique primarily by reference to the growing threat to the security of German troops in Poland. The 'current situation', he warned, would sow the seeds of a Polish military uprising and thereby make it impossible to 'exploit the country for the benefit of the German forces'.[24] The incorporation of this rationalization was crucial, because Blaskowitz's right, as Supreme Commander East, to intervene in administrative and 'interior political' questions was strictly confined to cases in which military security was affected.

To this report, Blaskowitz appended an anonymous communication forwarded to his command on 18 November. Signed 'the population of Łódż and Warsaw', this document referred to the atrocities inflicted by the SS and SD units on the 'Jewish and Polish population'. That elements of the Polish population in the occupied area should have seen in Blaskowitz an appropriate recipient for such a complaint is itself of some significance, since it suggests that local Poles were aware of the frictions between the German military and police. It is also striking that Blaskowitz should have been ready to offer himself, as it were, as the advocate of the Polish population vis-à-vis the organs of the Reich Security Main Office (RSHA). When the report was placed on Hitler's desk by Major Engel, however, the dictator flew into a rage, making 'trenchant attacks' on the 'childish attitudes' harboured by the military leadership. It was impossible, he vociferated, 'to wage a war with the methods of the Salvation Army'.[25] Whether Hitler's allusion to 'Salvation Army methods' was a reference to Blaskowitz's Christian piety, seen by other contemporaries as a conspicuous feature of his personality, is impossible to confirm, but highly likely.

Scarcely two weeks later, Blaskowitz compiled another report, no longer extant, in which further 'violations by the police, the SS and the [civil] administration' were listed. Blaskowitz went further: he had six copies made of the report and forwarded by Chief Quartermaster Erwin Jaenecke to the Army Supreme Command in Berlin. According to Blaskowitz's own later recollections, this report incorporated a list of criminal actions by German police units in Poland, including arrests of Jews, the forming of ghettos and the resulting local unrest. It was particularly critical of Hans Frank, chief of the civil administration in what was then known as the 'General Government of the Occupied Polish Areas'. Frank, Blaskowitz argued, had repeatedly authorized criminal actions in Polish cities, with the result that discipline among German troops was negatively affected, the threat of insurrection raised and the productive capacity of the Polish population compromised.[26] By this point, it seems, Blaskowitz was no longer merely informing his superiors of developments in the occupied zone – he was trying to effect a change in the attitude within the officer corps as a whole. The moment was well chosen. A decree issued by Himmler on 28 October 1939 declaring that the SS would support the illegitimate children of SS-men and that it was the high calling of German women to bear the children of departing SS-men, 'even outside the boundaries of bourgeois rules and customs', had caused deep irritation in the military, which saw in it a 'charter' allowing the SS and police to take part in illicit 'sexual activity on the home front'.[27]

On 18 December 1939, the Military Intelligence (Abwehr) officer Helmuth Groscurth travelled to the Western Front to distribute copies of the second Blaskowitz report (together with other materials) to the staffs of the three army groups. Among those who certainly saw the document were Generals von Witzleben, von Rundstedt and von Bock; Groscurth also took it to the Frankfurt Headquarters of General Ritter von Leeb, Commander-in-Chief of Army Group C, who passed the news to General Franz Halder, Chief of the Army General Staff, with the comment that the conduct of German units in Poland was 'unworthy of a cultured nation'.[28] The news of events in Poland threw an unflattering light on the comportment of Supreme Commander von Brauchitsch, who hoped by tolerating such excesses to achieve a harmonious relationship between the army, SS and police. In this way, Blaskowitz contributed to the crisis of confidence that undermined relations between the staff at the front and the Supreme Commander of the Army towards the end of 1939.

When incidents of arbitrary violence against Jews and Poles continued to accumulate in the General Government, Blaskowitz resolved to compile and submit a third report on the German occupation and its impact on the defeated population. In his notes for a presentation to the Army Supreme Command at Spala, scheduled for 15 February

1940, Blaskowitz depicted the consequences of German terror in uncompromising language. Several features of this complex document deserve emphasis. First, Blaskowitz did not merely accuse the police units in general terms of bad behaviour, but listed specific 'acts of violence'. These included thefts committed by members of the SS during house searches, the mistreatment of Jews and Poles on the streets and in shops, the illegal requisition of horses, with the result that the beet harvest had almost failed, the 'mistreatment of Jews and Jewesses', and the cohabitation of a certain SS-Untersturmführer Werner with the Jewish actress Johanna Epstein, who had changed her name to Petzold and was passing herself off as an ethnic German. The language was not sensationalist, but no effort was made to mute the horror and perversity of police actions. There was an account, for example, of the 'examination of sexual parts' that frequently took place when young women and girls were arbitrarily stopped and searched by German police. One particularly shocking account reported the case of two young Poles, a man and a woman, who were publicly beaten as they were made to dig their own graves in Tomaszow-Lublin. Traumatized, the woman began to menstruate, eliciting from a police official in a German uniform with a standard-issue military steel helmet the words: 'now she's got her period; we'll have to do without the fuckfest'. It turned out that the couple had been seized in error, in a case of mistaken identity.[29]

Secondly, Blaskowitz did not frame his report as the protest of an individual officer, but in the name of a broad stratum of German Wehrmacht commanders in occupied Poland, some of whom were named. The Wehrmacht liaison officer to General Governor Major von Tschammer und Osten, for example, was cited as reporting illegal death sentences issued by police officials, including some against Wehrmacht personnel. And the report included a letter from the Commander of Front Sector South, General Wilhelm Ulex, who had written to OberOst protesting against police atrocities and demanding the immediate dissolution of the police units. The appearance of Ulex's name will have surprised no one at Army Supreme Command. Ulex, a committed member of the Confessing Church, had already been removed from the active service list on account of political unreliability in March 1939 and was only reinstated when the invasion of

Poland was imminent and candidates for senior commands were scarce.

It has sometimes been noted that in building his case against the SS and police units, Blaskowitz made no appeal to notions of humanity or universal rights, but focused primarily on utilitarian arguments. From this, the Holocaust historian Raul Hilberg inferred that Blaskowitz was 'not outraged by the idea of drastic action, but only by the amateurish way in which the SS attempted to deal with such a massive body as 200,000 Jews'.[30] The Blaskowitz protest did not imply, Jochen Böhler has argued, a 'general rejection' of the regime's ethnic measures.[31] And Omer Bartov has emphasized that Blaskowitz's chief concern was not to prevent atrocities as such, but to keep the Wehrmacht uninvolved, 'so that the military did not have to get their hands dirty'. In this sense, Bartov suggests, Blaskowitz 'was actually legitimizing murder, just as his colleagues had done during the brutal "purge" of the SA in 1934'.[32]

Certainly, the moral compass of Blaskowitz's protest appears narrow from a present-day perspective. Among the reasons he offered for halting such police activity was the risk posed to the security of German troops by an increasingly hostile Polish population. Blaskowitz observed near the beginning of the report that the existence of an 'extensively networked organization for subversion and sabotage' supported by former cadres of the Polish army had recently been established in the Kamienna industrial district. It was 'the danger resulting from this discovery' that obliged Blaskowitz to 'formulate a general view on the question of the treatment of the Polish people'.

> Violent acts committed in public against the Jews arouse among the deeply religious Poles not just the deepest revulsion, but an equal measure of sympathy for the Jewish population, towards whom the Pole had previously adopted a more or less hostile attitude. In a very short time it will come to pass that our arch enemies in the east – the Pole and the Jew – supported, what is more, by the Catholic Church, will come together against Germany across the board in their hatred for their tormentors.[33]

Blaskowitz returned to this theme later in the document, noting that further terrorist measures would transform the Poles into a nation of resisters. It would be especially regrettable if the lower-middle-class Poles, who, 'with sensible treatment and effective German administration would peacefully and contentedly have worked for us' were to be 'driven, as it were, into the enemy camp'. In short, the main argument against the arbitrary and terrorist form of rule unfolding in German-occupied Poland appeared to be that it was and would continue to be an ineffective way of controlling Poland. It was 'absurd', Blaskowitz warned, to 'slaughter several tens of thousands of Jews and Poles, as is currently taking place'; this would neither kill off the idea of a Polish state nor 'eliminate' the Jews. 'On the contrary, the manner and means of the slaughter incurs the greatest damage, complicates the problems and makes them much more dangerous than they would be in the face of considered and target-oriented action.'[34]

In addition to these domestic worries, there was reason to fear the effect of the Polish outrages on international opinion. It was hard to imagine better material for enemy propaganda than the behaviour of the German police in Poland – and what the foreign broadcasters had already reported was 'but a tiny fraction of what has actually transpired'. 'We must expect,' Blaskowitz warned, 'that the howls of foreign protest will constantly increase, and work their damage, all the more so as these horrors really have occurred and cannot be disproven.'[35] Blaskowitz may or may not have been aware that he himself had already figured in foreign coverage of the Polish occupation. A short *New York Times* article of 30 January 1940 reporting on developments in Poland noted in a subtitle that 'Even General Blaskowitz Balks at Tactics Held Aimed at Virtual "Racial Extermination"', but provided no details on the source of this information.[36]

A recurrent theme in Blaskowitz's representations was the argument that police outrages undermined both the 'standing' and ethos of the Wehrmacht, which was 'forced to look on' as crimes and atrocities unfolded. It was not just a question of the reputation of the Wehrmacht in the eyes of the Polish population and of other outsiders, but of its internal values and standards. Particularly menacing, in Blaskowitz's eyes, was the prospect that the brutality of police behaviour might communicate itself to the troops of the regular army.

The worst damage wrought by the current conditions to the German ethnic organism is the measureless crudification and ethical degradation that will swiftly spread like a plague through valuable German human material. When senior officials of the SS and police call for violence and brutality and praise them in public, then power will very soon pass to the most violent individuals. With surprising speed, like-minded persons with disturbed personalities will gather, as has been the case in Poland in order to ventilate their bestial and pathological instincts. There is scarcely any means of restraining them, since they must feel, with some justification, that they have been officially authorized and entitled to commit any atrocity.[37]

The only solution, Blaskowitz insisted, was to immediately place the guilty individuals under the authority and jurisdiction of the military.

All of this suggests that Hilberg and Bartov were right to emphasize the limited quality of Blaskowitz's protest. There was a tendency to stress what Blaskowitz himself called the 'manner and means of the slaughter' rather than the politico-ethnic objectives underlying it. Particularly striking is Blaskowitz's own reference, as if in passing, to Jews and Poles as 'our arch-enemies in the east'.

Even so, a degree of caution is in order. Blaskowitz's official remit and his own emphatically soldierly understanding of his role as Ober-Ost encouraged him, as we have seen, to focus on issues of military security and effectiveness. But the details provided in the reports – such as the eyewitness account of German policemen torturing and mocking the young Polish woman – went beyond a merely utilitarian rationale; they were intended to awaken the rage and disgust of the reader. And while there was no principled appeal to human rights of the kind we would now expect, the invocation of humanitarian standards was implicitly present, especially in the text of the letter from Ulex, incorporated in Blaskowitz's report, which interpreted German crimes as indicative of 'a completely incomprehensible lack of human and ethical feeling'. These were not the words of someone who condoned the mass murder of men, women and children and merely wished to see it carried out in a more decorous way. And Blaskowitz presumably knew enough of his military superiors and of their political masters, who he must have assumed would be reading his report over the shoulders of the military commanders to whom it was addressed, to understand that humanitarian arguments would be less effective than utilitarian and prudential ones.

The report was a plea for a return to a traditional order of war and occupation focused on harnessing the conquered areas for German military and economic purposes. This did not preclude authoritarianism and draconian discipline. On the contrary, Blaskowitz was a hardliner in disciplinary matters and he was anxious that his superiors should understand this. Since the conquest of German-occupied Poland, he announced in the report of 15 February, German courts martial had ordered 'around one hundred executions by firing squad' for acts of sabotage and the illegal possession of weapons. Strict 'justice' of this kind was not incompatible, Blaskowitz insisted, with orderly rule in the occupied zone. The Polish population, he asserted, 'accepts this as our proper right'.

By contrast, the ethno-political campaign of extermination pursued by the SS and police would inevitably produce unending disruption and insurrection. Nowhere was his opposition to this paradigm more sharply expressed than in the proposal, at the close of Ulex's report to OberOst, that 'the entirety of the police units, together with *all their higher leaders and including all the leaders holding posts in the General Government*' who have been looking on for months as these acts of violence took place, be dissolved and replaced in one stroke by 'honourable and intact units'.[38] As these words suggest, the target of Blaskowitz's ire extended beyond Poland to the metropolitan apparatus of the SS and police empire. For all the narrowness of its moral compass, then, his protest amounted to more than a procedural critique. It was a comprehensive rejection of the terrorist exterminationism of the SS, articulated from within the boundaries of a narrowly military political consciousness and doubtless sustained to some extent – who can say for sure? – by a Christian conviction that 'was no mere inheritance from his father's rectory, to be carried about through life like a dusty inheritance', but 'a vital force that sought practical expression'.[39]

At the time when he composed his reports, Blaskowitz still hoped by this means to achieve change at the highest political level. He appears to have been unaware of the increasingly radical objectives of the political leadership, of Hitler's support for Himmler and his activities and of von Brauchitsch's almost unlimited willingness to bend the army to the will of its political masters. According to the later recollection of his staff chief in Poland, Colonel General Hollidt, the eastern command was 'at first poorly informed' about the development of policy for the eastern zone.

> Only bit by bit did it become clear from incoming reports that excesses were occurring on a large scale, but it remained unclear which acts were in accordance with orders and which were the crimes of demoralized units and groups ... Only after some time did the people around OberOst acquire the impression that all of these measures were ordered from above ...[40]

On 7 February 1940, however, only a day after Blaskowitz had compiled his third report, Walther von Brauchitsch circulated a statement to senior command posts that left readers in little doubt as to the attitude of the Army Supreme Command. 'Criticisms,' Brauchitsch warned, 'that endanger the unity and striking power of the troops', should be forbidden, since 'the solution ordered by the Führer of ethno-political tasks leads by necessity to otherwise exceptional and harsh measures against the Polish population of the occupied area'.[41] By the second week of March at the latest, it must have become clear to Blaskowitz that the atrocities committed in Poland were not excesses, but the logical consequence of the occupation policy of the SS leadership, supported by Hitler himself. On the evening of 13 March 1940, Himmler agreed, at the invitation of von Brauchitsch, to hold a lecture on racial-political measures in the occupied zone. Himmler was at first reluctant to speak on such an awkward theme in the presence of sceptics like Blaskowitz and Ulex, but ultimately agreed, with Brauchitsch's encouragement, in the interests of a fuller understanding between the army and the SS. That the address happened at all is evidence of how seriously Himmler took the deepening alienation of the military command in Poland, how anxious Brauchitsch was to restore his authority within the army, and of how eager the regime leadership was to close the fissure between army and SS in time for the assault on France.[42] The speech was a characteristically rambling and incoherent performance by the Reichsführer-SS, but it delivered a very clear picture of the regime's intentions, as Himmler's own surviving notes reveal:

> Executions – of the leading members of the resistance – very drastic but necessary – been present myself – no wild accusations by subordinates – none by me. Know exactly what is going on.[43]

It was on this occasion that Himmler made the famous assertion, noted by Ulex: 'I do nothing that the Führer does not know of.'[44] From this moment at the latest, Blaskowitz, who was present at the event with three colleagues from OberOst, could be in no doubt about the co-responsibility of the political leadership for the events in Poland. He later claimed that he had been 'unconvinced' by Himmler's address.[45] Yet the meeting also made it clear that there would be no final reckoning between the army and the SS, for the generals, far from confronting or challenging Himmler's right to act as he did, failed to question him at all on the Polish events. It was clear that, private expressions of solidarity aside, there would be no support for Blaskowitz or his arguments from the most senior military commanders.

All the same, Blaskowitz continued to compile dossiers on SS crimes in Poland. He was on the worst possible terms with General Governor Hans Frank, who resented the general's activities as an affront to his own authority and an 'infringement of his rights'. On 24 April he even appeared before the desk of Wilhelm Keitel, Chief of Wehrmacht Supreme Command, with two further dossiers, one of which contained shocking photographic evidence of Polish atrocities. Keitel refused even to open them on the grounds that these were matters for the SS that did not concern the military command.[46] A visitor to the General Government of Poland reported in late April 1940 that the Supreme Commander East continued to feel that he was still on top of the situation, that he was 'the man who in reality commands'.[47] But the truth was that Blaskowitz was now completely isolated within the top echelons of the German army.[48] On 14 May 1940 he was removed from his command. There was no protest from his military superiors.

Blaskowitz initially received the supreme command over the 9th Army, a reserve unit being prepared for the French campaign. But after only two weeks, he was removed from this post and transferred, on 30 May 1940, to the command reserve in Dresden. On 9 June 1940 came the appointment as Military Commander Northern France, but this posting, too, was terminated – apparently on the urging of Himmler – after only two weeks. From Brauchitsch came an evasive condolence letter announcing that Brauchitsch had decided to take on the role of MC Northern France himself and that no post remained that was suitable for a general of Blaskowitz's rank and seniority:

> I fully understand that this change, after such a short space of time, will be painful to you. I hope that the awareness that you rendered great service to the Fatherland at a decisive moment in this war will help you to cope with the fact that after the cessation of hostilities the possibility of an appointment of comparable significance no longer exists.

The letter ended with the assurance that only 'professional considerations' and 'no other interventions of any kind' had prompted this decision.[49]

Brauchitsch was lying: it was now evident that Blaskowitz's chances of further advancing in the service had been ruined by the Polish protests. What this meant became clear on 19 July 1940, when twelve other colonel generals were promoted to the rank of general field marshal. Each received from Hitler in person an opulent baton worth RM 6,000 paid for from the Führer's discretionary funds. In an address delivered at the ceremony, Hitler emphasized the importance of the unity of the German people and how 'absolutely necessary' it was 'that the Wehrmacht too declare itself completely for National Socialist thought'. Blaskowitz's absence was hard to overlook – he was the only colonel general not to receive promotion to general field marshal and he would remain in this position until the collapse of the regime. This was scarcely tantamount to personal ruin: as colonel general, Blaskowitz continued to receive from the regime the monthly tax-free gift of RM 2,000 assigned to officers of his rank, an arrangement introduced by Hitler in August 1940 on the model of the emperors of ancient Rome, who had doled out gifts to their generals as a means of purchasing their loyalty. Nevertheless, it was a clear sign that Blaskowitz had fallen from favour.[50]

Not until 25 October 1940 was a proper appointment found for Blaskowitz, this time as Commander-in-Chief of the 1st Army stationed in occupied northern France. This was scarcely the kind of job Blaskowitz was looking for. On 11 November 1942, shortly after the Allied landing in North Africa and following an agreement with the leaders of the Vichy government, the units of his army marched into unoccupied France without encountering any resistance. But apart from that, the Commander of the 1st Army was mainly concerned with running the military side of the occupation. Blaskowitz threw himself into training work with his usual commitment. He was tasked above all with preparing men who were destined to serve in Russia for the 'particular conditions of combat in the East'. These called for careful preparations in a range of areas, from 'practical instructions on winter hygiene' and 'the habituation of man and beast to the effects of cold and temperature change' to the special training of anti-tank troops, whose indispensability had been demonstrated by the fighting in the Soviet Union.[51]

For an officer stationed in the south of France, it was difficult, as Blaskowitz well knew, to stay abreast of the latest developments in Russia. In addition to the official reports of the Army Command, he drew on his correspondence with former colleagues now fighting in the east. In a letter of 15 September 1943, for example, Blaskowitz thanked his former quartermaster, Colonel General Jaenecke, who had supplied him with 'candid' descriptions of the situation in Russia. 'For me, having been kept away for years from the conflict, it is of course extraordinarily valuable to hear from well-informed sources how the conditions of combat have been shaped and changed with the passing years. Only [with this help] can I possibly provide my men with an approximate picture of how it may one day be with us.'[52]

In France, Blaskowitz attempted, as he had done in Poland under much less advantageous conditions, to build a constructive relationship with the local population. In the summer of 1941, Blaskowitz urged the German troops deployed to support French agriculture to 'think selflessly' about their task. It was 'not a matter of harvesting for the army itself, but far above and beyond this necessity of helping the country and its population'.[53] Here again, Blaskowitz invoked a principle he had formulated eighteen months before in his first Poland report, namely that 'acts of violence alone will not suffice to guarantee the safety and peace of the [occupied] country', which could only be secured 'through the creation of a pacified population supplied with the most necessary goods'.[54]

The first three and a half years in France were relatively uneventful. In May 1944, Blaskowitz was assigned the command of Army Group G, recently formed from the 1st and 19th Armies. The appointment coincided with an upsurge in resistance activity across the Massif Central. After the Allied landings in Normandy, resistance activity expanded dramatically. The German leadership responded with brutal counter-measures. On 17 June Blaskowitz received three letters from prefects in the Toulouse region protesting at crimes committed against French civilians by German soldiers involved in 'counter-terrorist' repressions. In his answer, Blaskowitz insisted on the right of the German army to defend itself against terrorism with all the means available to it. If fighting methods had to be applied that were 'new for western Europe', Blaskowitz went on, it should be borne in mind that terrorist methods of combat also represented a novelty for western European conditions. In such a 'treacherous struggle, where friend cannot be distinguished from foe', it was inevitable that 'from time to time innocent individuals would be among the victims'. The prevention of this shedding of innocent blood would thus be possible only if the French authorities and population themselves made the terrorist campaign impossible.[55]

Although it remained unlikely that the French population would assist the German forces in this way, Blaskowitz continued to insist that German counter-insurgency activity in the south of France be conducted as far as possible in compliance with the norms of international law.[56] In his army order of 17 June 1944, for example, he publicly distanced himself from the behaviour of those SS units that only a week before had murdered 600 women, men and children in Oradour-sur-Glane, on the pretext of a counter-terrorist campaign.

Army Group G was responsible for defending the southern French coast after the massed landings in the north. But Blaskowitz lacked the men, weapons and munitions he needed to make a success of this task. For years – first for the east and now for the Normandy front – he had been deprived of all available reserves. Only on 16 August

1944, a day after the Allied landing on the French Mediterranean coast and much too late to make a difference, did Hitler approve the necessary resources. Blaskowitz was now tasked with leading his armies back to the border of Alsace-Lorraine. Despite the efforts of the Americans to encircle the Blaskowitz armies through an outflanking pursuit, the retreat was a success.[57] Blaskowitz was rewarded with the Oak Leaves to the Knight's Cross of the Iron Cross. But at almost the same time, against Rundstedt's recommendation, he was relieved of his command and transferred once again (on 21 September 1944) to the command reserve, only to be reassigned on Christmas Eve 1944 to the command of Army Group G on the southern flank of the Western Front, and then transferred on 28 January 1945 to the command of Army Group H on the northern flank. Blaskowitz demonstrated impressive skill in managing large-scale withdrawals under heavy pressure and without air cover, but this did not suffice to earn him the respect of Hitler and his cronies, who concluded that the colonel general lacked the fortitude to 'stand and fight'.[58]

Motivated by the belief that 'we must prevail for the future of our people',[59] Blaskowitz sought to maintain the discipline of his numerically and materially inferior forces through the threat of draconian punishments. An order of 5 March 1945, signed by Blaskowitz, announced that soldiers who removed themselves from their units would be 'summarily condemned and shot' by newly created field courts martial.[60] While the armies of Army Group H were driven apart by units of the British–Canadian 21st Army Group and Holland was cut off from the Reich, Blaskowitz was appointed – on 7 April 1945! – Supreme Commander of the Netherlands, now known as 'Fortress Holland', comprising two very damaged general commands and the remains of the 25th Army. On 2 May, he collaborated with the local Allied commanders in measures designed to alleviate the subsistence crisis afflicting the civilian population of the Netherlands. But he remained strictly opposed to a separate capitulation for as long as there was still resistance in Germany. He surrendered to Lieutenant-General Charles Foulkes, Commander of the 1st Canadian Corps, on 5 May 1945, five days after Hitler had committed suicide in his bunker. His first act on returning from his meeting with Foulkes was to cancel the execution of thirty Dutch civilians who had been arrested after a skirmish with Dutch resistance fighters and were about to be shot.[61] Yet, even after the hostilities had ended and his army's weapons had been handed over to the Allies, Blaskowitz continued to order the execution of soldiers found guilty of deserting their units. On 17 May 1945, he ordered the execution of ten German soldiers who had tried to escape in civilian clothes, using borrowed Canadian rifles and ammunition.[62]

It may perhaps seem strange in retrospect that Blaskowitz neither approached the circles of the military resistance after his experiences in Poland, nor was approached by them. When he learned of the failed assassination attempt of 20 July 1944, he had a note sent to Führer HQ assuring the dictator that the soldiers of Army Group G would 'gather all the more closely around him after this appalling crime'.[63] Why he did this is now impossible to say. He may have feared that the memory of his stance over Poland would give rise to suspicion that he had been involved in the conspiracy, or he may simply have hoped to retain the monthly discretionary payments he was still receiving from the regime in the last year of the war.[64] There is no evidence to suggest that Blaskowitz ever protested against the deportation of Jews from occupied France. The army appraisal forms filed on Blaskowitz in May 1944 and April 1945 characterized his political outlook as 'National Socialist', but Rundstedt, who compiled both appraisals, may simply have been trying to protect his subordinate against further humiliating transfers – Blaskowitz certainly never joined the party.[65] In any case, it is unlikely that the reason for Blaskowitz's continuing loyalty to the regime lay in any ideological attachment to National Socialism. Much more significant was his conception of his calling as a German officer.

Blaskowitz's military professionalism enabled him to act in accordance with his principles, even when this placed him at odds with the political *Zeitgeist*. But this same professionalism also implied a narrowness of vision. Blaskowitz's avowedly apolitical stance and his military rigorism made him unsuitable for any form of political resistance. The diplomat Ulrich von Hassell, a key figure in the civilian resistance, recognized this when he visited Blaskowitz in France in October 1943, with a view to sounding out the author of the famous Polish dossiers. The result was disappointing. 'Discussion with

Blaskowitz not very fruitful', von Hassell noted in his diary. '[He] essentially sees things from a purely soldierly point of view.'[66] From this very bounded standpoint, questions about the moral character of the regime were inevitably overshadowed by duty – to his military superiors, to the troops under his command and to the German people whose fate, whatever one thought of the regime in Berlin, now hung in the balance.

Blaskowitz spent the last three years of his life in prison camps, initially at Dachau, where he spent time in a windowless isolation cell, later in the Steinlager Allendorf near Marburg and finally in the prison complex at Nuremberg. In February 1948, he was summoned to be heard as part of the 'Generals' Trial' in which 'Ritter von Leeb and Consorts' were to be tried for waging aggressive war and for war crimes committed in Poland and France. While in confinement, Blaskowitz was repeatedly interrogated on a range of questions relating to the prosecution case – his presence at summit meetings where aggressive campaigns were planned, the use of civilian forced labour on the fortifications in France, the techniques deployed in the battle against the French resistance, and the shootings of commandos and prisoners of war by units under his nominal command.[67]

The charge sheet against Blaskowitz included 'the waging of aggressive and illegal war', the forwarding and distribution of orders authorizing criminal acts against Allied military personnel (such as the Commando Order of 18 October 1942, which stipulated that enemy commandos were to be shot on capture) and the illegal employment of civilian labourers for fortification works. Blaskowitz was also accused of distributing to the units of Army Group G an order from Rundstedt stating that in sectors where resistance forces had been observed, all able-bodied men from eighteen to fifty-five years of age should be arrested for deportation to Germany. The prosecution cited the case of sixty French citizens who had been arrested in the summer of 1944 by 62nd Reserve Corps of the Army Group for deportation to Germany as labourers.[68]

Blaskowitz's defence counsel, Hans Müller-Torgow, got busy drumming up testimony in support of his client. Although there were witnesses prepared to testify to the Polish protests, the dossiers themselves could not be found. Supportive witnesses provided affidavits affirming Blaskowitz's deep Christian faith, his humane interventions on behalf of the civilians in the occupied zones under his control and his 'inner distance' from the political leadership – Müller-Torgow had assured character witnesses for the defence that statements addressing these three themes were most likely to help his client.[69] But Blaskowitz was in any case regarded as a comparatively light case and was advised by the American counsel appointed to oversee his defence that he could expect to be acquitted.

All the greater was the shock, then, when Johannes Blaskowitz, on the way back from a visit to the barber on the morning of the first day of his trial, leapt over the barrier and threw himself down the stairwell of the Nuremberg prison annexe. Friends and acquaintances puzzled over the reasons for the suicide. Some speculated that he sought by this means to avoid giving testimony that might have compromised fellow officers before the court; others suggested that even the prospect of an acquittal could not offset Blaskowitz's repugnance at the idea of acknowledging a court whose legitimacy he did not accept.[70] But these were pious projections. The defence counsel Hans Müller-Torgow, who saw more of Blaskowitz than anyone else during the last days of his life, surely hit the mark when he observed that his client had fallen prey during the last days before the trial to 'a pronounced pessimism that was out of all proportion to his actual prospects'.[71] We can glimpse this mood in a remark from one of the prisoner's last letters: 'Thinking of myself, I now see how kind God means to be when he hides our destiny from us.'[72]

In his partial and conditional rejection of specific features of the National Socialist regime, Colonel General Johannes Blaskowitz exemplifies the inadequacy of any paradigm that identifies 'compliance and resistance as the two distinguishable attitudes of the [German] population toward the Nazi state'.[73] Blaskowitz was not a resister, in the sense of someone who globally rejected and opposed the regime (by contrast both Helmuth Stieff and Helmuth Groscurth later joined the resistance and were executed for their role in it). Nor, on the other hand, does his comportment in Poland fall into the diffuse category of *Resistenz* (non-conformity), coined by Martin Broszat to capture fragmentary expressions of everyday discontent, the 'many

"small" forms of civil courage that could be expected from every contemporary'.[74] Richard Löwenthal's concept of 'refusal', denoting a
restricted resistance grounded not in principle but in less spectacular
forms of non-conformity, comes closer.[75] But Blaskowitz's protest was
not formulated in the idiom of everyday non-compliance; it was conspicuous and even provocative. Nor was it 'value-free', since it both
embodied and invoked a specific system of military values.[76] Although
we can discern certain continuities of principle in Blaskowitz's behaviour, such as his concern to operate wherever possible within the
norms of a traditional 'order of war', the episodic quality of his protest against the regime's ethno-political policies reminds us that the
relationship between compliance and non-compliance was not linear.
Many individuals 'zigzagged back and forth' between compliance and
various forms of dissent, exhibiting 'the permanence of different
modes of behaviour'.[77]

Rather than cutting the salami of non-compliance into ever thinner
taxonomical slices, we should perhaps enquire after the broader
impact of such partial rejections of regime policy. One of the distinctive features of recent work on the European dictatorships has been its
attention to the myriad alliances of convenience and modes of interaction that linked the governed with 'their' regime.[78] The Nazi regime,
like its Italian counterpart, depended for its stability and effectiveness
less on the backing of fanatical adherents than on the acquiescence
and conditional support of a majority whose interests and worldview
overlapped only partly with that of the political leadership. It has long
been understood that 'dissension and conflict' filled the lives of 'ordinary people' in the Third Reich, who were content to draw the benefits
from certain Nazi policies without wholeheartedly absorbing or
endorsing the party's doctrines, policies or propaganda.[79] The same
can be said of many of those who served the regime from positions of
high authority. In a suggestive passage of his diary, Joseph Goebbels
observed of the thuggish Waffen-SS commander Sepp Dietrich that
his value to the regime lay precisely in the fact that he was not a
National Socialist in the ideological sense and thus appealed to a constituency beyond the narrower confines of the party faithful.
Perhaps an analogous claim can be made for Johannes Blaskowitz,
a charismatic educator and leader of troops whose name remained a

byword among officers throughout the war for the determined defence of traditional military norms in the face of the most radical expressions of regime policy. Whether his troubled ambivalence and his bold stand in Poland actually weakened the regime may be doubted. The contrary may sadly be true, namely that individuals who were known for their principled objection to specific features of the regime but continued to serve it nonetheless had a subtle but important regime-stabilizing effect.

Psychograms from the Third Reich

In a diary entry for 11 August 1936, the German writer and journalist Friedrich Percyval Reck-Malleczewen recalled his first meeting with Adolf Hitler. It was in 1920, at the Munich home of his friend, the composer and conductor Clemens von Franckenstein. Among the Gobelin tapestries and the marble panels (Franckenstein lived at the time in the Villa Lenbach) sat Hitler, in a pair of gaiters and a floppy wide-brimmed hat, clutching a leather riding whip. He appeared – to Reck at least – uneasy in this opulent setting, and perched uncomfortably on the edge of a chair, oblivious to the nuances of his host's conversation, 'snatching hungrily at the words like a dog at pieces of raw meat'. Eventually he rose to his feet and launched into a long, ranting monologue, all the while thwacking his boot with the riding whip. Franckenstein's servants rushed in, thinking that their employer was being attacked. After Hitler had said his piece and left, there was a long and puzzled silence. Then Franckenstein stood up and opened one of the large windows looking onto the garden.

> It was not that our grim guest had been unclean, or fouled the room in the way that so often happens in a Bavarian village. But the fresh air dispelled the sense of oppression. It was not that an unclean body had been in the room, but something else, the unclean essence of a monstrosity.

Whether or not this scene took place as described (Reck-Malleczewen was given to fanciful embellishments), it would be a mistake to read the vignette as emblematic of Hitler's relationship with the old German elites. From the very beginning, as the French historian Fabrice d'Almeida has shown, Hitler networked with considerable success among the great and the good. His early sponsors included the Bechsteins, owners of the piano company. They invited him to receptions at their house in Munich and showered him with gifts, including his first luxury car, a red Mercedes worth 26,000 marks. Elsa Bruckmann, who was born Princess Cantacuzene of Romania, introduced Hitler to the wealthy industrialists who frequented the 'salon Bruckmann' and presented him with his first riding whip (until that point, he had carried a cane). Indeed, all three of Hitler's prized leather whips were presents from high society ladies. Throughout the 1920s, his access to elite society steadily increased. There was no need for Hitler to assimilate himself to the social norms of his hosts for his attractiveness lay precisely in his louche, somewhat uncouth manners and the 'aroma of adventure' that surrounded him. There was an undeniable frisson in welcoming a guest who left his pistol and bodyguards at the door when he entered a salon.

The Nazi movement acquired supporters as high up in the traditional social elite as it was possible to go. Among Hermann Göring's close associates was Prince August Wilhelm of Prussia, son of the Kaiser, who became interested in Nazism in 1926 and joined the Stormtroopers in 1930. Through August Wilhelm, Göring gained access to his brother Crown Prince Wilhelm of Prussia, and to the princes of Hessen, Christoph and Philipp. Göring was renowned (and resented by some Nazis) for his sycophantic attraction to the high-born, but he was not alone. Himmler, too, targeted the nobility, in the firm belief that they embodied the principles of selective breeding espoused by his SS. By 1938 nearly a fifth of all senior SS officers were titled noblemen (the figure for the lower officer ranks was 10 per cent). From a sample of 312 families of the old nobility, the historian Stephan Malinowski found 3,592 individuals who joined the Nazi Party, including 962 who did so before the seizure of power in January 1933. These Nazi nobles included members of the oldest and most distinguished East Elbian families: the Schwerins supplied 52 party members, the Hardenbergs 27, the Tresckows 30 and the Schulenburgs 41.

The very highest-born families, descendants of the ruling dynasties of the German principalities, were especially susceptible to the party's appeal. Duke Ernst August of Braunschweig (who was married to one of the princesses of Prussia) was a regular donor to the party and a close associate of several Nazi leaders (though he never became a card-carrying Nazi); Duke Carl Eduard von Sachsen-Coburg und Gotha (a grandson of Queen Victoria, born Prince of Great Britain and Ireland and known to his British friends as Charlie Coburg), joined the party in 1933 and became an SA-Gruppenführer in 1936. Some princely families flocked to the party en masse – 14 from the House of Hesse, 10 from the Schaumburg-Lippes, 20 from the Hohenlohes and so on. In all, it seems that between a third and a half of the eligible members of German princely families joined the party. As the American scholar Jonathan Petropoulos observed in his study of the princes of Hessen, if princes had constituted a profession, 'they would have rivalled physicians as the most Nazified in the Third Reich (doctors' membership peaked in 1937 at 43 per cent)'. Reck-Malleczewen himself was confronted with the extent of elite support when he visited a Berlin nightclub early in 1939 and found it heaving with 'young men of the rural nobility, all of them in SS uniforms'.

An interest in the relationship between the traditional elites of German society and the National Socialist movement developed only quite recently. There are various reasons for this: the celebration of German military resistance as the moral foundation stone of the new Federal Republic created an implicit linkage between high birth and principled opposition to Nazi criminality; many of the relevant archival sources are still in the hands of the families and some are less willing than others to support research; and for a long time it was widely believed that Nazism was in essence a movement of the downwardly mobile petite bourgeoisie – shopkeepers, clerks, tradesmen and minor officials, who saw in the movement's authoritarian racist politics a promise of rescue from *déclassement* and proletarianization. Nobles were too small a social group, of course, to make a significant contribution – as voters – to Nazi electoral success, but d'Almeida and Malinowski are surely right to suggest that the closeness between parts of the Nazi leadership and parts of the upper social stratum helps to explain why a coterie of senior German politicians of mainly noble descent were prepared to entrust the Nazi leader with high office in January 1933.

Once in power, the Nazis worked hard to attract the most compliant and enthusiastic elements of German high society. Of the 316 lunch guests at Göring's wedding to the actress Emmy Sonnemann in April 1935, for example, around 20 per cent were connected with noble families (the average for the population as a whole was about 1.5 per cent). The key figures in the Nazi leadership vied to throw the biggest and most extravagant parties. During the 1936 Olympic Games, Ribbentrop held a party for over 700 guests at his villa in Dahlem; Göring invited more than 2,000 to a garden party at the Aviation Ministry; and Goebbels trumped them all with a lavish evening on Peacock Island on the River Havel, to which guests were ferried in motorboats manned by crews in immaculate livery.

The Nazi high society that began to take shape at these events included celebrities from the worlds of film, music, art, the theatre, politics and sport. The regime associated itself with the most prestigious spectator sports, especially those involving planes, horses and fast cars. Hitler was present, along with 300,000 other spectators, at the German Grand Prix on the Nürburgring in 1935, when Manfred von Brauchitsch, nephew of the Walther von Brauchitsch who would serve from 1938 until 1941 as Army Supreme Commander, pulled into the lead in a W25 Mercedes-Benz ahead of Tazio Nuvolari's ponderous Alfa Romeo. Hitler shared the bitter disppointment of the German crowd when a rear tyre of the Mercedes burst only five miles from the finish and Nuvolari stormed past to take the prize. So certain had the organizers been of a German victory that they had no recording of the Italian national anthem to play over the loudspeakers; happily, Nuvolari was able to lend them his own record of the 'Marcia Reale', which he carried as a good-luck charm.

Horse-racing was especially favoured because of its association with selective breeding. Göring transformed the Berlin Grand Prix into the hugely hyped Grand Prix of the Capital of the Third Reich. The winner received 100,000 marks, the largest prize ever awarded at a racecourse, and the event was supported by a press campaign coordinated by Goebbels and his Propaganda Ministry. In March 1938, Hitler himself created a new grand prix, the Union Klub Prize of Honour, worth 40,000 marks and endowed with enough capital to last a century. At these glittering events the socialites of the Third Reich showed off their outfits and displayed their success before the cameras of the international press.

In the process of linking arms with the elites of birth, wealth and sporting accomplishment, the new leaders reinvented themselves as a privileged caste, defined by conspicuous luxury. Göring owned houses in Berlin, Munich and the Obersalzberg, as well as a sprawling country house called Karinhall, which was done up like an oversized hunting lodge. Bormann and Speer also had extensive properties and Ribbentrop owned a large number of mansions, urban apartment buildings and country estates. Virtually all the big men in the party acquired substantial art collections. Göring had his art agents hunt down paintings all over Europe. There were several hundred pieces in his gallery at Karinhall, including works by Dürer, Cranach, Fragonard and Boucher. By the time of his arrest, he had collected 1,375 paintings, 250 sculptures and 168 tapestries. Hitler, too, surrounded himself with paintings in all of his residences – including Cranachs, Dürers and Holbeins. The occupation of France enabled Ribbentrop to snap up paintings by Utrillo, Monet, Degas, Bonnard and Braque at bargain-basement prices. Even the relatively modest Himmler collected Etruscan bronzes and acquired a Brueghel masterpiece.

Ruling elites, of course, have often sought to distinguish themselves by the acquisition of prestigious cultural objects. But these collections had a political as well as a cultural function. This was the glitzy upside to the troglodytic philistinism that underlay the denigration and blacklisting of 'degenerate art'. Art collections projected the cultural pretensions of the regime; all the Nazi leaders used them as propagandistic resources, inviting journalists and photographers whenever they made acquisitions or official donations.

Above all, putting together and displaying such immense piles of loot demonstrated the personalization of power that infiltrated German society after 1933, and not just at the summit of the regime. The giving of gifts and the dispensing of favours, Fabrice d'Almeida has suggested, was one of the crucial tools of Nazi authority. A customized policy of tax rebates was devised for the performing arts; the beneficiaries included the screen actor Hans Albers and the conductor Wilhelm Furtwängler, but also many less prominent figures from provincial centres. Cultural administrators and the artists themselves were left in no doubt that these were individual settlements, through which each beneficiary entered into a personal relationship with the holders of power. This had little to do with formal party membership; it was a form of clientelism that transcended the party and its ideological support base. The same mechanisms were at work in the German army, where Hitler used huge gifts of cash and real estate to co-opt senior officers. Many of those commanders (Manstein, Rundstedt, von Kluge and Guderian come to mind) who later claimed that they had been restrained from joining the resistance by moral compunctions about their oath of loyalty omitted to mention that they had also been bribed with large, secret monetary gifts from Hitler.

The exchange of gifts also helped to cement the internal structure of the party and its organs. Hitler was constantly giving presents: vases, tea sets, sweets, lamps, books, cigars, his own watercolours. In 1935, Goebbels was gifted a stereophonic record player (at that time the acme of German sound technology) and Göring received a painting by Adolf Ziegler, an artist lampooned as the 'Reich Painter of Pubic Hair' for his waxy depictions of eugenic nudes. Himmler, too, became an assiduous trafficker in gifts. His office kept a file on eighty senior members of the SS whose birthday and Christmas presents were all meticulously logged. On Christmas Day 1933, Obergruppenführer Prützmann received a portrait of Himmler: one can only imagine the expressions of pleasure on his family's faces as the countenance of the Reichsführer-SS emerged from the wrapping paper. Like the princes of an earlier era, Nazi leaders dispensed hunting privileges to favoured subordinates. Göring, whose many titles included Reich Master of the Hunt, stalked stags with groups of dignitaries, and a hunting party led by Himmler went on a killing spree at Joachimshof in the autumn of 1938, shooting rabbits, hares, foxes, buzzards, deer, birds of prey and anything else they could set their sights on – miraculously, the beaters escaped unharmed.

Excluded from this dolce vita, of course, were the Jews of the old Weimar high society. D'Almeida writes about the millionaires' colony on Schwanenwerder, an island in the River Havel favoured by the wealthiest Jewish families. Before the formation of the Hitler government in January 1933, Israels, Karstadts, Schlitters, Goldschmidts, Salomonsohns, Sobernheims and Monheims had all built or bought villas in this charming spot. Schwanenwerder was the most expensive street in the interwar German version of Monopoly. After the elections of March 1933, the island was invaded by SA men from nearby Zehlendorf and a Nazi flag hoisted over the water tower. In the year or so that followed, Jewish families were forced to sell up and move out. Into their houses came the Nazis. Goebbels bought the villa owned by the banker Schlitter for a very modest sum; the Salomon-sohns' villa was purchased by the Reich Chancellery and reserved for Hitler's use; Albert Speer snapped up Baroness Goldschmidt-Rothschild's house in 1939 for only 150,000 marks and sold it at a huge profit only three years later. Nothing could better illustrate the intimate link between the hedonism of the new elite and the logic of theft, expropriation and exclusion that was central to the regime's character.

Anthropologists have long been fascinated by gift-giving. They have shown how in many different kinds of human society the exchange of gifts can function as a vehicle of political manoeuvre, a prototypical contract whose purpose is to establish social bonds founded upon the expectation of reciprocity and obligation. The gift-giving behaviour of the most powerful Nazis exposes the crucial importance of those networks that connected the party with people who possessed various forms of authority or influence, but were not directly affiliated with National Socialism. These networks – in society, sport, the arts and public life in general – made an important contribution towards stabilizing, domesticating and normalizing a regime whose ideological substance and political morality were in many respects exotic to mainstream Germany. Winning them over was an enterprise in which Hitler and his coterie of chieftains invested much effort and imagination. It may have been one of the cleverest things they did.

The ascent (if that is the right word) of Heinrich Himmler to become the chief architect of Nazi genocide is one of the strangest strands of the regime's story. There was nothing obvious or predictable about Himmler's rise to absolute power over the life and death of millions. Himmler played no role in the strategizing of the party before the seizure of power in 1933 and was not one of Hitler's intimates. He lacked the acerbic charisma of Goebbels, the suave intelligence of Speer and the unforced bonhomie of Göring. His attempts to make a success of himself outside the party were a miserable failure. Despite his diploma in agronomy, Himmler's efforts at farming were a resounding flop (the hens refused to lay and the plants kept dying). His early ventures into regional party administration were not a success. He was physically unprepossessing. The pretentious paramilitary haircut could not compensate for the pudgy, unathletic body and the drastically receding chin – a matter of some import in a milieu obsessed with racial phenotypes. 'Why have you got your hand in front of your face?', his fiancée commented on a photo he sent her around 1929. 'Did you want to cover up your chin?'

Most importantly, young Himmler was not well liked. He did not impress his fellow fraternity students at the Technical University in Munich, who repeatedly refused, despite Himmler's importuning, to elect him *Fuchsmajor*, an office assigned to a respected senior student who is entrusted with overseeing the recruitment of new members. Even his Bavarian fellow Nazis loathed him. They were repelled by his attention-seeking and by the hectoring, pompous criticisms he enjoyed parcelling out to peers. Fortunately for Himmler, none of this mattered. In the NSDAP, what counted were not plaudits from the provinces, but the support of the leadership, and particularly of the Führer himself. And this Himmler was assiduous in cultivating. Though he never became intimate with the dictator, he acquired a reputation as Hitler's most dedicated and ruthless servant. Whereas the SA possessed a powerful and charismatic leader of its own in Ernst Röhm, Himmler fashioned the SS (originally a small offshoot of the much larger SA) into an instrument of the Führer's will alone.

His chance to demonstrate the unconditional quality of his loyalty came in the summer of 1934, when Himmler authorized the murders of Ernst Röhm and the dissident Nazi Gregor Strasser, both of whom had helped in the mid-1920s to lay the foundations of Himmler's career within the party. He manoeuvred his way around various sceptical Nazi bigwigs to secure an ever larger share of power over the policing agencies of the German federal states, before amalgamating them into a Reich-wide security apparatus. Göring belatedly recognized the threat posed by Himmler, but his attempts to reimpose control over the police leader were a failure. Himmler did not win every power struggle he entered into, but he won enough of the battles to bypass all of his rivals, including sceptical commanders within the German army. From the summer of 1941, as the Nazi empire expanded eastwards, his police apparatus would grow like a malignant tumour, infiltrating military and civil chains of command and unleashing a wave of exterminatory violence unique in world history.

As the historian Peter Longerich shows, the mature SS of the later 1930s and 40s became a kind of monument to the grotesque personality of its leader. The pseudo-military structure reflected the attitudes and tone of the Bavarian paramilitary milieu in which Himmler had spent his early twenties. The clerical black garb spoke to the mysticism of a man who had forsaken the Catholic faith of his childhood to embrace a raft of esoteric post-Christian fads. In the summer of 1940 Himmler instructed the head of the Ahnenerbe (Ancestral Heritage), a research organization within the SS, to investigate references to thunderbolts in the ancient Germanic myths, on the grounds that these were surely evidence that the ancient Germans had possessed 'a highly developed weapon' requiring 'an extraordinary knowledge of electricity'. The Ahnenerbe spent thousands of man-hours compiling a massive file index on the witch trials of early modern Germany, because Himmler believed witches to be the custodians of an occult 'old knowledge' that might still be recoverable. An expedition was despatched to Tibet to confirm the postulations of 'cosmic ice theory', another of Himmler's hobby-horses. From the desk of the Reichsführer-SS poured a stream of letters on the correct preparation and ageing of mead, a suitable design for mineral-water bottles, the nutritional potential of seaweed, the baking of crispbreads using 'a special form of algae' and so on. As late as November 1944, Himmler was urging SS boffins to look into the possibility that the remains of meteors might be lodged inside Europe's highest mountains.

To an extraordinary degree, the proclivities of the leader shaped the public life of the organization. Even as a very young man, Himmler had demonstrated an almost compulsive need to police and control the lives of others. After his political ascent, this trait was given free rein. Letters went out to SS-men across the Reich ordering them to father children, to stop using curse-words, to have their brides inspected for their child-bearing potential by gynaecologists, to stop being 'hen-pecked' by their wives. One man was told to check his mother-in-law into a lunatic asylum, another to go on a diet: 'I regard it as unheard-of that a man of thirty-six is so phlegmatic and fat and complacent. It is in your interest to change this as quickly as possible.'

There was a streak of punitive malice in many of these communications. In the summer of 1944, Himmler, furious at the news that some SS and police leaders in Russia were failing to treat pest control as seriously as they should, proposed that a 'Fly and Gnat Room' should be established to discipline delinquents:

> All SS leaders and police who are either uninterested in the nuisance created by flies and gnats or even dismiss it with a superior smile will find they will be taken into care there for some considerable time, during which they will have the opportunity to study the question of flies and gnats from a theoretical angle as well as to enjoy the attentions of the thousands of flies and gnats in the room itself.

Particularly striking is the rabidity of Himmler's homophobia. In a speech to a gathering of SS functionaries in February 1937, Himmler estimated that there were 2 million male homosexuals in Germany. If one added to that the 2 million 'healthy' men killed in the First World War, he proposed, that made 4 million males who were in effect incapable of reproducing. 'If things stay the same,' he warned, 'our nation is going to be wiped out by this plague.' Homosexuality unsettled Himmler's sense of his own identity, in part because he found it difficult to repress a latent self-identification with homosexual men. The idea of homoeroticism infiltrating the paramilitary, pseudo-clerical and intensely homosocial environment of the SS filled the Reichsführer with frissons of pious horror.

Direct extermination orders from the Reichsführer himself are rare, but, as Peter Longerich has shown, Himmler's role in the destruction of European Jewry was central throughout. Himmler's whistlestop inspection tours of the eastern occupied areas were followed again and again by waves of mass murder that engulfed first men, then women and children. On 14 March 1942, for example, Himmler visited Lublin for discussions with Odilo Globočnik, the leading figure in Jewish policy in the General Government of Poland. The 'clearance' of the ghetto began two days later. Many were shot in the ghetto itself, a few thousand were selected for forced labour, and the rest, numbering about 30,000, were sent to be murdered at the extermination facility in Bełżec (whose construction Himmler had ordered in October 1941). The pattern was reproduced across Poland, the Baltic states, Belorussia, Central Russia and the Ukraine.

Peter Longerich has despatched the myth, widely trafficked in television documentaries, that Himmler was personally nauseated by the sight of open-pit executions. According to the testimony of a police lieutenant in charge of one of the killing squads at Minsk in November 1941, he assumed the pose of an attentive and businesslike observer:

> After the first salvo, Himmler came right up to me and looked personally into the ditch, remarking that there was still someone alive. He said to me: 'Lieutenant, shoot that one!' [...] Himmler stood beside me while I did it. [...] For Himmler and his entourage, the whole thing was simply a spectacle.

This performance of neutrality and detachment corresponded to one of Himmler's deepest and most perverse convictions, namely that it was possible, while overseeing the slaying of blameless children, women and men, to remain 'decent'. 'Decency' was an abiding theme of Himmler's letters and speeches. He believed that the stomach pains that plagued him were psychosomatic and attributed them to his untiring efforts to be 'good and decent'. The 'decency' of the SS manifested itself in the priggish honour code that supposedly regulated the daily life of its members, who were informed, for example, that 'an SS man buys nothing he cannot pay for' and 'never buys anything in instalments', but it also applied to the administration of mass murder, which was to be implemented under the most scrupulous discipline. The idea that SS or police personnel might be stealing watches or jewellery from the people they were killing was enough to drive Himmler into a fury. A 'decent' killer did his work 'objectively' and without relish or the prospect of personal advantage. This, Himmler declared in his notorious 'Posen speech' of 1943, was the greatest achievement of his SS: to have seen thousands of corpses 'lying side by side', 'to have coped [sic] with this and – except for cases of human weakness – to have remained decent'. That is why the prim little face beneath the peaked cap had to remain unmoved as the bodies tumbled into the pit at Minsk.

Between 23 April and 2 May 1942, a series of meetings, some very protracted, took place between Himmler and his deputy, Reinhard Heydrich, and between Himmler and Hitler. Although little is known of what exactly was said, it can be inferred from the timing and intensity of these summit discussions that they ratified the transition from local and regional mass killings to a Europe-wide extermination programme. After the assassination of Heydrich at the end of May 1942, the pace of the killing increased yet further. Under the auspices of Operation Reinhard, named for Himmler's deputy and pushed forward with vengeful determination by Himmler, 2 million people, most of them Jews, perished at Bełżec, Sobibor and Treblinka.

Staggering as these concentrated assaults on the lives of millions are, we should resist the presumption that the Holocaust unfolded from a single 'fundamental decision'. A close analysis of the narrative, Peter Longerich has proposed, suggests rather a sliding scale of expanding and increasingly lethal violence. The Holocaust was not, in other words, the foreordained and defining objective of the SS programme for the occupied eastern zones. It was simply the preliminary phase of an even vaster plan, unrealized at the end of the war, that would have taken decades to accomplish and would ultimately also have involved the extermination of tens of millions of Slavs. We get a glimpse of this vision in Himmler's announcement in July 1943 that vast 'dead zones' would be created in northern Ukraine and 'Russia-Centre', from which all Slavs of all ages were to be removed for concentration and 'forced labour'. Any that remained would be classed as 'bandits' and 'shot on sight'. The lands that had once been their home would become immense plantations, whose purpose would be to supply the German Reich with food and other products – Himmler earmarked some areas for the planting of Kok-Sagys, a rubber-like plant from Central Asia that was another of his 'research' hobby-horses.

Even as the regime hurtled towards the abyss, Himmler's power continued to soar. As Reich interior minister (from 1943), head of the Waffen-SS with privileged access to military matériel and head of a growing armaments manufacturing apparatus, Himmler secured a concentration of power he had never before achieved. But this further expansion of his activities also revealed his limitations. Himmler was and remained a master at the deployment of terror against defenceless civilians abroad and at home. But his ventures into armaments produced a litter of white elephants. Massive Kok-Sagys plantations took valuable arable land out of food production without ever producing a viable source of plant-based rubber. The shale oil refineries and peat-based fuel extraction plants were a costly irrelevance. Himmler's success in securing a foothold in Luftwaffe armaments production came too late to offset the overwhelming air superiority of the Allies. As the commander of an Army Group from January 1945 – an appointment that came as the fulfilment of a boyhood dream – Himmler was an abject failure (Hitler sacked him from his command after only two months).

Yet, even in the face of impending ruin, Himmler's self-belief remained strong. In the final phase of the war, he began planning for the peace ahead. In the spring of 1945, orders went out to the camps to end the shooting of Jewish inmates. Communicating through his former personal physician, Felix Kersten, now in Stockholm, Himmler informed the World Jewish Congress that he was willing to release 10,000 Jewish prisoners to Sweden or Switzerland. A similar offer was made to Count Folke Bernadotte, vice-president of the Swedish Red Cross. When Bernadotte met Himmler in person in February and March 1945, he found the Reichsführer courteous, genial and keen to convey a good impression. Himmler was aware, he told Bernadotte, that the world regarded him as 'brutal'. But the reality was exactly the contrary: he loathed brutality! An even more surreal encounter took place on 19 April, when Himmler met with Norbert Masur, an agent of the World Jewish Congress, to discuss prisoner transfers. When the conversation touched on the regime's treatment of the Jews, Himmler denied that there had been any mass killings. His own preference, he claimed, had always been for a policy of emigration, which he had supported 'in conjunction with Jewish-American organizations'. Yes, a number of Jews had perished during the war with Bolshevik Russia, but this could hardly have been avoided, given the intensity of the conflict. As for the camps, these were harsh but fair – one needed only look at Auschwitz, where 150,000 Jews still survived in good health.

How Himmler expected his interlocutor to believe these gross false-hoods is anybody's guess. The Allied press was already full of photos of the liberated camps and detailed reports on the gas chambers at the extermination facilities. Himmler clearly still hoped to reinvent himself as the honest broker and 'decent fellow' who might even be welcomed into an advisory function of some kind by the Western Allies. The Reichsführer-SS remained, as Longerich aptly puts it, 'versatile'.

With the Third Reich collapsing around him, Himmler embarked on a last bizarre adventure. Slipping into mufti and donning an eye-patch in place of the trademark rimless pince-nez, he made his way with a small incognito entourage in the direction of Meinstedt in Lower Saxony, where he was arrested by British troops, to whom he introduced himself, using a forged paybook, as a Sergeant Heinrich Hitzinger of the Wehrmacht. He acknowledged his true identity a few days later, still apparently confident that he could talk his way out of trouble. When it became clear in the course of a medical examination that an attempt would be made to remove the phial of cyanide concealed between his teeth, he pulled his head away, bit open the phial, swallowed the poison and was dead within fifteen minutes.

The biographical gaze, when it is directed at the perpetrators of great evil, sometimes has an attenuating effect on our hostility to the subject – either because mitigating circumstances are brought to light, or simply because the narrative of childhood and youth confronts us with the person who was not yet guilty of the adult's misdeeds. This effect is strikingly absent in Himmler's case. There was no tyrannical paterfamilias, no scenario of childhood neglect or abuse that might explain the inhumanity of the adult. And the controlling, pedantic goody-two-shoes of the youthful diaries is too obviously the larval form of the mature Reichsführer-SS. Nor is there any evidence that the slightest beam of moral insight into his own villainy ever penetrated Himmler's awareness. He was like those malefactors in Dante's hell who must remain there for ever, precisely because they are completely unable to understand why they are there.

How much explanatory historical weight can the biography of this personality carry? Himmler's ascendancy makes sense only when we connect him with the changes unfolding in German society after 1918.

In the narrowness of his horizons, Himmler reflected the inwardness of a conservative Catholic Bavarian milieu that had been on the cultural defensive for several generations. He was one of many thousands of young Germans drawn to the post-war paramilitary networks, a perfervid milieu in which the First World War seemed never to have ended. In exchanging Christianity for a hodge-podge of pseudo-science and new-age esoterica, he walked on well-trodden paths. Finally, in his conscious cultivation of a form of political reason entirely denuded of empathy, Himmler revealed his affinity with that generation of German men whose understanding of the Great War was shaped not by direct experience, but by the shock of the defeat and the political turbulence of the early post-war years. In a close reading of the career of the senior Nazi functionary Werner Best, the Freiburg historian Ulrich Herbert showed that Best belonged to a cohort of middle-class youth who were respectable, polite and well-off and yet completely rejected the commitment to law that was supposed to be the preserve of the bourgeoisie. Best aspired instead to 'heroic realism' – the cool, rational, merciless pursuit of the interests of the *Volk*. It was this mindset that explained the willingness of so many upper- and middle-tier planners and administrators – the German historian Michael Wildt called them 'The Generation of the Unconditional' – to embrace great brutality in the name of the people, and to combine it with careful planning and administration. Himmler shared with this generation an ambition to achieve total self-mastery in the name of the defeated nation, to be hard, 'rational', immune to pity and self-doubt. And this in turn explains the contemporary political resonance of his thought and action. The truly extraordinary aspect of Himmler's story is not the wickedness of the persona at its centre, but the unique political and cultural constellation that gave such a man the resources to turn his sordid, incoherent fantasies into other people's real-life nightmares.

Like many of my male friends and colleagues, I have spent the last couple of years working my way with immense pleasure through Karl Ove Knausgaard's titanic Norwegian work of self-description *Min Kamp* (*My Struggle*). In the middle of *The End*, the sixth and last volume, something very strange happens. At around page 482, the book swerves away from the pitch-perfect genre scenes of family and social life that have made this author world famous and plunges, like a car crashing through a safety barrier, into a prolonged reflection on Adolf Hitler. For over 360 pages Knausgaard circles around the German dictator, his youthful longing and seriousness, his love for his mother, the struggle with an authoritarian father, his refusal of the destinies prescribed for him by convention. Long passages are given over to summarizing, or simply quoting at length, the first volume of *Mein Kampf*, written while Hitler was in prison in 1925. He ponders (twice) on that moment, memorable because it was preserved on film, when Hitler emerges, 'his hands shaking with sickness', from a bunker beneath Berlin 'with the world in flames and millions of people dead as a result of his volition' to greet a line of young boys who have been called up for the defence of the collapsing capital city. In that perilous moment, Knausgaard writes, Hitler reveals, 'in a fleeting glimpse of his eyes, [...] something warm and kind, his soul'. 'He was a small person,' Knausgaard concedes, 'but so are we all.' And out of these and many other thoughts about the German dictator spiral long cascades of reflections on modern life, interwoven with high-end literary and cultural references, from James Joyce to Hermann Broch, Olav Duun, Knut Hamsun, Leonardo da Vinci, Jorge Luis Borges, René Girard, Michel Serres, Ernst Jünger, Theodor Adorno, Martin Heidegger, Bruno Latour, Emmanuel Levinas, Jesus Christ, Hannah Arendt and Giorgio Agamben (this list is not exhaustive).

Not until page 848 does *The End* escape again from Hitler's orbit. In the meanwhile, the reader has trekked across a massive, crater-like depression in the book's structure. It is like coming up for air when, on page 849, we are allowed once again to inhabit the body of the writer: 'I sat down again, poured myself some tepid coffee from the vacuum jug and lit another cigarette.' The Hitler-spectre is banished and the 300 pages that remain contain some of the most luminous and touching passages of the entire Knausgaard cycle.

What, one might ask, is Hitler doing in this book? I suppose his appearance at some point was inevitable, given the fact that the cycle's Norwegian title, reluctantly accepted by Knausgaard's Norwegian publisher, was *Min Kamp*. (The German translator refused to use *Mein Kampf*, and the German edition appeared instead under the

clunking collective rubric *Das autobiografische Projekt*.) Asked why
he chose to adopt the title of Hitler's autobiographical essay, Knausgaard has tended to fudge. A friend suggested it, he told one interviewer.
It was better than his other working titles, 'Argentina' and 'Parrot
Park'. The Hitler essay at the heart of volume six doesn't answer the
question either, or at least not directly. We have to infer its purpose by
examining the services Hitler performs for the one who has summoned him back from the dead.

Mein Kampf, Knausgaard writes, is 'literature's only unmentionable
work'. To read its pages is to travel into a forbidden zone. But perhaps
the strangest thing of all is that the Hitler Knausgaard finds when he
breaches the taboo is a crumpled, Hitler-shaped reflection of himself.
The hated father, the beloved mother, the fear of intimacy, the sense of
outsiderhood and ponderous seriousness with which he approaches
life, all these fixtures of the self on display throughout *Min Kamp* are
also present in the author of *Mein Kampf*. Even Hitler's abstention
from masturbation, recalled by the future dictator's youthful room-
mate August Kubiczek and much discussed in the Hitler literature,
chimes with Knausgaard's belated and laborious efforts at onanism,
bleakly recorded in book four of the cycle. No need for detail here –
suffice it to say that we are worlds away from the joyful and anarchic
evocations of the same act in Philip Roth's *Portnoy's Complaint*.

To frame the journey towards Hitler as an encounter with oneself
is an unexpected thing to do. It naturally does not mean that Knausgaard endorses Hitler's acts or worldview. But he insists that it must
be possible to distinguish between who Hitler was and what he did.
In the case of the young Hitler, who was already himself but not yet
the author of a genocidal war, the distinction seems (at least to Knausgaard) impossible to deny. Hence the rage he expresses towards the
British historian Ian Kershaw, author of the classic English-language
biography of the Nazi leader. Kershaw, Knausgaard charges, adopts a
dismissive attitude towards the young Hitler; he fails to warm to the
passion and innocence of his subject. The historian's excessively 'negative' view, Knausgaard suggests, is not just 'immature', it makes his
biography of Hitler 'almost unreadable'.

These strictures against Kershaw are among the most bewildering
sentences in the entire Knausgaard cycle. It is one thing for a male

Norwegian writer to emote empathetically in the direction of an image of Adolf Hitler he has pieced together in his own mind after reading half a dozen books. But the task of Ian Kershaw, an historian who has immersed himself over decades in treatises and archival records on his subject, can scarcely be to sound out his own spiritual affinity with Hitler. It must rather be to understand what it was about him, even in his youth, that might help to explain his later impact on history. The care and lucidity with which Kershaw addressed that task established his reputation as the doyen of the Hitler biographers. Yet the distanciated, analytical perspective of the historian is precisely what disgusts Knausgaard.

What exactly is driving this effort to engage empathetically with Hitler? Part of the answer must lie in the furtive pleasure that comes with the breach of a taboo. I was reminded of the smirk on the face of the Danish director Lars von Trier when he announced to an audience at the Cannes Film Festival in May 2011 that he 'understood' Hitler, that he could imagine him sitting in his bunker and could 'sympathize' with him. Knausgaard's musings on Hitler soon lead him to thoughts on the constraining effects of 'political correctness' on public utterance. If, he asks, he were to use racist epithets about black people in his writing, or to espouse unequivocally racist views, would he still be accepted as an author of serious fiction? The Holocaust, he suggests, 'has taken on all the characteristics of a taboo'; 'even as I write about it, I sense its unmentionable nature' (p. 821). Woven around these thoughts are wisps of cultural and moral-philosophical commentary. We have lost touch with 'the authentic'. 'The holy has vanished from our lives', leaving us with nothing but 'the sublime', its secular echo. 'Oh, for crying out loud,' Knausgaard laments, 'what do I even know of the divine?' (pp. 633–4) 'Reason,' he notes, 'is the same to us as profitability' (p. 838). He regrets the 'regimentation of the human that all ideological thinking creates' (p. 841). Tear aside the veil of rationality, he proposes, and you will see that 'we are not modern at all, we are as old as the dolmens and barrows, kin to the grass and the trees' (p. 661).

Some of this is interesting, some of it is banal and some of it is simply untrue. Is the Holocaust really an 'unmentionable' taboo? Obviously not, even if denying that the Holocaust happened at all is a punishable offence in some jurisdictions. Is reason really 'the same to us as profitability'? Has 'the holy' really departed from our lives? Was it ever the overwhelming force in the lives of believers that Knausgaard imagines? Reading him on this subject, I was reminded of the Italian pilgrim in Dante's *La Vita Nuova* who visits the Church of the Holy Sepulchre in Jerusalem, but finds himself unable to respond in an unmediated way to the scenes and relics around him, because his mind keeps playing through the narratives he will share with his friends when he returns from this long journey – that was in 1294! As for the claim that the authentic has vanished, this is surely not true, even of Knausgaard himself. Consider the following passage:

> I drove with John [the author's youngest child], who slept, an hour and a half beneath towering fells, through the valleys where the shadows of approaching night grew long, past the racing rivers and gushing water-falls, and all the time I sang out loud, drunk on the sun and death. What else could I do? I was so happy. (p. 644)

A Norwegian among towering fells, drunk on the sun and death. What could be more authentic than that? It is odd to see this humane and intelligent writer pose as the advocate of intuition and feeling against rational cognition and enlightenment, as if that were a choice we are obliged to make.

Whatever one thinks of all the culture-critical sermonizing, it is clear that Hitler is working hard for this text. He elbows aside the 'I' of autobiography, creating a *mise en abîme* that exposes the structural limitations of the genre. In fixing on Hitler as the disturbing doppel-gänger of the authorial ego, Knausgaard expands the moral remit of his oeuvre by folding into it the arc of modern history. Hitler becomes the test case for the fool's liberty of the contemporary novelist. Readers with a better understanding than mine of the Norwegian context will doubtless discern other, local resonances. But it might be worth bearing in mind that the impact of the Nazi occupation on Norwegian post-war society was especially deep. In a sequence of trials extending from 1945 to 1957, over 90,000 cases were investigated (3.2 per cent of the country's entire population) and 46,000 persons were sentenced by the Norwegian courts on counts of collaboration. Far from stabiliz-ing the country, as the returning Norwegian government-in-exile had hoped, the trials had a profoundly polarizing effect. This was the most expansive juridical reckoning with former collaborators anywhere in post-war Europe. Knausgaard makes no mention of these events, beyond registering his surprise upon discovering a Nazi pin among the belongings of his dead father, who was neither a Nazi nor a Nazi sympathizer. But the controversy around the Norwegian trials resonates in the author's need to express both the attraction and the repulsion awakened in him by Nazism and its enigmatic leader.

To turn from Knausgaard to Peter Longerich's *Hitler: A Life* is to re-enter that world of sober, appraising diction that Knausgaard deplores in the writing of Ian Kershaw. Longerich is in no doubt that his subject was emotionally 'retarded' and unable to feel empathy (p. 950). The study of Hitler's early life reveals 'a lack of feeling in his dealings with others', a 'marked egocentricity' and a tendency to seek refuge in a 'fantasy world focused on himself'. Even as a soldier during the First World War he stood out as a markedly isolated figure, an 'eccentric loner'. The only being with which he had an emotionally binding relationship during his wartime service was his dog Foxl, which was allowed to sleep with him.

Longerich's meticulous account of the dictator's life touches on many issues, from Hitler's management of dissension within his party to his thoughts on foreign policy, rearmament, the economy, the tactical skill with which he handled the relations between his movement and the political elites and his understanding and consolidation of his own leadership role. He has little time for the notion that Hitler's 'charisma' was crucial to sustaining the regime's authority. The monopolistic control of media and public communications, Longerich argues, was more important to sustaining the dictator's authority than the 'Hitler Myth' explored by Ian Kershaw, or, for that matter, the spiritual-erotic union imagined by Knausgaard between the 'we-less I' of Hitler and the 'I-less we' of the German people.

Two strands of Longerich's argument are particularly worthy of note. The first is that, notwithstanding the claims he made throughout his life, Hitler's early career was not a lonely mission to save his country. On the contrary, his entry into politics was orchestrated by powerful interests pursuing their own objectives. It was the Reichswehr Information Department in Munich that arranged for Hitler to be trained in public speaking and then employed him as an agitator to immunize the soldiers still serving in Munich against the appeal of socialism. As a naturally talented popular speaker who stood out for the vehemence of his antisemitism, Hitler soon merged into a network of army officers, racist journalists and extreme right-wing organizations, all of them united in their aim of building a platform for anti-socialist agitation. And these forces were also sponsored and encouraged by conservative elements in the Bavarian state government under Gustav von Kahr, who worked hard to transform Bavaria into a 'cell of order' in which right-wing groups could flourish.

Longerich has less to say about the role played by conservative collaborators in the seizure of power by the Nazis, but the same observation applies. Throughout the Weimar years and especially in the period 1930–33, Hitler and his movement continued to be seen as a potentially valuable asset by conservative interests who hoped to use him as a weapon against the political left in Germany. The so-called 'seizure of power' was as much an achievement of the conservative elites as it was of the Nazi leader and his movement. It was the conservative political leadership of the late Weimar Republic who prematurely dissolved two parliaments in 1930 and 1932 at a time when support for the Nazis was growing; it was they who brought down the Social-Democrat government of Prussia in the summer of 1932 through a coup that replaced the elected Prussian state government with an imperial commissariat. And it was the absorption of Prussia into the federal government that enabled Hermann Göring to secure control of the Prussian police force – the largest in Germany – after the appointment of Hitler to the chancellorship. Here, too, the conservatives provided the Nazis with key tools for the consolidation of their own power. Even the Reichstag Fire Decrees that suspended civil and political rights and the Enabling Law that made it possible for the Hitler cabinet to override parliament were devices initially concocted by the conservatives and merely inherited by the Nazis. Electoral success and control over a large political movement with a formidable militia were important assets, but it was the combination of these advantages with the support of the old elites that gave Hitler and his party the edge they needed in 1933.

Once in power, Longerich argues, Hitler gradually secured

unchallenged control of the regime's political life. There has long been debate over Hitler's capacity to shape the continuing evolution of his regime. 'Intentionalists' argued that he enjoyed a plenitude of authority and used it to pursue a consistent programme. 'Structuralists' argued that the chaotic interplay between poorly coordinated power centres within the regime opened the system to influence from below, meaning that the leaders were as often as not carried along on a tide of 'cumulative radicalization' generated by negative energies released by the regime but not ultimately under its control. Ian Kershaw's biography famously balanced the two perspectives, recognizing the many forms of local and regional initiative that shaped policy but also insisting on Hitler's role as the umpire who decided which ideas and policies prospered and which did not.

Longerich pushes hard in the intentionalist direction, identifying Hitler as the key decision-maker at virtually every key juncture in the regime's history. It was Hitler who personally directed the putsch against the SA and other opponents of the regime in the summer of 1934, enabled the forcible sterilization of the 'Rhineland bastards' (children of French colonial troops and German women) in 1937 and triggered the murder of 70,000 persons under the 'euthanasia' programme of 1939–41. Hitler ensured that the war against the Soviet Union would be a war of racial conquest and annihilation, insisting that the forthcoming campaign was not just an armed conflict, but 'a confrontation between two ideologies' in the course of which 'the Jewish-Bolshevik intelligentsia [. . .] must be eliminated' (p. 731). And Hitler was implicated in every stage of the expanding campaign of genocide against the Jews, though his growing suspicion of written communication means that his interventions became more informal and less easily traceable in the documents. In April 1943, Hitler personally hectored the Hungarian leader, Admiral Horthy, to send the Hungarian Jews to German death camps. 'Jews', he told Horthy, had to be 'treated like tuberculosis bacilli'. The Slovaks, the Croatians and other satellite leaders were likewise taken to task for dragging their feet over the deportation of 'their' Jews.

Longerich's is a meticulous and compelling account of its subject that draws on stupendous reading in the archives. If there is a weakness, it lies in the author's decision to focus his enquiry so tightly on

Hitler alone, occluding from view the many forms of synergy and collusion that made the dictator's power so devastating in its effect. Whereas the early part of the book is scrupulously attentive to context and to the young Hitler's dependence on a multitude of helpers, the full-blown adult dictator appears on the stage almost alone. And this, of course, makes it harder to verify the claims Longerich makes for Hitler's completely dominant place within the regime's decision-making structure.

Longerich's book moves steadily over its terrain, like one of those cleaners on the floors of swimming pools that roll about collecting drowned insects and leaf debris. The tone of Brendan Simms's *Hitler: The World Was Not Enough* could hardly be more different – written with passion and verve, this book grabs the reader by the elbow and propels her from the first page until the last towards a single conclusion. The central argument can be summed up as follows: at the centre of Hitler's worldview was a profound preoccupation with 'Anglo-America'. It started on the Western Front during the First World War when his unit faced British, Canadian and Australian troops and found them to be tough fighters. It deepened in 1918 when he encountered American prisoners of war, freshly arrived from across the Atlantic, and noticed that some of them had German names. These 'seminal' experiences, Simms argues, seared two interconnected life-long preoccupations into Hitler's mind. He became obsessed with the power, size and global reach of capitalist Anglo-America. And he came to believe, secondly, that the Anglo-Saxons enjoyed these advantages in part because their racial value had been elevated by the influx over several centuries of German emigrants who, by leaving their country, had siphoned off some the best hereditary material available to the German people and placed it in the hands of a superior power.

Simms is not the first historian to stress the importance of America to the arc of Nazism's history. Adam Tooze's *Wages of Destruction* highlighted the crushing asymmetries between the American and German war efforts in 1941–5 and his next book, *The Deluge*, proposed a rethinking of the twentieth century as an era marked not by the fragility, but by the immense power of the liberal Anglo-American order. Tracing the lineaments of Hitler's thinking on the Anglo-world across an impressive range of different sources and utterances over the entire span of his political career, Simms is able to show that the United States and Britain were more important reference points for the German dictator than has been acknowledged, and that his geopolitical vision was genuinely global. If persuading us of this were the book's purpose, we could simply note the originality of the finding, record our approval and retire, tired but happy, to bed. But Simms has a much larger objective in view.

His book, Simms announces in the introduction, is not intended to be 'additive', in the sense of merely bringing new ideas to an existing literature. Rather it aims to be 'substitutive'. The book is not offering a new perspective *on* Hitler, it is proposing a new theory *of* Hitler. In Simms's reading, Hitler's antisemitism, his quest for *Lebensraum* (living space) in the East, his aspiration to overcome class antagonisms through the creation of a harmonious 'people's community' (*Volksgemeinschaft*), and even his architectural preferences – all of these preoccupations become subordinate functions of the overriding obsession with Anglo-America. The 'people's community' becomes Germany's attempt to match the American dream, the war with Russia is about denying resources to the Anglo-Americans; antisemitism is merely an articulation of Hitler's loathing for Anglo-American 'plutocratic capitalism'.

Rethinking Hitler in this way means that Simms has to shunt the Soviet Union, the decisive theatre of the military struggle with Nazi Germany, to the margins of his analysis. Even when Hitler is bogged down in his attritional conflict with the Red Army, Simms insists, it is Anglo-America he has in his sights. Not all of these claims are new. In a controversial study published in 1987, the German historian Rainer Zitelmann argued that Hitler was contemptuous of radical antisemites, admired Stalin and pursued eastern 'living space' chiefly as a means of achieving parity with the United States. What sets Simms apart is his determination to answer every question with one argument.

The monocausal paradigm means that Hitler has to be uncoupled from the idea of anti-Bolshevism and aligned instead with the enemies of 'plutocratic capitalism'. But was Hitler really an 'anti-capitalist'? There was an anti-capitalist 'left wing' within the NSDAP, but Hitler never made any serious effort to follow through on their demands: the banks were never nationalized, corporate profits stayed buoyant, the department stores remained in business, and the power of those

Nazis who espoused a 'second [social] revolution' was destroyed by the putsch of 1934, in which Hitler played a central role. As for Hitler's frequent expressions of loathing for Bolshevism and the German left (not to mention his regime's murderous attacks on both), these have to be palmed aside as aberrations or decoded as indirect references to world Jewry and its capitalist schemes.

Hitler's antisemitism, too, becomes a dependent variable. But while it is certainly true that Hitler played on occasion with the idea of using the Jews as 'hostages' to deter Washington from entering the war, Simms's reasoning makes it impossible to see why the intensity of the extermination increased in the last years of the conflict, when America was already in the fight and nothing could be gained through further killing sprees within the shrinking area under German control. Here, I found Longerich's account more convincing. For Hitler, the extermination of the Jews was an end in its own right, Longerich argues, but over time it also became a tool of German power politics, drawing satellite governments into a web of criminal complicity from which there could be no escape. As Lucy Dawidowicz argued many years ago and Saul Friedlander reminded us more recently, Hitler's 'war against the Jews' really was a war against the Jews.

Simms's insistence on the overriding importance of one guiding idea means that his narrative is strangely inert. The protagonist at the centre of the story, having been shaped for life by his seminal wartime encounters, is immune to change. That Hitler acquired a set of enduring convictions or key ideas fairly early in his life is plausible, but that he fixed them into an inalterable hierarchy and stuck to this order of priorities throughout seems much less likely. Hitler's political commentaries, memoranda and monologues – and, for that matter, his political behaviour and decision-making – are full of moments at which the dictator seems to be switching from one priority to another, playing with the same general objectives but arranging them differently in his thoughts as the circumstances change. In Longerich's account, Hitler confronts thresholds that force him to retreat from one commitment and assign priority to another. But for Simms, Hitler's mind is as unreactive as argon gas: he never yields an iota to the pressure of events. The closing sentence of the last chapter says it all: 'As in the beginning, so at the end.'

Hitler got a lot of things wrong, Simms tells us, and his career was ultimately a 'catastrophic failure'. But he got two things right. He was 'exactly right' about 'the overwhelming power of Anglo-America'. And he was 'entirely accurate' in his conviction that the Germans were too weak to prevail against 'the "Anglo-Saxons", the global "master race"'. It was a fatal error, Simms observes, to muster a continental-European 'coalition of cripples' against the awesome might of Anglo-America, whose exploits against the Third Reich are recorded with knee-hugging gusto throughout the book. Simms's suggestion that Hitler was fundamentally an anti-capitalist has earned him a sharp rebuke from Richard Evans, who has accused him of using the Nazi leader to besmirch the reputation of the left and thereby importing into British academic discourse the extremist polemics of the American alt-right. This seems to me a misunderstanding. There is politics here, to be sure, but it is not the anti-leftist animus of the alt-right, it is the *geo*political vision of a post-Brexit world in which Anglo-America stands aside from a weak and fragmented Europe too lacking in political cohesion to project real power on the global stage. It is no accident (and no joke) that the book's subtitle refers to the 1999 James Bond blockbuster *The World Is Not Enough*, in which the famous British secret agent and an American nuclear physicist together save the world from a dastardly scheme cooked up by an ex-KGB officer. Simms is a prolific contributor of political commentary on current affairs and he has repeatedly criticized the EU partner states (and especially Ireland) for failing to see that Britain, like America, is, by tradition and character, an 'ordering power', not a power that can ever be subordinated to an order greater than itself. It is, quite simply, a country of a different, stronger and better kind. On this question, it seems that Simms and the protagonist of his book are in agreement.

Karl Ove Knausgaard recalls the sensation of near-nausea that overcame him as he began reading *Mein Kampf*: 'Hitler's words and Hitler's thoughts were thereby admitted to my own mind and for a brief moment became a part of it.' Brendan Simms confesses a similar apprehension: 'the author,' he writes, 'has tried throughout to get into Hitler's mind, without letting [Hitler] get into his'. Whether Hitler gets into our minds, or we mislay something of our own inside his, it is clear that this strange and hateful man, who has now been dead for seventy-six years, is still playing with our heads.

History, like the present, is full of controversial figures. But there is surely nothing to compare with the swarm of avatars who throng the Hitler literature, from the 'unperson' of Joachim Fest, to the wily, pragmatic tactician of Alan Bullock, the fixated ideologue of Eberhard Jaeckel, the programmeless improviser of A. J. P. Taylor, the 'weak dictator' of Hans Mommsen, the 'revolutionary' modernizer of Rainer Zitelmann, the 'psychopathic God' of Robert G. L. Waite, the 'artist' and political aesthete of Wolfram Pyta and the repressed homosexual of Lothar Machtan (to mention just a few). He has sometimes ruled the roost and he has sometimes drowned in structures. Every new cultural current since 1945 has brought forth new Hitlers. They have proliferated across popular culture too, from video-game Hitler-zombies and the endless parodic recycling of bunker-scene clips from the movie *Downfall* to the scores of Hitlers spawned by sci-fi and schlock fiction and cinema. In Timur Vermes's comic novel of 2012, *Look Who's Back*, Hitler, having accidentally slipped through a time warp into the twenty-first century, earns popularity as an impersonator of himself on German TV and becomes the star of a YouTube video that goes viral, scoring 700,000 hits. Hitler continues to demand our attention. Is this evidence, as Ron Rosenbaum has suggested, of our 'continuing inability to process Hitler'? Or does it suggest precisely the opposite, the hypertrophic over-processing of something that continues to provoke us, but also in some ways to fuel our culture?

The Futures of War

The Reign of George VI, 1900–1925, published anonymously in London in 1763, makes intriguing reading today. In this eighteenth-century vision of the future, twentieth-century France still groans under the despotism of the Bourbons. America is still a British colony. 'Germany' still means the sprawling commonwealth of the Holy Roman Empire. As the reign of George VI opens, the British go to war with France and Russia and defeat them both. But after a Franco-Russian invasion of Germany, the war reignites in 1917. The British invade and subdue France, deposing the Bourbons. After conquering Mexico and the Philippine Islands, the Duke of Devonshire enters Spain and a general peace is signed at Paris on 1 November 1920.

The impact of revolution on the international system lies far beyond this author's mental horizons and he has no inkling of how technological change will transform modern warfare. In his twentieth century, armies led by dukes and soldier-kings still march around the continent re-enacting the campaigns of Frederick the Great. The *Britannia*, flagship of the Royal Navy, is feared around the world for the devasting broadsides of its '120 brass guns'. The term 'steam-punk' comes to mind, except that there is no steam. But there are passages that do resonate unsettlingly with the present: English politics is mired in factionalism, Germany's political leadership is perilously weak, and there are concerns about the 'immense sums' Russian Tsar Peter IV has invested in British client networks, with a view to disrupting the democratic process.

Predicting future wars – both who will fight them and how they will be fought – has always been a hit-and-miss affair. In *The Coming War with Japan*, published in 1991, George Friedman and Meredith

LeBard solemnly predicted that the end of the Cold War and the collapse of the Soviet Union would usher in an era of heightened geopolitical tension between Japan and the US. In order to secure untrammeled access to vital raw materials, they predicted, Japan would tighten its economic grip on southwest Asia and the Indian Ocean, launch a massive rearmament programme and begin challenging US hegemony in the Pacific. Counter-measures by Washington would place the two powers on a collision course and it would merely be a matter of time before a 'hot war' broke out.

The rogue variable in the analysis was China. Friedman and LeBard assumed that China would fragment and implode, just as the Soviet Union had, leaving Japan and America as the rivals in a struggle to secure control over it. It all happened differently: China embarked upon a phase of phenomenal growth and internal consolidation, while Japan entered a long period of economic stagnation. The book was clever, well written and deftly argued, but it was also wrong. 'I'm sure the author had good reasons in 1991 to write this, and he's a really smart guy,' one reader commented in an Amazon review of 2014 (having failed to notice Meredith LeBard's co-authorship). 'But here we are, 23 years later, and Japan wouldn't even make the list of the top 30 nations in the world the US would go to war with.'

This is the difficult thing about the future: it hasn't happened yet. It can only be imagined as the extrapolation of current or past trends. But forecasting on this basis is problematic in the extreme. First: the present is marked by a vast array of potentially relevant trends, each waxing and waning, augmenting each other or cancelling each other out; this makes extrapolation exceptionally difficult. Second: neither for the present nor for the past do experts tend to find themselves in general agreement on how the most important events were or are being caused – this too, bedevils the task of extrapolation, since there always remains a degree of uncertainty about which trends are more and which are less relevant to the future in question. And finally: major discontinuities and upheavals seem by their nature to be unpredictable. The author of *The Reign of George VI* failed to predict the American and French Revolutions, whose impact on the international system would be profound and lasting. None of the historians or political scientists expert in central and eastern European affairs predicted the collapse of the Soviet bloc, the fall of the Berlin Wall, the creation of a new Germany or the dissolution of the Soviet Union. And Friedman and LeBard failed to foresee the current ascendancy of China – economic, political and military.

Lawrence Freedman's wide-ranging book *The Future of War* is aware of these limits of human foresight. It is not really about the future at all, but about how societies – mainly in the anglophone West – have imagined it. The book doesn't advance a single overarching argument; its strength lies rather in the sovereign presentation of a diverse range of subject matter situated at various distances from the central theme: the abiding military fantasy of the 'decisive battle', the place of peace conferences in the history of warfare, the impact of nuclear armaments on strategic thought, the quantification of wars and their human cost, the place of cruelty in modern warfare and the changing face of war in a world of cyberweapons and hybrid strategy.

In modern societies, the business of imagining wars to come has been done not just by experts and military planners, but also by lay autodidacts and the writers of fiction. The most influential early description of a modern society under attack by a ruthless enemy was H. G. Wells's bestseller, *The War of the Worlds*, in which armies of Martians in fast-moving metal tripods poured 'heat rays' and poisonous gas into London, clogging the highways with terrified refugees who were subsequently themselves captured and destroyed, their bodily fluids being required for the nourishment of the invaders. The Martians had been launched from their home planet by a 'space gun' borrowed from Jules Verne's *From the Earth to the Moon* (1865), but the underlying inspiration came from the destruction of the indigenous Tasmanians after the British settlement of the island, an epic of rapes, beatings and killings that, together with pathogens carried by the invaders, wiped out virtually the entire black population (a few survived on nearby Flinders Island). The shock effect of Wells's fiction derived not from the novelty of such destruction, which was already familiar from the European colonial past, but from its unexpected relocation to a white metropolitan setting.

The most accurate forecasts of the stalemate on the Western Front in 1914–18 stemmed not from the hands of a professional military strategist, but from the Polish financier and peace advocate Ivan

Stanislavovich Bloch (1836–1901), whose six-volume study *The War of the Future in Its Technical Economic and Political Relations* (1898) argued that not even the boldest and best-trained soldiers would be able to cut through the lethal fire of a well dug-in adversary. The next war, he predicted, would be 'a great war of entrenchments' that would pit not just soldiers but entire populations against each other in a long attritional struggle.

Bloch's analysis of the larger strategic picture was unmatched, but no one imagined the *experience* of stationary warfare using modern weapons more precisely than the Hamburg schoolteacher Wilhelm Lamszus. His book, *Das Menschenschlachthaus*, published in 1912 and translated into English, French, Danish, Finnish, Czech and Japanese, foresaw the horrors of the Western Front with clairvoyant precision. A young man, the father of a family, leaves his home amid celebrations and marching music and makes his way to the front with his comrades:

> There rises a noise of screams and yells, an uproar so unnaturally wild and unrestrained that we cringe up closer to one another . . . and, trembling, we see that our faces, our uniforms, have red, wet stains, and distinctly recognize shreds of flesh on the cloth. And among our feet something is lying that was not lying there before – it gleams white from the dark sand and uncurls . . . a strange dismembered hand . . . and there . . . and there . . . fragments of flesh with the uniform still adhering to them – then we realize it, and horror overwhelms us. Outside there are lying arms, legs, heads, trunks . . . they are howling into the night; the whole regiment is lying mangled on the ground there, a lump of humanity crying to Heaven . . .

Bloch's meticulously detailed scenario was an argument for the avoidance of war. Lamszus was a pacifist, a Social Democrat and a critic of chauvinist imperialism. If this kind of thinking failed to have much impact on official planning, it was partly because such warnings tended to be written off as the whining of anarchists, traitors and neurasthenic cowards, and partly because military planners foresaw a different future, one in which determined offensives and shock tactics would still carry the day against defensive positions. The truly astonishing thing is that their optimism survived the First World War. It waned during the early years of the conflict, in the face of immense slaughter for minimal gains, but revived in 1917–18, with the return to a war of movement marked by massive offensive strikes and break-throughs into enemy terrain.

The advent of aerial warfare – more than any other early twentieth-century military innovation – stimulated visions of transformation, though contemporaries were divided on the question of how exactly it would shape future conflicts. The first actual war to see the use of aerial bombardment took place in the context of the Italo-Turkish War of 1911, a conflict that began when the Kingdom of Italy attacked and invaded the Ottoman territory known today as Libya. Before many major actions in the Libyan War, Italian aeroplanes went up in reconnaissance, signalling the enemy's position and strength, so that the Italians could shell the Turkish guns from field batteries or from ironclads moored offshore. In February 1912, an Ottoman retreat between the Zanzur oasis and Gargaresch to the southeast of Tripoli became a rout when the Italian Dirigible *P3* dropped bombs among the retiring troops. Dirigibles could carry up to 250 bombs charged with high explosive. Bombs could be dropped in small numbers from aeroplanes, too, though this was an awkward business, since the aviator had somehow to steer the machine while gripping the bomb between his knees and using his free hand to insert the fuse, before aiming it by hand at the troops below. Elsewhere, the gross technological imbalance between the Italian armies and the Ottoman subjects whose province they were invading had less lethal effects. George Frederick Abbott, a British observer with the Ottoman forces, recalled seeing Italian planes bombard Turco-Arabic encampments with bundles of proclamations, which fluttered in the sunlight 'like so many flakes of toy snow'. These were the verbose missives of Italian government propaganda, composed in an antiquated Arabic that most of the troops engaged in the fighting below could not read. The Arabs, Abbott recalled, 'left off firing and, stooping, picked up the sheets eagerly, in the hope that they might be bank-notes'.

The application of air power was hardly conclusive in Libya: it would take the Italians twenty years to 'pacify' the hinterland of the coastal cities. But its potential was already obvious to contemporaries. H. G. Wells's *The War in the Air* (1908) imagined a form of airborne campaigning so devastating for all sides that a meaningful victory by any one party was unthinkable. He depicted an America under attack in the east from German airships and *drachenfliegers* and in the west from an 'Asiatic air fleet' equipped with swarms of heavily armed 'ornithopters' (lightweight one-man flying machines). The book closed with a post-apocalyptic vision of civilizational collapse and the social and political disintegration of all of the belligerent states.

Others saw aerial warfare as a means of recapturing the promise of a swift and decisive victory. One of the first military analysts of its potential was the Italian officer and air power enthusiast Giulio Douhet, who had been tasked in 1911 with reporting on the significance of the Libyan campaign for the future deployment of planes in warfare. As commander of the Italian aviation battalion at Turin from 1912, Douhet composed one of the first air force manuals, the *Rules for the Use of Airplanes in War*. The first draft was heavily edited by Douhet's conservative military superiors, who objected to his characterization of aircraft as 'weapons'. But Douhet continued to espouse the value of aircraft in increasingly visionary terms. 'To gain command of the air,' he wrote in an essay of December 1914, 'is to be able to attack with impunity any point of the enemy's body.' Aware of the power of fiction as a tool for the imaginative exploration of possible futures, he wrote a novel entitled *The War of 19–*, in which he foresaw a war between Germany and a Franco-Belgian alliance. In it, Douhet described German bombers striking cities immediately after the commencement of hostilities in order to demoralize their populations. His influential study *The Command of the Air* (1920) aimed to show how an aerial attack, if conducted with sufficient resources, could carry war to the nerve centres of the enemy, breaking civilian morale and thereby placing decision-makers under pressure to capitulate. To this day, scholars disagree on the role played by aerial bombing in bringing the Allied war against Nazi Germany to an end, and the Vietnam War remains the classic example of a conflict in which overwhelming air superiority failed to secure victory.

The ultimate twentieth-century weapon of shock was the atomic bomb. The five-ton device dropped by an American bomber on Hiroshima on 6 August 1945 flattened four square miles of the city and killed 80,000 people instantly. The second bomb, dropped three days later on Nagasaki, killed a further 40,000. The advent of this new generation of nuclear armaments – and above all the acquisition of the same weapon by the Soviet Union – opened up new futures. In 1954, a team at the RAND Corporation led by Albert Wohlstetter warned that if the leadership of one nuclear power came to the conclusion that a pre-emptive victory over the other was possible, these devastating weapons might actually be used in a surprise attack. On the other hand, if the destructive forces available to both sides were in broad equilibrium, there was reason to hope that the fear of nuclear holocaust would itself stay the hands of potential belligerents. 'Safety', as Winston Churchill put it in a speech to the British parliament in March 1955, might prove 'the sturdy child of terror and survival the twin brother of annihilation'.

And this line of argument gained ground as the underlying stability of the post-war order became apparent. The 'function of nuclear armaments', the Australian international relations theorist Hedley Bull suggested in 1959, was to 'limit the incidence of war'. In a nuclear world, Bull argued, states were not just unlikely to conclude a general disarmament agreement, they would be 'acting rationally in refusing to do so'. In an influential paper of 1981, the political scientist Kenneth Waltz elaborated this line of argument, proposing that the peacekeeping effect of nuclear weapons was such that it might be a good idea idea to allow more states to acquire one: 'more might be better'. In a lecture delivered at the University of Cambridge, the Israeli military historian Martin van Creveld argued that nuclear weapons were the single most important reason for the peace that had prevailed among the great powers since 1945. 'These awesome weapons,' he declared, 'are the most beautiful gift mankind has ever given to itself.'

Most of us will fail to find much comfort in this Strangelovian vision. It is based on two assumptions: that the nuclear sanction will always remain in the hands of state actors and that state actors will always act rationally and abide by the existing arms control regimes. The first axiom still holds, but the second looks fragile. North Korea's nuclear deterrent is under the single-handed control of one of the most opaque personalities in world politics. In January 2018, Kim

Jong-un reminded the world that a nuclear launch button is 'always on my table' and that the entire United States was within the range of his nuclear arsenal: 'This is a reality not a threat.' For his part, the president of the United States taunted his Korean colleague, calling him 'short and fat', 'a sick puppy' and 'a madman', warning him that his own 'nuclear button' was 'much bigger and more powerful' and threatening to rain 'fire and fury' down on his country. Then came the US–North Korea summit of 12 June 2018 in Singapore. The two leaders strutted before the cameras and the American president spoke of the 'terrific friendship' between them. The 'sick puppy' was now a 'smart cookie'. But the Singapore meeting was diplomatic fast food. It lacked, to put it mildly, the depth and granularity of the meticulously prepared summits of the 1980s. And since then, the temperature of relations has plummeted again: 2020 opened with a New Year's Day speech in which Kim Jong-un announced a 'new strategic weapon' and threatened to initiate, in the curious parlance of North Korean policy statements, a 'shocking actual action' if the US did not scale down its sanctions against North Korea. We are as yet no closer to the denuclearization of the Korean Peninsula than we were before.

Russia has installed a new and more potent generation of intermediate-range nuclear missiles aimed at European targets, in breach of the 1987 INF Treaty, and the US administration has responded with a Nuclear Posture Review that loosens constraints on the tactical use of nuclear weapons. The entire international arms control regime so laboriously pieced together in the 1980s and 90s is falling apart. In a climate marked by resentment, aggression, braggadocio and mutual distrust, the likelihood of a hot nuclear confrontation either through miscalculation or by accident seems greater than at any time since the end of the Cold War.

In a compellingly argued and influential essay, 'The Better Angels of our Nature', Steven Pinker proposed that the human race, notwithstanding these grim omens, is in fact becoming less violent, that the 'better angels' of our nature are slowly gaining the upper hand as more and more societies come to accept the view that 'war is inherently immoral because of its costs to human well-being'. During the 'long peace' since 1945, there has been a decline in every kind of organized conflict. And this has been accompanied by a fall in more spontaneous forms of violence: in present-day Europe, your chances of being murdered are between one-tenth and one-fiftieth of what they would have been had you lived 500 years ago. Lawrence Freedman, emeritus professor of war studies at King's College London, is sceptical of these claims and of the optimism that seems to be licensed by them. Pinker's principal yardstick of progress, the declining number of violent deaths per 100,000 people per year across the world over the span of human history, strikes Freedman as too crude: it fails to take account of regional variations, phases of accelerated killing and demographic change; it assumes excessively low death estimates for the twentieth century, and ignores the fact that deaths are not the only measure of violence in a world that has become much better at keeping the maimed and traumatized alive.

However the numbers stack up *in toto*, there has clearly been a change in the context and distribution of fatalities. Since 1945, state-*vs*-state conflicts have been a less important source of mortalities than various forms of civil war, a mode of warfare that has never been prominent in the fictions of future conflict. It is estimated that 2 million died under the regime of Pol Pot in Cambodia in the 1970s, though 'only' 80,000–100,000 of these were actually killed by regime personnel; the rest perished through starvation or disease. In a remarkable spree of low-tech killing, the Rwandan genocide took the lives of between 500,000 and 1 million people. The relationship between military and civilian mortalities has also seen drastic change. In the early twentieth century, according to one rough estimate, the ratio of military to civilian deaths was around 8:1; in the wars of the 1990s, it was 1:8. One important reason for this is the greater resistance of today's troops to disease: whereas 18,000 British and French troops perished of cholera during the Crimean War, in 2002 the total number of British soldiers hospitalized in Afghanistan on account of infectious disease was twenty-nine, of whom not one died. On the other hand, civilians caught up in modern military conflicts, especially in contexts where medical services and humanitarian supplies are disrupted, remain highly exposed to disease, thirst and malnutrition.

A further reason for the disproportionate ballooning of civilian deaths is the tendency of military interventions to morph into chronic insurgencies and civil wars. Counting the dead is extremely difficult in the context of a dysfunctional or destroyed state riven by civil strife, but the broad trends are clear enough. Whereas the total number of Iraqi combat deaths from the air and ground campaigns in the 1991 Gulf War appears to have been between 8,000 and 26,000, the total number of consequent Iraqi civilian deaths was around 100,000. Whereas several tens of thousands of Iraqi military personnel were killed in the Second Gulf War, the total civilian death toll may have been as high as 460,000 (the *Lancet* estimate of 655,000 is widely regarded as too high). The deaths incurred by the coalition forces in these two conflicts were 292 and 4,815 respectively. So the problem may not be warfare as such, but the fact that even the most determined and skilful applications of military force, rather than definitively resolving disputes, inaugurate processes of escalation or disintegration that exact a much higher human toll than the military intervention itself.

The resulting deterritorialization of violence in regions marked by decomposing states makes the kind of 'decision' Clausewitz associated with battle difficult to achieve or even to imagine. 'With the change in the type and tactics of a new and different enemy,' Robert H. Latiff writes in *Future War*, 'we have evolved in the direction of total surveillance, unmanned warfare, stand-off weapons, surgical strikes, cyber operations and clandestine operations by elite forces whose battlefield is global.' In pithy, flip-chart paragraphs, Latiff, a former US Air Force major general, sketches a vision of the future that resembles the fictional scenarios of William Gibson's *Neuromancer*. In the wars of the future, he suggests, the 'Metabolically Dominant Soldier' enjoying the benefits of immunity to pain, reinforced muscle strength, accelerated healing and 'cognitive enhancement' will enter the battlespace neurally linked not just to his human comrades but also to swarms of semi-autonomous bots. 'Flimmers', missiles that can both fly and swim, will menace enemy craft on land and at sea, while undersea drones will seek out submarines and communication cables. Truck-mounted 'Area Denial Systems' will deploy 'painrays' that heat the fluid under human skin to boiling point. Enemy missiles and aircraft will buckle and explode in the intense heat of chemical lasers. High-power radio-frequency pulses will fry electrical equipment across wide areas. Hyersonic 'boost-glide vehicles' will ride atop rockets before being released to attack their prey at such enormous speeds that shooting them down with conventional missiles will be 'next to impossible'. 'Black biology' will add to these terrors a phalanx of super-immune pathogens. Of the more than $600 billion the US spends annually on defence, about $200 billion are allocated to research, development and the testing and procurement of new weapons systems.

Latiff acknowledges some of the ethical issues here, though he has little of substance to say about how they might be addressed. How will the psychology of 'human–robot cooperation' work out in practice? Will metabolically dominant warriors returning from war be able to settle back comfortably into civilian society? What if robots commit war crimes, or children get trapped in the path of pain rays? What if radio-magnetic pulse weapons shut down hospitals, or engineered pathogens trigger epidemics? Will the growing use of drones or AI-driven vehicles diminish the capacity of armed forces personnel to perceive the enemy as fully human? 'An arms race using all of the technologies I've described,' writes Latiff towards the end of his book, 'will not be like anything we've seen, and the ethical implications are frightening.'

Frightening indeed. It's hard not to be impressed by the inventiveness of the weapons experts in their underground labs, but hard, too, not to despair at the way in which such ingenuity has been uncoupled from larger ethical imperatives. And one can't help but be struck by the cool, acquiescent prose in which the war studies experts portion out their arguments, as if war is and will always be a human necessity, a feature of our existence as natural as birth or the movement of clouds. Pondering on these matters, I found myself recalling a remark made by the French sociologist Bruno Latour when he visited Cambridge in the spring of 2016. 'It is surely a matter of consequence,' Latour said, surprising the emphatically secular colleagues in the room, 'to know whether we as humans are in a condition of redemption or perdition.'

Over the last few years, as the INF treaty architecture of the 1980s has fallen apart and the Russians, the Chinese and the US have announced new generations of weaponry, I have often thought of Latour's words. The advocates of peace will always be vulnerable to the argument that since the enemy is whetting his knife, the talk of peace is unrealistic, even dangerous or treacherous. The quest for peace, like the struggle to arrest climate change, requires that we think of ourselves not just as states, tribes or nations, but as the human inhabitants of a shared space. It demands feats of imagination as concerted and impressive as the sci-fi creativeness and wizardry we invest in future wars. It requires the use of reason to ascend from the narrow standpoint of a particular interest to a vantage point from which we can see, as Peter Singer, professor of bioethics at Princeton University, has put it, 'that our own interests are similar to and, from the point of view of the universe, do not matter more than, the interests of others'. It means connecting the intellectual work done in Centres of War Studies with the research conducted in Peace Institutes, and applying to the task of avoiding war the long-term pragmatic reasoning we associate with 'strategy'. 'I don't think that we need any new values,' Mikhail Gorbachev told an interviewer in 1997. 'The most important thing is to try to revive the universally known values from which we have retreated.' And it must surely be true, as Pope Francis remarked in April 2016, that the abolition of war remains 'the ultimate and most deeply worthy goal of human beings'.

High in the Joyful Air

In January 2018 I travelled to Sydney on a family errand. During my stay there I read Jürgen Osterhammel's *The Transformation of the World: A Global History of the Nineteenth Century*. Like virtually all of my colleagues in modern history, I had often delved into this book in search of passages addressing whatever questions were preoccupying me. But now I read the book from beginning to end as a *book*, or rather as a Kindle text – since *Transformation* was much too heavy for a long-haul flight. It was my first Kindle reading experience and it took some getting used to. One tracked one's progress through the text not by what Jane Austen once called 'the tell-tale compression of the pages', but by a small percentage indicator at the bottom of each page. After many hours of reading pleasure the device announced that I had reached 4 per cent. Of the bound mass of paper that perches like a flightless bird in the reader's hand, only an abstract quantity of words remained.

As I made my way across this quantity of words, I was overcome by a pleasant sensation. I seemed to be floating over a world full of people, over mountains and bridges, over valleys crossed by railways, over battlefields and libraries, hospitals and steamships. I saw plagues and sheets of water spread out across the land. I saw the violence of nature break into the history of human beings: earthquakes, tsunamis, volcanic eruptions, droughts, rain, the changing patterns of climate. I saw how humans came into the world and how they died, how they moved in great numbers, or were moved, spurred on by wars and revolutions: refugees, exiles, convicts, migrants, travellers.

I was reminded of the American poet Walt Whitman, a man of the nineteenth century. Think of how Whitman's eye floats over persons and things, how his glance touches hurrying pedestrians, old women, harbour workers and waitresses, mothers giving birth, slaves on sugar plantations. He doesn't call them by name, he sees them in categories, but he knows how they make a living, how broad or narrow is the spectrum of their opportunities, whether they go to sleep with a full belly or hungry. He is interested in the connections people build, the things that bring them together. In 1865, in 'Crossing Brooklyn Ferry', he observes the evening masses of office workers from Manhattan board little ferries to cross the East River to their homes:

Flood-tide below me! I see you face to face!
Clouds of the west – sun there half an hour high – I see you also face to face.

Crowds of men and women attired in the usual costumes, how curious you
     are to me!
On the ferry-boats the hundreds and hundreds that cross, returning home,
     are more curious to me than you suppose,
And you that shall cross from shore to shore years hence are more to me,
     and more in my meditations, than you might suppose.

Later, in 1883, the Brooklyn ferries were replaced by the Brooklyn Bridge. In an essay about borders and bridges, Osterhammel reflects on the difference that a bridge makes:

A world without bridges would be slower, damper, more resistant, composed of smaller parts, a world of fords, ferries and ravines into which one must first descend and from which one must climb back out. In many thinly settled areas outside Europe this world still exists. To this day, there is not a single bridge that crosses the Amazon.

To compare Jürgen Osterhammel with Walt Whitman may seem far-fetched, but in fact it is not. After all, Osterhammel is interested in the big connections that frame our existence. He is interested in the restless movement of people and things. 'The history of human-kind is present to [Whitman's] spirit,' declared W. Schlösser in the foreword to the 1948 German edition of Whitman's *Leaves of Grass*. 'His thought is wrought from the myths of humanity's great teachers; the knowledge of his time submits in good order to his reason.' We could say much the same of Jürgen Osterhammel, although in his case it's the *theories*, rather than the myths, of the great teachers that inform his thinking. Whitman's enthusiastic German translator, the naturalist playwright and author Johannes Schlaf, described the American poet as 'broad-chested and sunburned, the white-haired head raised above the highest summits, his feet fixed fast to the earth, his gaze piercing the states from sea to sea'. Here, too, one can discern a certain resemblance between the poet and the historian, with exception of the white-haired head, which doesn't yet quite apply to Jürgen Osterhammel.

The reference to the height of summits is suggestive. 'The view from the summit', Osterhammel observes on page 1279 of his book (yes, it's a long book), 'is an impressive experience.' And in an essay entitled 'The Altitude of Eagles', published in 2017 in a book with the same title, Osterhammel discovers an interesting commonality between the enigmatic poet Friedrich Hölderlin and the naturalist Alexander von Humboldt: both men loved mountains. Humboldt was among the most intrepid and successful mountain climbers of his era. But Hölderlin, too, found in the bridges of the Swiss Alps a 'concentrated metaphor for the mobile mastery of life in the high ranges': 'with fearless steps, the sons of the Alps pass across the abyss / on lightly constructed bridges'. And Humboldt admired the intricate rope bridges of Equador – robust, economical, terrifying – across which the traveller was advised to run 'as fast as possible and with the upper body bent forward'. Hölderlin and Humboldt, who, as far as we know, never met each other, come together, Osterhammel writes, 'in a pictorial world of heights, bridges and the defiance of separation'.

The summit is immobile, of course. It offers the observer just one breathtaking panorama. Eagles and cranes are more fortunate, because 'the liberty of the bird resides not only in the infiniteness of its airy medium, but also in the capacity to view things from a range of distances'. Hence Hölderlin's affinity for birds: 'High in the joyful air, the falcon looks about him'. It was precisely this vertiginous feeling of altitude, combined with an eagle's eye for the details on the ground that struck me as I read Jürgen Osterhammel's *Transformation*.

I'd like to focus on a few aspects of the book that seem to me particularly important. But first I should say that Osterhammel has written other books, not to mention many articles and essays. *China und die*

Weltgesellschaft (China and World Society), published in 1989, pioneered a new approach that would shape his later work, because it was concerned both with China's entry into the 'global system of states' and with its integration into 'that form of global economy that emerged in the eighteenth century and was dramatically extended and deepened from the last quarter of the nineteenth century onwards'. Osterhammel fixes his gaze on the variety of regional linkages – for example, the contrast between the Canton trade, which was oriented towards the West, and the very different conditions obtaining along the Chinese borders with Russia. He attempts to overcome the Eurocentrism latent in the European archival records and in the Western historical literature by 'switching seamlessly' between 'sinocentric' and 'eurocentric' perspectives. By this means he recuperates a sense of the room for manoeuvre available to the Chinese, notwithstanding the asymmetry of the forces engaged, and at the same time explaining why the Western powers succeeded, at long last, after the Treaty of Nanking in 1842, in saddling the Chinese with agreements that seriously curtailed their sovereignty.

The book was also about overleaping infradisciplinary boundaries. The history of China in the modern era, Osterhammel wrote, can be told along two parallel narrative tracks: that of the political integration of China into the international community and that of its economic incorporation into the world economy. Both strands can in theory be developed separately and independently of each other, were it not for the fact that, in China, trade and the international legal framework within which it took place were always and with good reason 'understood primarily as a *political* matter'. It is precisely the interweaving of different factors, mixed in varying proportions, Osterhammel wrote, that gives rise to 'the specificity of particular historical situations'.

The boundaries between disciplines are as a rule even more energetically guarded than the boundaries within them, and here too Osterhammel wanted to build bridges. As late as the 1980s, the history of Asia was largely written by specialists in Islamic studies, sinologists and indologists, rather than by historians. And this tended to conceal from view the multifaceted interactions between Europe and the rest of the world. What was needed was a scholar who was not merely an historian and a political scientist but also a sinologist (even if Jürgen Osterhammel prefers not to apply this latter term to himself).

In *The Disenchantment of Asia. Europe and the Asian Empires in the Eighteenth Century*, Osterhammel focused on eighteenth-century European discourses about Asia. Here, too, there was a bridge to be built, a bridge extending back over the violence and divisions of the nineteenth century towards an older literature that was seriously interested in global experience and in a general science of humankind. Today, when so many of my younger colleagues want to be world historians (this is the case in Cambridge, at least), it is easy to forget how fresh and innovative the early work of Jürgen Osterhammel was, and I am not referring here just to the studies of China, but also to his essays on the history of the League of Nations – the works he published on this subject in the 1970s are still regarded as reference texts and are cited everywhere. Osterhammel was a pioneer.

It's interesting in this connection to note the many parallels with the professional path of my friend and colleague Christopher Bayly. In his great study of 1983, *Rulers, Townsmen and Bazaars: North Indian Society in the Age of British Expansion, 1770–1870*, Bayly succeeded, like Osterhammel in *China and World Society*, in doing justice to the drastic asymmetries of imperialism without occluding from view the extraordinary variety and irrepressible dynamism of Indian society. And much the same can be said both for Bayly's 1996 study *Empire and Information* and for Osterhammel's *Disenchantment of Asia*. Osterhammel focused primarily on the literary genre of the travel narrative in the age of Enlightenment, Bayly on the emergence of 'colonial knowledge' within the framework of the British colonial administration in India between 1780 and 1880. But both books distanced themselves from the thesis, increasingly fashionable in the 1980s, that the knowledge of Asia cultivated by Western observers was rooted exclusively in the fantasies of an Orientalist imaginary largely detached from reality. And Bayly's *Imperial Meridian*, in which he reconceived the global history of the axial era between 1770 and 1830 as a multi-imperial, interactive global history, intersected at many points with Osterhammel's enmeshed histories of the Imperial 'civilizing missions'. For both historians, this gradual expansion of the field of vision led in the direction of a spectacular, career-crowning modern and global synthesis – even if Osterhammel rejects the word 'synthesis' on the characteristically self-effacing grounds that a narrative drawn from the expert knowledge and arguments of hundreds of living and dead colleagues is not really a synthesis, but a 'composite analysis', a mosaic.

One especially striking feature of *Transformation* is the clarity and precision of the language. Jürgen Osterhammel describes, for example, how the increasingly systematic and institutionalized storage of knowledge gave rise to new forms of erudition while rendering others obsolete. 'Learnedness was decoupled from feats of personal memorization; the once admired knowledge-accumulating polymath became a pitiable curiosity.' What is pleasing about this sentence is not its literary beauty but the conceptual clarity of its distinctions and the density of its intellectual substance. Was China's present-day ascendancy 'preprogrammed long in advance'? No, Osterhammel replies. The 'Rise of China' that fills our headlines today is not a single homogeneous state of affairs, but a composite and multilayered phenomenon, each of whose strata possesses its own prehistory. Different factors will come into focus if we examine the problem from the perspective of, say, 1930, than if we adopt the turn of the twentieth century as our vantage point. 'Every different temporal horizon,' Osterhammel writes, 'brings its own explanatory mechanisms into play.' Again and again, there are formulations one would like to note down, because they convey complex claims with insurpassable precision. And this brings us back to Walt Whitman, about whom the radical poet Ferdinand Freiligrath, living in English exile, wrote: he possesses a 'plain language', calling 'each thing by its right name without renouncing that sonority that gives pleasure to a refined ear'.

Osterhammel has a fine feeling for the tension between Leopold von Ranke's respect for the unique particularity of every epoch and the anticipatory character of past constellations. 'The telegraphy [of the nineteenth century],' writes Osterhammel, 'was much too cumbersome, overloaded and expensive (in 1898 the Times paid 15% of its annual revenue for telegraphy fees) to qualify as a "Victorian internet", but at least the underlying patterns of an historically unprecedented *world wide web* had been laid.' What Osterhammel does here diachronically, between one age and the next, he also achieves synchronically, by means of comparison. One could cite hundreds of examples. Suffice it to say that Osterhammel is constantly weighing commonalities and differences against each other. He steers his boat with a steady hand between the Scylla of axiomatic contrast and the Charybdis of an 'ecumene' grounded in the presumption of a common human condition.

Again and again, Osterhammel invites us to reflect on the fundamental categories of historical understanding, on the conceptual repertoire of historical reasoning. Is the wet space of the oceans different from the mostly dry space of continents? How are space and time connected in historical thinking? What is an era? 'The thresholds between eras,' Osterhammel writes, 'cannot be discerned by enquiring more deeply into the objective "meaning" of specific epochs. They only emerge when numerous finely calibrated chronologies are superimposed. Thresholds become visible, one might say, when such fine dividing lines accumulate into thickened embankments, or when we observe a compression in the frequency of change.' The answers that Osterhammel finds to these and other fundamental questions should be mandatory reading for all growing historians.

'Numerous finely calibrated chronologies': *The Transformation of the World* is marked throughout by an acute awareness of temporality, a feeling for the experienced duration of time, for the texture of time. Does it flow fast or slowly? Does it flow at all, or is it apprehended in discrete intervals and moments? Does the future crash into the present, or is the present driven forwards into an empty future, still to be filled with events? And Osterhammel understands that temporal horizons stretch not only into the future, but also into the past. How far back did human memory extend in the nineteenth century? In one of my favourite passages, Osterhammel reflects on the temporal range of memory. 'Only quite recently,' he writes, 'did the ninetenth century [. . .] sink below the horizon of what was personally recallable. We can date this moment back to the death in an Australian zoo in June 2006 of the giant tortoise Harriet, who had got to know the young naturalist Charles Darwin on the Galapagos Islands in 1835.'

There is so much to enjoy in this sentence. Quite apart from the fact that an Australian heart must swell at the thought of this plucky tortoise, an immigrant who had crossed oceans, the sentence invites us to reflect, at least fleetingly, on the question: what does it mean when a tortoise remembers something? And in what sense did this patient and clearly very adaptable animal 'get to know' the young Charles Darwin? I found myself thinking of the wonderful first line of the 'Baby Tortoise' poem by D. H. Lawrence: 'You know what it is,' Lawrence writes to a newly hatched tortoise, 'to be born alone.' Only to poets and historians falls the gift of spying into the souls of tortoises. There are many such pleasing moments in this book. Let me cite just one more: 'the formation of diasporas as a consequence of mass migration was omnipresent in the nineteenth century, it was almost the default condition. Only the French stayed at home.'

Finally, this book poses in the most pointed way the question at the heart of the best writing in world history: to what extent can the world historian of Western provenance leap over the shadow of her own Eurocentrism? One can, of course, expand the frame by inserting non-Western actors additively into the narrative. One can offer comparisons and parallels. But there remains the problem identified by the art historian James Elkins in 2007 in a book with the title *Is Art History Global?* Art historians who set themselves the task of writing a global art history have to come to terms with the fact that the entire methodological armature of their discipline is Western in origin; indeed that it hails almost exclusively from one specific region of the European continent, namely Germany. In order to offset this disadvantage, Elkins writes, the better colleagues make an effort to integrate the hermeneutic traditions of their subjects. A sophisticated study of Chinese art, for example, might draw on the repertoire of Chinese art criticism and apply indigenous ways of seeing to the analysis of Chinese works of art. But what, as a rule, they do not do is interpret objects from the European canon by the criteria of Chinese art reception. No serious art historian in a Western institution would apply the concepts of Confucian art criticism to the interpretation of a painting by Monet. It is precisely by integrating non-Western works and concepts into their field of vision, but not into their interpretative or narrative technique, that such historians underscore the Eurocentric character of their enterprise.

The Cambridge historian of science Simon Schaffer spoke some years ago in a wonderful lecture with the title 'Histories of Astronomy and Empire' about the journey that the astronomer John Evershed made to the Wallal Mission on the coast of Western Australia in order to observe and record with an array of instruments the total eclipse of the sun on 21 September 1922. The astronomers were interested in measuring the displacement of stars that could be seen in the sky near the totally darkened disc of the sun. And their results confirmed fairly exactly what Albert Einstein had predicted seven years before in his General Theory of Relativity. What never appeared in the official report of the expedition, Simon Schaffer reminded us, were the Nyangumarda men of the area, about forty in number, whose help was essential to the success of the entire project; after all, it was they who built the huts and the kitchen and saw to the needs of the male and female strangers engaged in the observations.

Now, one can say that by integrating these people into the narrative, we have partially overcome the Eurocentric vantage point. On the other hand, it would be better and more interesting if the optical perspective were itself inverted, at least temporarily. If one succeeded in doing that, one might understand the history of the Wallal Expedition as a story about how the Nyangumarda people, with their own traumatic Australian history, viewed the work of the astronomical strangers through the lens of their own cosmology. The cosmology of the Australian peoples, their knowledge of the heavenly bodies, has in recent years been the subject of intensive research. But, of course, no one asked the Nyangumarda what they made of the busy intruders with their instruments. The sources that would allow us to undertake such a retelling do not exist, at least not in this case. But even the thought that one could reorient perspectives in this way alerts us to what is lost from view when we tell modernity in our way.

Jürgen Osterhammel knows this. He lets non-European experiences and ways of seeing speak in his text. But it is one of the strengths of his work that he also acknowledges the limits of history's field of vision, that he doesn't bracket out the dark matter of the past, but acknowledges its presence as the inscrutable companion of our thoughts.

In Memory of Christopher Bayly

Christopher Bayly's books didn't document results, they tracked intellectual journeys. 'This book,' Chris wrote at the opening of *Rulers, Townsmen and Bazaars* (1983), a study that transformed historical understanding of the impact of British rule in India, 'grew out of a fascination with the rich pattern of commercial life still to be found in the tangled lanes of brass-smiths' stalls and ancient merchant houses which lay behind the water-front of the city of Benares.' The stately water-front mansions of the *ghats* (bathing wharves) of Benares (Varanasi) were just a point of disembarkation. What interested him were the tangled lanes behind.

These steps away from the waterfront into the recesses behind elite networks and smooth historiographical surfaces can be traced in every book Chris wrote. Chris was acutely aware of the intricately layered quality of human societies. Again and again, he offered his readers vertiginous views through superimposed social textures. Nothing in what unfolds before our eyes is obvious, because everything is in motion. Clans and occupational fraternities coalesce into class-like structures; power changes hands: cosmopolitan oligarchs yield to merchants, Nanakpanthi Khattris take over from their Islamicized caste fellows; Kannada merchants and Chettis slip into positions once occupied by Armenians and Jews. Chris saw a piece of agency, a spark of resilience and hope, in everyone who entered his field of vision.

And consider this passage from the introduction to Bayly's *Empire and Information*, one of my favourite books:

> [This book] is a study of social communication in the sense used in Karl
> Deutsch's pioneering work. It considers those specialists who helped to

articulate indigenous systems of knowledge and keep information, ideas and gossip flowing: the astrologers, physicians, experts in the philosopher's stone, midwives, marriage makers, and other knowledgeable people who brought news from one community and region to another. It was the density and flexibility of indigenous routines of social communication which explains why north Indians were able to make such striking use of the printing press, the newspaper and the public meeting once those innovations finally began to spread rapidly amongst them in the 1830s and 1840s.

What a characteristic passage! It opens with an appeal to theory – in this case Karl Deutsch's *Nationalism and Social Communication* of 1953. Then we catch an extraordinary glimpse of the people and networks who are going to animate the book, the profusion and variety conveyed through the poetry of a list (Chris loved lists, but his lists are never hierarchical – he was equally interested in and equally attentive to every item in the sequence). And then out of this synchronic commotion, the forward surge of modernization: the printing press, the newspaper, the public meeting. Chris's thinking breathes in these words.

When he died unexpectedly of a heart attack in Chicago on 18 April 2015, Sir Christopher Bayly was the pre-eminent historian of India and the British Empire and a pioneer in the field of global history. He was also the first British academic ever to be knighted 'for services to history outside of Europe'. Chris's distinction was international, as the long list of his appointments and honours testifies, but his career was centred on St Catharine's College, where he was elected in 1970 to a fellowship and college lectureship in history and became director of studies in history. We talked and worked there together for twenty-five years. In 1992 Chris Bayly was appointed to the Vere Harmsworth Professorship of Imperial and Naval History. At the time of his death, only two years after his retirement from Cambridge, he held concurrent professorships at the University of Chicago, the University of Copenhagen and Queen Mary University of London.

Chris was born in Tunbridge Wells, Kent, to a family entangled with the history of empire. He remembered childhood conversations with his London cockney grandfather, who had fought during the

First World War in Egypt, Palestine and Turkey. His father had seen service all over the world as a merchant mariner, including on ships running copra from India. 'So I had an early introduction to colonial and world history,' he would later say. The history Chris learned at the Skinners' School in Tunbridge Wells and as an undergraduate at Balliol, Oxford, from 1963, was broad in its intellectual horizons but strongly European in focus. The turn towards a career in Indian history came in 1965, when Chris embarked on a long vacation journey across land to India, passing through Turkey, Iran, Afghanistan and Pakistan. Forced to avoid the Indian–Pakistani warzone, he travelled south to Karachi and caught a Shia pilgrimage boat to Basra. 'I got a sense of India from the other side,' he recalled in a July 2014 interview. 'Not dropping out of an aircraft. India in West Asia, and particularly the Muslim dimension. So that was a very formative experience.'

At St Antony's, Oxford, his graduate college, Sarvepalli Gopal and Albert Hourani guided his reading in the histories of India and the Middle East; the supervisor of his doctoral thesis was Jack Gallagher (also of Balliol), who was then overseeing a transformation in British imperial history. Chris came to Cambridge in 1970 at the invitation of Eric Stokes, Smuts Professor of British Commonwealth History, who had been at St Catharine's College since 1963. The transfer to Cambridge was arranged, as Chris later recalled, in the strikingly relaxed way typical of those times: 'Jack phoned Eric: "Eric, have you got a job there for this funny person called Bayly that I've got?" He said: "Maybe we do," and that was it.'

Eric Stokes was to be Chris's most important mentor. In the 1970s, Stokes was moving away from the issues of principle and ideology that had commanded the attention of his earlier work towards an approach to Indian history that stressed the importance of landholding structures and the pressures exerted on them by British systems of revenue management. An interest in the dynamic interaction between local elites and imperial governments would also be an abiding feature of Chris's work on India. Stokes's unpretentious and likeable scholarly persona was another inspiration. In a touching piece for the *Oxford Dictionary of National Biography*, Chris found words for Stokes, who had died in 1981, that one might use of Chris himself:

'His influence as a historian was accomplished not with domineering patronage, but through humour, self-deprecation, and intellectual inquisitiveness.'

The seething, ever-present mobility of the people in his narratives makes it impossible to think of India as something stagnant or passive, something to which history or empire simply happened. Chris's eye was fixed on those forces of self-organization and self-reinvention that predated the arrival of the British and would survive their departure to shape the India of today. Already in the earliest books on India, Chris had discerned parallels with peasant Egypt, small-town Meiji-era Japan and the striving professional classes of nineteenth-century China. These expansive reflections later fed into the two breakthrough books that shaped and deepened the new field of world history – *Imperial Meridian* and *The Birth of the Modern World* – establishing Chris as one of the foremost historians of his generation worldwide. *Imperial Meridian* (1989) marked a transition from highly textured work on the Indian subcontinent to a new kind of history focused on how the interactions between great imperial power complexes shaped and were shaped by processes of change within them. *The Birth of the Modern World, 1780–1914: Global Connections and Comparisons* (2004) not only did much to establish world history as a scholarly discipline, but also altered the conceptual framework of the subject by decentring the West.

The forging of that new kind of history reflected both an appreciative engagement with the work of other historians across the widest possible span of specialisms and an eagerness to build bridges with neighbouring disciplines. Anthropology was a subject that loomed especially large on Chris's intellectual horizons. There was, of course, a personal dimension to this encounter. Thirty-four years of marriage to Susan, an anthropologist of India and Vietnam, took shape as a life of perpetual travel and reunion, sustained and nourished by passionate argument and keen enthusiasm for one another's work. Anthropology was important, because once you began seeing Indian peasants as peasants rather than as imperial subjects and objects of British policy, the portals opened to a comparative and synoptic awareness of peasantries in other locations. The same opening of lateral perspectives enlivened Chris's writing on small business people, mercantile networks, religious confraternities and the other social groups who occupied his attention.

At a time when many other historians regarded official state archives as the only important source, Chris searched out the privately archived north Indian collections of commercial family record books from which he derived the most important insights in *Rulers, Townsmen and Bazaars*. Once deciphered, these complex texts allowed him to reconstruct the social and religious life of the merchant networks and thus to peer into worlds whose inner life had left little trace on the grand narratives of official reportage. He was probably the first scholar to make use of the *bahi khatas* (account books) that all significant mercantile families had kept for centuries. In these, Chris found not just a meticulous record of revenues and expenditures, but also entries documenting the constellation of relationships and affiliations that sustained the economic and moral life of merchant networks across much of the subcontinent. Alongside the double-entry bookkeeping were salutations to various deities, lists of temple accoutrements and accounts of expenditures on worship, bathing in the Ganges and gifts to Brahmins. And what struck him most as he worked with those difficult, handwritten texts was what he saw and heard when he lifted his gaze from the faded pages and observed what the banker-merchant families were doing all around him: especially the visits they hosted from the naked *sadhu* holy men who were still – in Chris's time – consigning their brotherhoods' assets to the trusted men of business whose forebears their own precursors had dealt with in centuries past. As Chris put it, in words reminiscent of Max Weber, whose work he had read closely, 'Notions of credit, piety and commercial security were closely tied together.' A nexus connecting commerce and religion announced itself here that would be a central theme in his subsequent work.

Chris learned as much from his dealings with the twentieth-century custodians of these mercantile depositories as he did from the documents themselves. He was impressed by anthropologists' insistence that intimate and everyday transactions can be the key to a sympathetic understanding of the world's people and places. He responded with particular excitement to the work of those anthropologists who brought to the exploration of social and cultural life in both familiar and far-flung settings a recognition that human existence is experienced dynamically, in a world of continual change.

Nowhere is the imprint of anthropology more clearly discernible than in the essay he wrote on Indian cloth, 'The origins of swadeshi (home industry)', published in 1986 in a groundbreaking volume, *The Social Life of Things*, edited by the anthropologist Arjun Appadurai. In this innovative piece, Chris charted the array of meanings ascribed to the production and consumption of cloth. In the early twentieth century, Indian nationalist leaders focused on the need to support artisanal Indian-made textiles against industrially produced British imports, which were seen as destroying indigenous weaving and the culture and communities sustained by it. But what was remarkable about this essay was the way Chris exposed the deep history of cloth as a product embodying various forms of non-commercial value. From the beautiful shawls ceremonially exchanged by rulers and courtiers in India's precolonial princedoms to Gandhi's famous khadi homespun cotton, over time Indians had invested cloth with cultural meaning. Chris did not treat Indian tastes and styles as the expressions of an ancient and unchanging culture, but as matters of economic, political and moral choice and initiative that were responsive to the changing horizons of Indian political expectations. What resulted was a 'collective biography' of Indian cloth over a period of 300 years. 'If slavery,' he wrote, 'was an example of how persons could be made "things", the history of cloth in India also showed how things could retain the quality of the people who fashioned and exchanged them.' Chris's was never an exoticizing or orientalist gaze; he never collapsed his historical protagonists into the inert contours of an unchanging tradition. His writings on Indian temple and trading cities, on the involvement of Hindu spiritual ascetics in the early colonial economic life of north India's networks, and his explorations of Hindu and Muslim statecraft in the transition from precolonial to colonial rule were brilliant studies in the flux and transitions of a complex society.

At the heart of *The Birth of the Modern World* was a narrative of convergence. The book opened with a powerful evocation of the diversity of bodily practices across the world's societies at the beginning of the modern era; the nineteenth century, Bayly argued, saw the rise of global uniformities in the structures and articulations of states, religions and economic life, visible not only in great institutions but also in modes of dress and the consumption of food. The book shrank the distance between 'the West' and 'the rest'; industrialization, urbanization, nationalism and the development of the state were for him ultimately global processes, notwithstanding local specificities. The book registered moments of heightened difference and antagonism, but, for Chris, these were always subordinate phenomena. Antagonisms flourished precisely because societies were becoming more connected and more alike. An intriguing example, much discussed in recent years, is the Islamic *burkah*, the full body covering of Muslim women. Often regarded in today's West as a mark of medieval obscurantism, Chris wrote, the *burkah* was originally 'a modern dress that allowed women to come out of the seclusion of their homes and participate to a limited degree in public and commercial affairs'.

The answers Chris found gave rise to new questions. If the history of the modern world was (or is) a history of convergence, what or who drove that process? Did convergence have a subject, or should we think of converge as an impersonal, subjectless verb? Is convergence something that just happens, like the rain? ('Oh, look outside – it's converging!') And how important are coercion, force and violence in the process? To what extent was convergence *driven* by violence, by the imposition of alien norms? The answers world history gives to these questions are equivocal. Generally speaking, world history has tended to favour tropes of exchange and interaction over those of subordination and imposition. And this, incidentally, is even more true of 'global history', which has sometimes proselytized energetically for a coercion-free scenario. 'Globalization,' Bruce Mazlish announces in his *New Global History* of 2006, 'is not something that the West has imposed upon the rest of the world, but the result of the interplay of many factors across continents.'

Chris Bayly's narratives allowed for what he described as 'the brute fact of western domination', but his book also stressed the limited and temporary character of that domination and insisted on the 'interdependence' of processes of changes that derive from many causes. What emerges is a picture in which modernity does not figure as something which some people or some regions did to others less favoured or deserving, but rather, as R. I. Moore put it in the fore-word to *The Birth of the Modern World*, 'as a series of transformations in which most of the people of the world participated, and to which most of them contributed, not simply as the objects or victims of the successes of others, but actively, independently and creatively'. There is no doubt about the attractiveness of this approach: by subdividing and distributing agency as widely as the sources will allow, it favours a more complex and encompassing analysis. But the question remains of how we should balance the wars of conquest and the ambient vio-lence that are clearly central to the making of modernity in many parts of the world with processes of exchange and relations of reci-procity that appear to presume a more level playing field. However we answer these questions, no one who reads *The Birth of the Mod-ern World* can fail to be impressed by the subtlety and lucidity of the reasoning, the breadth of compass, the attention to reciprocity in pol-itical, economic and social relationships and the well-oiled analytical gears that enabled Chris to travel elegantly between the local and the global.

Even as he enlarged the scope of his attention, Chris continued to generate fresh insights into Indian history. *Empire and Information* (1996) offered a compelling account of intelligence-gathering in India between 1780 and 1870, showing how 'native informants' recruited by the British actively shaped the process. In India, British administra-tive personnel encountered an 'information order' of great sophistication and complexity. And the networks sustaining this order were not simply reservoirs to be tapped by the imperial power: they shaped and filtered what could be known of the cultures and societies of the subcontinent. Whereas Edward Said's *Orientalism* (1978) had suggested that Western knowledge of the Orient was a process of sys-tematic misrepresentation, in which European cultural conventions, fantasies and fictions were superimposed wholesale onto subordi-nated societies, Bayly described a dialogue between indigenous and imperial knowledge-gathering systems. In analogous fashion, *Origins of Nationality in South Asia* (1998) and *Recovering Liberties* (2011) elucidated how Indians responded as autonomous agents to Western nationalism and liberal political and economic thought.

Chris's books bore the imprint of wide and humane interests; they were also methodologically eclectic. As Richard Drayton, Rhodes Professor of Imperial History at King's College London, put it in an obituary for the *Guardian*: Chris Bayly had 'an astonishing capacity to respond quickly to new perspectives and had the knack, in particular, of grafting historical ideas from one specialism to another. He read widely across the social sciences and had a magpie's eye for something brilliant in another discipline.' Conversation was a crucial part of the gathering and comparing that drove Chris's historical thinking: when discussions with students or colleagues got interesting, Chris would pull out a small crumpled notebook and start scribbling down ideas.

As these observations may suggest, Chris lived in his work. Not for it, but in it. The 'Bayly *mahal*', as he sometimes affectionately called the home he and his wife, Susan, founded when they married in 1981, was a place of conversation over work and wine, a conversation anchored in shared passions, complementary interests and pride in each other's achievements. And C3 on Main Court, the room Chris occupied for decades at St Catharine's College, was much more than an office. Eloquent objects were gathered there. The model ship his father had built. The eighteenth-century tall-heeled Venetian rosewood slippers decorated in mother of pearl – witnesses to the cultural links between northern Italy, the Ottoman Empire and China. The beautiful Gandhara head of the Buddha, 1,500 years old and carved by Greek and South Asian artisans in a style native to eastern Afghanistan – of all the things Chris and Susan had found together, this was his favourite.

It was in C3 that so many conversations happened, conversations that never failed to take Chris's guests to new places. And this was not just a matter of the sparks that were always falling from Chris's forge, but also his other gifts – gifts of unassuming and attentive friendship. Just a few days after his death, one of Chris's former St Catharine's graduate students, Jayeeta Sharma, wrote: 'I will never forget how awkward I felt, as a provincial student from a little place in Northeastern India, how he helped me to find my moorings, with C3 as a welcoming, warm and beautiful space for talk, laughter, and hospitality.' Even now, whenever I walk into the main court of St Catharine's College of an afternoon, I look involuntarily across to the window of

C3, on the off chance that Chris might be leaning in his shirt sleeves on the windowsill and call out: 'Clark! Drink?'

After Chris had declined the offer by his former students to produce a volume of essays in his honour, a conference was organized in Varanasi in January 2015 to honour his achievements, though, of course, the participants had no inkling of how little time he had left to live. Here one could see Chris at ease and happy in the setting of the civilization that had absorbed and rewarded his attention for so many years. It is hard to imagine a more fitting acknowledgement: it was on the stone *ghats* of this beautiful, thronging city that the young Chris Bayly had begun his journey into the history of India and the world.

Brexiteers, Revisionists and
Sleepwalkers

In the first days of 2014, a debate broke out in Britain over the origins of the First World War. It was not a debate among historians. It was a debate among politicians and journalists. It was the then education secretary, Michael Gove MP, now Minister for the Cabinet Office, who fired the first shot of the anniversary year. In a piece published on 2 January for the right-wing tabloid *Daily Mail*, Gove asked a bizarre question: 'Why does the Left insist on belittling true British heroes?' The heroes he had in mind were the soldiers who had fought in the British Army during the First World War. A skein of 'left-wing' myths, he argued, had obfuscated the true nature of the war, belittling Britain and clearing Germany of blame.

One culprit in disseminating the myth, Gove suggested, was the BBC television comedy *Blackadder*, whose final series presented trench warfare as a cruel and ultimately meaningless ordeal. But his principal targets were those 'left-wing academics' (his term) who insisted on downplaying the glory of Britain's war effort. 'The First World War may have been a uniquely horrific war, but it was also plainly a just war.' It was the Germans who had started it and resisting them was the only decent thing. It is 'always worth remembering', he added, 'that the freedom to draw our own conclusions about this conflict is a direct consequence of the bravery of men and women who fought for, and believed in, Britain's special tradition of liberty'.

Gove's sally did not go unanswered. Labour's shadow education secretary, Tristram Hunt, a published historian, replied with a counterattack in the *Guardian*. In his piece, Hunt observed, among other things, that the origins of the First World War were more complex than Gove's broadsides acknowledged. 'Michael Gove,' intoned the headline, 'using history for politicking is tawdry.'

At this point, stomping and puffing were heard from behind the scenes and Boris Johnson, then mayor of London, emerged to defend his friend Michael Gove. 'Germany started the First World War,' declared the *Telegraph* headline, 'but the Left can't bear to say so.' 'In this centennial year,' Johnson added solemnly, 'it's more important than ever that we treat the truth with respect.' It was a 'sad but undeniable fact', Johnson went on, 'that the First World War – in all its murderous horror – was overwhelmingly the result of German expansionism and aggression'. This, Johnson insisted, was a 'truism' – a claim so obviously true that it needed no defending. And it had recently been 'restated by Max Hastings, in an excellent book', and 'echoed by Michael Gove, the Education Secretary'. 'I believe that analysis to be basically correct,' Johnson wrote. It was 'all the more important, in this centenary year, that we remember it'. Then came the body blow to the Labour MP: 'If Tristram Hunt seriously denies that German militarism was at the root of the First World War, then he is not fit to do his job, either in opposition or in government, and should resign. If he does not deny that fact, he should issue a clarification now.' Here was a prominent British Conservative declaring in public that a political opponent's failure to endorse the thesis of German war guilt in 1914 ought to entail his removal from political office. Johnson's article appeared on the *sixth of January*. The anniversary year was not yet one week old and already the politicians had commandeered the First World War.

This was how the 1914 debate unfolded in the opening hours of the anniversary year. The terms in which it was instrumentalized politically contrast interestingly with the debate that unfolded in Germany in 2014. In Britain, questions about what happened in 1914 became intertwined with questions about British identity. In Britain, any utterance that relativized German war guilt, even marginally, was denounced as a leftist project whose purpose was to unsettle national certainties. Even the gentle parody of the BBC comedy *Blackadder*, which in reality was deeply respectful of the suffering and sacrifice of the ordinary soldiers caught up in the conflict, could be inflated by Michael Gove into an assault on national self-respect and honour. It was tantamount to defiling the mass graves of British soldiers and burying the nation's honour along with them.

It was ludicrous, of course, to claim, as Gove did, that Britain fought for democracy in 1914. Did that apply to the Bengali lancers or Nepali Ghurkas who fought on the Western Front? Or to the Zulu and Chinese labourers toiling in the supply lines? Did it apply to Britain's Russian allies, who fought for the tsarist autocracy? Britain fought, like every other power, to defend and magnify its position in the world. But that was not good enough for the jingoes, who insisted on a narrative of sacrifice and redemption capable of meeting present-day needs. Particularly striking was Michael Gove's claim that Britons owe their freedom to debate the past to the victory of 1918 over Wilhelmine Germany: a claim that would be true if the victory over Nazism in 1945 was backdated to the very different context of 1914–18. This was history read backwards: 1914 through the lens of 1940.

At the very least, the British case suggested that there is a contingent character to the politics of the debate over the origins of the First World War. Because in Germany, the political polarities of the debate were and are inverted. It seemed that anyone who threatened to unsettle the consensus on Germany's culpability as the author of this conflict was vulnerable to the suspicion that he or she was a right-wing revisionist who intended to dismantle the entire apparatus of historico-critical self-scrutiny that had transformed German political culture after 1945 and particularly from the late 1960s onwards.

Let me illustrate this observation by focusing for a few minutes on the critical response to my own book on the subject. And here I'd like simply to boil the more hostile responses down to a few salient points. The first relates to the threat supposedly posed by the book to the consensus underpinning the political culture of present-day Germany. I would highlight Heinrich August Winkler's full-page piece for *Die Zeit*, which opened with the words: 'An effect is haunting Germany. It is the Clark Effect.' When I read these words, there was an eerie ring to them – until, of course, I realized that Winkler was evoking with the metrics of his sentence the sonorous opening words of Marx and Engels's Communist Manifesto.

But what exactly *was* the Clark Effect? Professor Winkler went on to explain: 'He has found a large, mainly older and conservative-minded public, in which some positively celebrate him as a redeemer.' Why this cultish veneration? The answer, Winkler suggested, lay in 'a deep-seated need for national vindication' in the German reading public, though he acknowledged that it was not yet clear whether the book had itself triggered a change in awareness or merely exposed a sea-change in cultural attitudes.

My British (Anglo-German) colleague John Röhl, also writing for *Die Zeit*, took a similar view. He, too, was shocked by the 'overwhelming response to the book in Germany'. The book had been welcomed as an acquittal – *Freispruch* – for the German leadership of 1914. It was conceivable, Röhl conceded, that the author of *The Sleepwalkers* might have been surprised by the public response to it. But this did nothing to diminish the book's harmful effect. 'The impact of this book on the German public,' Röhl suggested, 'threatens to lure Germany onto an historiographical special path.' Both critics proceeded from the assumption that the book's success in terms of sales was a uniquely German phenomenon. Winkler referred, for example, to the 'overwhelmingly positive response Clark has met with in Germany – and *only* here'. Hans-Ulrich Wehler agreed: 'The commercial success [of *Sleepwalkers*] in the German book market – and not at all in the English one! – betrays a deep-seated need for vindication that has now been washed to the surface.' The historian Lothar Machtan, too, focused on the commercial success of the book. Only a phenomenal effort of organization by all stakeholders could explain such an anomaly, Machtan suggested: 'Everybody who was involved in this marketing campaign – the author, the agent, the publisher – naturally knew one thing: namely that a monograph running to 1000 pages about Europe's path into the First World War can only reach a broad public if it is rendered highly visible by the media.' And in order to achieve that, such a book would have to connect in some way with 'the psychological condition of the present' – in this case, 'the notoriously bad conscience of the Germans in relation to their own history in the twentieth century'.

Another strand of the critique related to its position in relation to the existing historiography. Since Germany's primary responsibility for the outbreak of war had already been established by Fritz Fischer, the argument went, my book must in effect be a reversion to the pre-Fischerian naiveté of the 1950s, or worse still, to the revisionism of the 1920s and 30s, when historians paid by the German foreign office to unpick the legitimacy of the Versailles settlement argued that the Germans of 1914 were innocent lambs, sprung upon by the voracious powers of the Triple Entente – my book had, in effect, pushed the state of knowledge backwards. John Röhl made this claim explicit: 'It seems that we are not moving forwards, but backwards. As if the current state of research were that of the 1920s and 1930s!' In short: the book was a whitewash, whose effect, and also whose *purpose*, was to clear the Germans of co-responsibility in the outbreak of war. And that, in turn, raised questions about my fitness to operate as a professional historian. 'An historian who consciously pulls back from the position established by the latest research,' Röhl wrote in *Die Zeit*, 'breaks the fundamental rules of historical writing.'

I've only commented on a few of the critiques prompted by the book's appearance, but I think I've captured the central strands of the case played out in the press by an influential part of the German historical 'guild', the *Zunft*, as it is suggestively called in Germany. And these were the themes animating a demonstration that took place against the book in Munich on 4 June 2014. A group calling themselves 'The Society Against Historical Revisionism' had staged the event and many of the participants turned up in their pyjamas, although it was four o'clock in the afternoon. At first I thought this was rather touching – perhaps they had just got out of bed. The sleepy expressions on their faces suggested that might be the case. But then I realized that the pyjamas were there to ridicule the book's title. And indeed many of the posters bore a standardized motif showing a sleepwalker with his arms extended in front of him, stepping blindly forward into the darkness.

The critics have focused a lot of fire on the book's title. It has been argued that the metaphor 'sleepwalkers' implies that the actors involved in the decisions that brought war in 1914 must have been unconscious or asleep. In a warm review for *Die Zeit* of Ian Kershaw's excellent history of Europe in the first half of the nineteenth century, *To Hell and Back*, my Freiburg colleague Jörn Leonhard contrasted Kershaw's differentiated handling of the outbreak of the First

Figure 5. 'Slithering, Sleepwalking and Bending into Shape'. A Rosa Luxemburg Foundation poster advertising a discussion of recent debates on the outbreak of the First World War, October 2014. Poster by Toni Püschel (*www.tonipueschel.de*)

World War with the untenable thesis, supposedly expounded in my book, that this war was brought about by 'unconscious sleepwalking'. In fact, of course, the actors, as I understood and depicted them, were not 'unconscious'. On the contrary, they were all constantly scheming and calculating, plotting virtual futures and measuring them against each other. I called them 'sleepwalkers' not because I thought they were actually asleep or unconscious – it's amazing that I have to explain this! – but because I was struck by the narrowness of their vision. But I have to concede that the title makes it easy to parody the book on the basis of a wilful misunderstanding of the metaphor.

The effect – and often also the purpose – of this misreading was, of course, to place the book in the vicinity of Lloyd George's famous and patently erroneous claim that the European powers had 'slithered' into a war by accident in 1914. My own view was, and is, that this war was anything *but* an accident. It was the consequence of hugely complex chains of decisions made within a range of executive structures, decisions made in full consciousness of the risks involved.

However false or misleading, the association with Lloyd George's slithering has remained at the core of critical responses, especially from the hard left. In 2017, Klaus Gietinger and Winfried Wolf published a study of the 'Clark-Effekt' under the title *The Comforter of Souls. How Christopher Clark Redeemed the Germans from their Guilt for the First World War*. I first became aware of Mr Gietinger when I heard from German colleagues that he had been emailing them with requests for advice on how to attack my book. The book's cover was decorated with a painting of a field chaplain celebrating a religious service before kneeling soldiers. But the altar adorned with a crucifix and two candles that can be seen in the original painting had been removed. There was no God and no crucifixion, just a clerical proxy for Christopher Clark absolving the members of his congregation from all sin. To my knowledge, Gietinger and Wolf had not collaborated before this study appeared, though they already shared a passionate political hostility to motor cars. Klaus Gietinger was the author of *Totalschaden: Das Autohasserbuch* ('Write-Off: The Book for Car-Haters'). And in a readable and well-argued study, *Eisenbahn und Autowahn* ('Railways and Car-Madness'), Winfried Wolf described himself as a 'sworn enemy of the automobile'. Wolf was also the author of *Sackgasse Autogesellschaft* ('The Dead-end of Car Culture') and Gietinger had published an accessibly written volume under the title *99 Crashes. Prominent Accident Victims*.

The thesis of their joint book is easily summarized: I had 'submerged myself in the depths of the German collective soul' and 'tickled it with fine words'. My book on the outbreak of the First World War was 'ideologically motivated'; my intention was to whitewash the Germans by means of an 'historical rollback', using 'distortions', 'omissions' and 'falsifications' to pave the way for an intensified German participation in the 'new imperialism (Afghanistan, Iraq, Libya, Syria)'. On the German domestic political scene, I had contributed to the emergence of a 'salon-fascist' party. And why all this mischief?

'One might assume that he is as naïve and innocent as he appears during public appearances, or perhaps he has relatives among those [Australians] who died at Gallipoli [...] and is traumatized by it. Or perhaps it's because he has a German wife?'

I have to confess to finding all of this a little bit odd. Firstly: it is simply not the case, as the critics implied, that the book was a great success in Germany and a flop everywhere else. In making this claim, the critics were suggesting that only the Germans were needy and uncritical enough to swallow the book's arguments. But the book did well in other countries, too. I'm much too modest to go into the detail, but the book was a *New York Times* bestseller and was translated into over thirty languages.

More importantly, the book did not 'acquit' the German leadership of co-responsibility for the outbreak of war. On the contrary, it referred explicitly to the growing support for a preventive war among the highest echelons of the German military, and to the 'several dozen occasions' on which senior German commanders explicitly demanded a war 'sooner rather than later', even if this meant taking the initiative and accepting the odium of the aggressor. It referred to the danger inherent in a form of preventive war thinking that 'allowed commanders to sanction even the most aggressive initiatives as essentially defensive'. I tried to show how the logic of preventive war fed into Chancellor Bethmann Hollweg's thinking, and specifically into his willingness to risk a war with Russia, as the July Crisis unfolded. I warned against minimizing the belligerence and imperialist paranoia of the Austrian and German policy-makers that rightly absorbed the attention of Fritz Fischer and his historiographical allies.

How odd it was to find the Fischer thesis held up as the established and consensual position on the outbreak of war, the high-water mark of historical interpretation, such that any position dissenting from Fischer's arguments must necessarily be damned as a reversion to some earlier, more primitive state of understanding. Published in the years 1961–73, the works that came to comprise the 'Fischer thesis' had argued that Germany pursued uniquely aggressive war aims in 1914, and that the German political leadership had deliberately engineered the outbreak of war in pursuit of German hegemony on the continent and a dominant place in world affairs. The Germans,

Fischer argued, had not merely caused the war, they had planned it in advance, initiating a countdown in 1912 that would expire in the summer of 1914.

But a great number of studies had appeared in the decades since Fischer that nuanced our understanding of what happened in 1914. These were not attacks on Fischer, they were just scholarly studies of various facets of the 1914 problem. No one who read Jean Claude Allain's 1976 masterpiece, *Agadir 1911: une crise impérialiste en Europe pour la conquête du Maroc* ('Agadir 1911: An Imperialist Crisis in Europe for the Conquest of Morocco'), could come away thinking that Germany was a uniquely aggressive or provocative presence in European international politics before 1914. On the contrary, Allain was sharply critical of the French leadership of the pre-war, a position he had already refined in his meticulous study of the irenicist politician Joseph Caillaux. In an immense and learned analysis of the war aims of the principal belligerents called *L'Or et le sang* ('Gold and Blood'), published in 1989, Georges-Henri Soutou, professor at Paris IV, came to the surprising conclusion that, whereas the war aims of the Central Powers were in essence defensive, those of the Entente Powers were offensive and focused on securing permanent global economic hegemony. Neither Allain nor Soutou was translated into German and Soutou's 966-page study was scarcely discussed in Germany.

Holger Afflerbach, now professor at the University of Leeds, is no revisionist and did not seek to lead an attack on Fischer, yet his 983-page book on the Triple Alliance between Germany, Italy and Austria perhaps inevitably complicated the unipolar paradigm expounded by Fischer, indirectly undermining the plausibility of his thesis. The reaction of *Die Zeit* was perhaps predictable: Volker Ullrich, the *spiritus rector* of *Die Zeit*'s historical Feuilleton and later the foremost coordinator of the critical response to *The Sleepwalkers*, praised Afflerbach's study as a 'great research achievement', but attacked with particular energy his 'criminal understatement' of the influence of the German military on the outbreak of the First World War, coming to the paradoxical conclusion that the book, although it was 'one of the most important recent works of diplomatic history', represented a 'backwards step' from the established state of the research.

In a collection of essays co-edited with his London colleague David Stevenson, Afflerbach opened up the possibility that this war, far from being inevitable, might have been improbable, that it might have been becoming less likely, even as it became more imminent. There is no need to go into the detail of this argument – suffice it to say that it does not sit easily with the Fischer thesis, whose central claim was that the German war party not only caused, but deliberately planned the outbreak of this war. How could a planned war be improbable? By insisting on the role of contingency in the aetiology of the war and and on the open-endedness of the situations faced by the key decision-makers, Afflerbach opened up the problem in a way that I found hugely inspiring.

I could keep listing such studies: Dominik Geppert's *Pressekriege* ('Press Wars') showed that the highpoint of the Anglo-German antag-onism was reached before 1912 and that 1913 and 1914 were years of relative détente, not of a constantly building sense of threat. Frie-drich Kiessling showed that the interactions among the powers on the European continent in the last years before the outbreak of war gave rise not only to risks and tensions but also phases of genuine relax-ation, in which the danger of a major conflagration seemed to recede, though he also pointed out that phases of détente could heighten objective risks by muting the key actors' awareness of the dangers attendant upon their decisions. Sean McMeekin's *The Russian Origins of the First World War*, which came out with Harvard University Press in 2011, explored Russia's designs in the Balkans and on the Dardanelles and the growing willingness of the Russian leadership to risk, if necessary, a European war. Stefan Schmidt's study of French foreign policy in the July Crisis shed fresh light on the thinking of Raymond Poincaré and the men around him, revealing a more pro-active posture than many earlier studies had suggested. For decades, the American historian Sam Williamson's subtle studies of Austro-Hungarian foreign policy had exposed a complex picture, in which the volatility of Balkan politics and the evolution of Austrian threat analysis posed a danger to peace that lay beyond the interpretative horizons of the Fischer thesis. And one could make the same general point about Günther Kronenbitter's massive analysis of Austro-Hungarian defence policy before 1914, or Konrad Canis on the foreign policy of the German Empire before 1914 and many other studies.

These historians were and are not revisionists with an axe to grind and a campaign to fight; they don't belong to a club or a gang; they are *historians*. And over the years, they have pulled at various strands of the immense bundle of arguments, contentions and assumptions that we call the 'Fischer thesis', until the point was reached where not very much of the original structure was left. This is not to say that Fischer's books had lost their value or were no longer worth reading: they remain a powerful portrait of the aggression and paranoia of large parts of the German leadership before 1914. Fischer did not invent his sources! They are also a powerful rejoinder to the argument that Germany slithered helplessly into war. But the case Fischer made for his view that the Germans planned this war in advance, that they carried a unique responsibility for the outbreak of war, had shed much of its plausibility.

So I was astonished to see Fritz Fischer's work held up by the critics as if it remained the newest and best interpretation of the problem of 1914. They were saying that anyone who failed to reconfirm Germany's status as primary culprit in the outbreak of war was in effect rolling the wheel of history backwards, back over and behind the great watershed of *Germany's Aims in the First World War* and *The War of Illusions*. But wasn't it *they* who were pushing the historiography backwards, or at least trying to? Surely it was they who were ignoring or overlooking the recent work in this field, not the so-called revisionists. They seemed to be suggesting that the acme of historical understanding had already been reached: the only path beyond Fischer led back into the revisionism of the 1920s.

The very implication that there was no way forward out of the Fischer paradigm suggested that the fixity of the Fischerite view was rooted in politics rather than in an impasse generated by the disciplinary logic of historical research and interpretation. The revisionists were accused of feeding German nationalist apologetics. It was time, Heinrich August Winkler announced, for the revisionists to undergo a process of 'self-revision'. It was said that my book would single-handedly seduce the Germans onto a 'new *Sonderweg*' – a reference to the thesis of the 'special path' that led Germany from the failure of revolution in 1848 to the catastrophe of Nazism. Once emancipated from the yoke of guilt in the outbreak of the First World War, the critics implied, the Germans would disinter their ancestral totems and sing their old war songs. Without the continuity provided by German guilt for the events of 1914, Hitler and his regime would be stranded in a shrinking pocket of time. Hitler would be downgraded to a mere accident, with no larger significance for Germany's road to modernity. In the worst-case scenario, the process of revision would eat its way forwards through time towards 1933 and 1939, unsettling the moral consensus around German culpability in the *Second* World War. The paedagogical benefits of the old consensus would be lost. A new arrogance and self-certainty would make itself felt. The logic of revisionism would eventually arrive at that 'specifically German understanding of Realpolitik that helped to lead Germany onto the road to the First World War' (Winkler).

These claims take us back to the observation with which I began this essay. The presumption had seemingly established itself that those who tampered in any way with the verities of the Fischer paradigm must be arguing from the right, while those who defended it must be doing so from the left. Certainly my most prominent critics counted themselves among the critical historians of the academic left. But as I have already suggested, this was a highly contingent, not a necessary linkage. The connection between left-oriented politics and German war guilt reflected the specificities of the Federal Republic's political and academic culture, rather than anything intrinsic to the arguments. I certainly did not understand or write the book as an assault on the left or a vindication of the right. I understood and understand it as an attempt to make sense of pre-war Europe in terms of the interplay between a plurality of aggressive and imperialistic power centres. My book was not born of a desire to vindicate the Germans or anyone else, but of an impatience with the glib and self-serving anglophone memory of 1914 with which I grew up. I found endless hints and inspiration in the monumental Russian source volumes *International Relations in the Age of Imperialism*, published in the 1920s by a team of Bolshevik scholars, precisely because they, as intelligent exponents of Marxism-Leninism, were alert to the existence of more than one imperialism in pre-war Europe.

Particularly puzzling was the claim that questioning the Fischer thesis would ultimately unsettle the consensus around German responsibility for the outbreak of the *Second* World War. But why? There has never been a debate around 1939 to compare with the century of wrangling over 1914, precisely because the causation of the First World War was ultra-complex in a way that the inception of the Second was not. It cannot be the case that we need to saddle the German leadership of 1914 with primary responsibility for the outbreak of war in order to provide the criminality of the Hitler regime and its many helpers with an adequate historiographical anchorage. There must surely be continuities between the NS-regime and the German past that bypass the question of war guilt in 1914 entirely. Antisemitism, nationalism, revanchism, Aryanism and race theory, the vision of a violent fellowship among men sworn to a redemptive struggle, *völkisch* anti-modernism, anti-globalist and anti-cosmopolitan sentiment, anti-communism, the cult of the strong leader and other ideological components of the NS-regime all have more or less deep histories that are not rooted in the events of 1914.

As for the revival of national longings for vindication, today this is a global problem. Whether a change of this kind is underway in Germany is hard to say. But if it is, it surely has very little to do with the publication of books on the First World War. My own book has not, as a rule, been instrumentalized for reactionary political objectives, at least not by people in positions of influence. Inasmuch as the political class of Europe have picked it up at all, they have tended to use its arguments, along with the term 'sleepwalkers', as a means of arguing for caution and circumspection in international relations. Foreign Minister Frank-Walter Steinmeier, a keen reader of history, cited it in this sense. So did the former chancellor Helmut Schmidt, who warned that he could see sleepwalkers at work in the escalation of the Ukraine Crisis. He didn't mean, of course, that the political actors in question were actually asleep or unconscious! And beyond Germany, the same inference has been drawn. In his annual address to his ambassadors, the then president of the French Republic, François Hollande, urged French policy-makers not to be sleepwalkers ('Ne soyons pas des somnambules') and so did Emmanuel Macron. For the Greek finance minister Yanis Varoufakis, responding to the Greek financial crisis of

2009–19, it was the 'troika' (the IMF, the European Commission and the ECB) who were the sleepwalkers. These were readings of the book's argument that I could live with, because they referenced the complexity of the aetiology advanced in it; the parody version, in which the actors become will-less zombies slithering towards doom, is not.

I want to close by expressing my gratitude to the critics. Among them were some of the historians whose work I most admire. I have been reading and learning for many years from the works of Wehler, Winkler, Leonhard, Röhl, Ullrich, Machtan and their colleagues. I appreciate the sincerity of the objections raised. I am deeply grateful to everyone who contributed to this debate over the last few years. It was a reminder of how deeply history matters in Germany and how passionately historical debates are pursued across the media and in public life. It can get rough at times, but for an historian, this appetite for historical controversy makes Germany a very special place.

The moralizing and polemical tone that sometimes enters such discussions, the habit of imputing political motivation, isn't always helpful, but it may be part of the price we pay for taking part in a culture that takes history seriously and believes in its power to improve the quality of citizenship. The process of historical self-scrutiny that took place in Germany after 1945 and especially after the cultural transformation of 1968 is a unique and profoundly valuable achievement, in which the critical historians played a crucial role. Today the negative effects of the absence of such a process of global self-scrutiny in the United States are widely remarked. I personally value and admire the self-critical culture of German academic history, but I do not believe that debating the causation of the First World War in an open-ended, respectful and empirically transparent way will undermine or damage it. In any case, I am confident that my colleagues in Germany and elsewhere will continue to worry away at the task of making sense of what happened in 1914, even as we move beyond (because there *is* a beyond!) the parameters of the controversy triggered half a century ago by the books of Fritz Fischer.

Uncertain Times

Everyone seems to agree that these are uncertain times. But how uncertain are they and why do we feel so unsettled? Elements of unpredictability and risk have been present in all historical situations. Is the objective character of events in the world to blame for our sense of disquiet? Or does it arise from our own historical sensibility, our shared awareness as historically acting subjects in twenty-first century Europe? In this essay, which was written before the crisis generated by the COVID-19 pandemic, I explore some of the reasons for contemporary uncertainty and for our heightened sensitivity to unpredictability.

We could begin with the geopolitical constellation of today's world. One of the things that prompted me in the early 2000s to write a book about the outbreak of the First World War was that the July Crisis of 1914, the summer crisis that brought war, was starting, paradoxically, to feel fresher and more relevant than it had twenty or so years before. When I was growing up in Sydney, Australia, we studied the First World War at school. And to us, and our teachers, in the 1970s, it seemed that the Europe of June 1914, the Europe in which the heir to the Austro-Hungarian throne and his wife, Sophie Chotek, made their way to Sarajevo after the summer manoeuvres in Bosnia, was as old as ancient Egypt. The wonderful books of Barbara Tuchman, *The Proud Tower* and *The Guns of August*, focused on the effete hierarchies and ornamentalism of a bygone era: the intricate rules of precedence at processions and dinners, even for children and infants, the glittering costumes and sumptuous menus, the expansive and disinhibited personalities of grandees born to high privilege. Sophie Chotek von Chotkowa, the wife of Archduke Franz Ferdinand, was forbidden to sit beside him in the Habsburg royal carriage with its golden wheels because their marriage failed to meet the exacting criteria of the protocol chiefs of the House of Austria – this was one reason why she insisted on sitting beside him in the open car that drove them through the Bosnian capital on 28 June. And then there were the green ostrich feathers on the hats of the chief protagonists – iridescent fronds, floating above the crowds, that helped the assassins gathered in Sarajevo on that day to locate their target.

These brilliant, garish period details had an alienating effect. They seemed to pull the people and events of that era into a very remote past. And we thought: if their hats had absurd bright green ostrich feathers, then their dreams and arguments and hopes must have had ostrich feathers on them too. They must have been bygone men and women, people with obsolete ideas, characters from a history painting, people who could say nothing to us. They seemed far away because their world, a world agitated by the competition between great powers, appeared so different from ours which, in the 1970s, was a world full of violence and agitation – Vietnam, Cambodia, Iran, Afghanistan – but also disciplined by an extremely simple structure: the stand-off between two nuclear superpowers.

Events were unpredictable then, yes – remember the words of Prime Minister Harold Macmillan at the time of the Suez Crisis in 1956. The Egyptian head of state, Gamal Abdel Nasser, had unilaterally nationalized the Suez Canal. With the support of the British and the French, Israel attacked Egypt on the Sinai Peninsula and the Gaza Strip. The hope was that, with the help of the Israelis, it would be possible to bring the Canal back under international control. But the plan went terribly awry, exposing London and triggering consternation in Britain. Asked by a young journalist to explain why everything had gone so disastrously wrong for the British, Macmillan replied with characteristic *sang froid*: 'Events, dear boy, events.'

So events had the power to upset the best-laid plans, even then, as in all times. But the outer framework was stable. And after all, the Suez Crisis was very quickly resolved. The whole thing came to an end when the United States, the Soviet Union and the United Nations joined in insisting that the three intervening powers withdraw. They did so without demur. The whole thing lasted nine days.

From the perspective of that Cold War framework, the pre-1914 world looked hair-raisingly unpredictable. But all this began to change as the Cold War came to an end and something different took its place. What that thing is, is still under discussion. We are still working it out.

But there is one thing we shouldn't forget. The era we are now in got off to a beautiful start, at least in Europe. In 1989–90, the dissolution of the eastern bloc produced a profound transformation in the geopolitical structure of Europe. A new German state emerged (the Germany of 1990 was not the old Germany reunited but an entirely new state with new territorial boundaries). This was the second great territorial unification of German-speaking Europe and the third great popular uprising (1848–9, 1918–19, 1989. It is astonishing how these German uprisings take place at seventy-year intervals).

And this happened *without a war*. It is worth reflecting on how extraordinary that is. The Peace of Westphalia in 1648, the emergence of a unified German Reich in 1871, the reordering of Central Europe after 1918 under the terms imposed by the treaties of Versailles, Saint-Germain-en-Laye, Trianon and Sèvres, and the partition of Europe after 1945 – these transformations were all brought about by wars, and were paid for in millions of human lives. When you add them all together – the Thirty Years' War with 8 million dead, the German Wars of Unification with more than 250,000, the First World War with 16.5 million (estimates range from 15 to 22 million) and the Second World War in Europe with perhaps 43.5 million dead – when you add them all together, they come to the fearsome total of over 68 million people whose lives had to be consumed in order to accommodate the European state system to the latest shifts in the balance of power.

It was different in 1989–90. A forty-year-old security system was dismantled, an empire dissolved, the balance of power on the continent placed in question, a new German state created – all without a war. Europe breathed a huge sigh of relief and one could and did look back with a certain pride on what had been achieved.

It's what came next that created the world we are in now: the collapse of the Soviet Union, the Yugoslav wars, the Chechen wars, the 9/11 terror attacks on New York and Washington, the Afghanistan War, the Second Iraq War and its apparently endless aftershocks, the

Georgian crisis, the global financial crisis, the Ukraine crisis, the Greek financial crisis, the European migrant crisis and, most recently, the COVID-19 crisis.

The US political scientist George Friedman has observed that we need to distinguish between two periods since 1989. The first we could perhaps call the 'post-Cold War'. It extended from 1990 until the years between 2004 and 2007. It was marked by an overwhelming focus on American power. The world seemed to revolve around Washington. The phrase 'new American century' was in vogue and decision-makers in Washington spoke of 'full spectrum dominance'.

That was the post-Cold War. But it didn't last very long. The disasters that followed the initial successes of the Second Iraq War raised doubts about how well the US would be able to translate its full spectrum dominance into durable outcomes. The Putin regime disavowed and repudiated the politics of the Gorbachev and Yeltsin era and began pushing back against the USA, against NATO and against the EU. Far from fragmenting or collapsing, as many in Washington had predicted after Tienanmen Square, China entered a phase of breathtaking growth, acquired a new sense of direction and began challenging the inherited geopolitical order in the South China Sea.

This last point brings to mind a feature of our epoch whose importance remained hidden in the early years. In the West, it was assumed that the global ascendancy of capitalism and the triumph of liberal democracy were twinned, interdependent. There was a sense that the summit of a long historical evolution had been reached. As the new American century dawned, it was easy to feel that history itself had accomplished its task and come to an end. In an influential and widely discussed essay of 1992, the political scientist Francis Fukuyama spoke of the 'end of history'. The locomotive of history, he proposed, had reached its terminal. The West had prevailed as a political and social order and as a system of values. The peaceful worldwide extension and elaboration of this system could begin under leadership.

But the reality was different, because the resolute crushing of an incipient democracy movement by the Chinese government in 1990 was just as important in shaping our present as the fall of the Berlin Wall in 1989. That our present is dually imprinted by the almost simultaneous transformations in Beijing and Berlin is the central thesis of the book *Post Wall, Post Square* by the LSE historian Kristina Spohr. China followed a different road out of the Cold War from Europe. The Communist Party of China held fast to the one-party system at the same time as pressing ahead with the conditional integration of the country into the world economy. Contentious claims to islands in the South China Sea were soon joined by a tranche of initiatives whose purpose was to establish China as a globally dominant power.

Amid all this flux, the post-Cold-War era came to an end. And what replaced it? George Friedman proposed the rather ungainly rubric 'post-post-cold war era'. The Russian foreign minister Sergei Lavrov spoke of a 'post-Western' or 'post-liberal' order. The Chinese government's official term for the current era is 'The Epoch of Strategic Opportunity'. But the names don't matter. What marks the contemporary era is the re-emergence of authentic multipolarity.

This multipolarity has many dimensions. The isolationism of the United States is one of them. Under Donald Trump, the White House administration managed to alienate many of its traditional partners. 'I think the European Union is a foe, what they do to us in trade,' he told CBS *Evening News* anchor Jeff Glor in July 2018. 'Now you wouldn't think of the European Union, but they're a foe.' Donald Trump even picked fights with the Canadians. At the G7 summit of 2018, Trump described the Canadian prime minister as 'weak' and 'dishonest', while at the same time touting for the rehabilitation of Vladimir Putin. The man whose predecessors were thought to lead the Western world appeared to have no interest whatsoever in the West as a community of political values and standards. Trump raised doubts about the depth of America's commitment to NATO and repeatedly appealed to the idea of a world order based entirely on the pursuit by each state of its own interests.

Long before the Trumpian non-linearity collided with the White House, the Putin regime had begun pushing back hard against NATO and the EU, creating in the process a frozen conflict in East-Central Europe for which a resolution is nowhere in sight, and establishing in the ruins of Syria a platform for Russian policy. New regional powers emerged, determined to assert dominance in their respective areas: Turkey and Iran being the most important examples.

If the cohesion and credibility of NATO appear under threat, the same can be said of the EU. One might have imagined that the EU would have responded to the Yugoslavian, Georgian, Greek financial, Ukrainian, migrant and COVID-19 crises by tightening and strengthening its decision-making structures and developing more coordinated responses to new emergencies. But the opposite was the case. The worse the crises got, the less coordinated were the responses.

The Greek financial crisis exposed the dysfunctionality of a customs union without real political traction, in which political imperatives and economic imperatives could wind up drifting in opposite directions. In a penetrating analysis of that crisis, the German sociologist Jürgen Habermas pointed to the absurdity of a situation in which the representatives of one sovereign democracy addressed the representatives of another simply as defaulting creditors. The immigration and refugee crisis placed political office-holders under pressure to act without consultation and swelled the sails of right-wing populist movements. In those countries where these have taken power, they have begun to pick at the fabric of norms that sustain the EU as a composite political culture, the most important being the independence of the judiciary.

And as if this were not already enough, Brexit has opened many new questions. Britain's departure has torn a gap in the power structure of the EU. Who will fill this gap – federalists in the Franco-German mould, middle-way pragmatists such as the Finns and Swedes, or nationalists like the Poles and Hungarians – is still completely unclear.

As these examples remind us, the risks Europe faces in this era are not all exogenous. Some of them Europeans helped to fashion for themselves. Remember what happened in spring 2008: Georgia and Ukraine applied to be put on a NATO fast-track Membership Action Plan (MAP). Had this gone ahead, it would have made them the fourth and fifth Soviet republics to join the Western coalition. With Ukraine's large population and economy, its resources, its strategic location on the Black Sea and historic significance for the Russian empire, its recruitment to the Western coalition would have been a devastating blow to Russia. Putin had only just given a series of increasingly clear warnings that he wouldn't stand for it. And yet President Bush threw his weight behind the bid, announcing that welcoming Ukraine and Georgia into the MAP would make it clear to Russia that 'these two nations are and will remain sovereign and independent states'. He even made a flying visit to Kiev.

The EU member states were divided on the issue. Poland, the other East European and the Scandinavian member states were excited by the idea. Germany and France were opposed, and so eventually were Italy, Hungary and the Benelux countries. The membership process was not initiated. But Mrs Merkel conceded that the Bucharest summit at which the matter was discussed should issue a statement endorsing the aspirations of Georgia and Ukraine and declaring: 'These countries will become members of NATO.' It was a fudge, but it triggered a phase of further escalation. And what did the EU do? In May, at the pressing of Poland, it adopted the idea of an Eastern partnership for Ukraine as one of the key elements of the new EU foreign policy to be developed under the terms of the Lisbon Treaty. Swallowing their doubts for the moment, Berlin and Paris fell into line. The EU and NATO stayed, at least for the time being, in lock step.

Even a very cursory overview of the key elements in this situation reveals that all was not well. First, there was the very poorly articulated relationship between the EU and NATO, which were and are, in any case, two completely different kinds of organization with fundamentally different purposes and capabilities, NATO being a heavily armed alliance and the EU a civil structure with no army and an extremely stunted security apparatus; there were the usual low levels of internal consensus within the EU on key foreign policy and defence questions; there was a gross mismatch between implied commitments and the political or military will to fulfil them; and there was a spate of ill-coordinated international signalling that managed to be both ambiguous and provocative. It was not a good mix. It goes without saying that none of this justifies the illegal interventions of Russia in Georgia or Ukraine, or diminishes the threat posed by Russia to those entities (they include the EU!) that it identifies as its enemies. Neither does it excuse the lies, obfuscation and gross insults handed out to Western states in the aftermath of the shooting down of MH17 by a Russian guided missile or the botched attempt on the life of Sergei Skripal by two agents of the GRU. But when we in the West ponder on how we got to where we are, it is as well to be aware of our own role in the events that brought us here.

A second point about home-generated risk relates to the other big story of 2008, the financial crisis. And here I draw on arguments advanced in Adam Tooze's *Crashed*, a magisterial analysis of the financial crisis in its world-historical setting. In Europe, this story is often told as the history of an American crisis, rooted in the securitization of immense volumes of questionable assets, principally subprime mortgages. But in fact the EU grew its very own financial crisis. European investment funding was much more deeply implicated in the US crisis than is often acknowledged. And in some ways, the Eurozone economy was more crisis-prone even than the United States, because, although there was a unified currency, there was, in contrast to America, no unified regulatory structure for banking. Nor did the key decision-makers seem to feel there was any reason to hurry in creating one.

The European Central Bank was of little help in this respect. It internalized the logic of the markets to an even greater degree than the Fed or the Bank of England. Instead of imposing discipline on Europe's banks, it allowed a feedback loop to emerge in which the ECB depended upon the banks to exercise self-discipline, while the banks saw the ECB as providing an implicit European guarantee for even the weakest borrowers. The result of this and other missteps was a sequence of credit-fuelled booms that bore next to no relation to the geography of the real European economies. And the size of the problem was phenomenal: the balance sheets of the three largest banks in the world – all of them European: RBS, Deutsche and BNP Paribas – came to 17 per cent of global GDP. The liabilities of the Irish banks added up to 700 per cent of Irish GDP! The figures for Germany and Spain were 300 per cent.

By this standard, every member of the Eurozone was, on average, at least three times as 'overbanked' as the United States. And Europe's banks were far more dependent than their US counterparts on the volatile forms of 'wholesale' market-based funding we associate with the subprime mortgage crisis. Yet the Eurozone lacked anything resembling a financial fire department.

The risks that resulted and are still resulting were not merely financial – there was a link with broader questions of politics and European order, because nothing explains better than 2008 the current crisis in democratic legitimacy, the hostility to experts and elites and the rise of illiberal, anti-globalization populist movements, the dwindling cohesion and success of traditional parties and even the electoral success of Trump, whose victory was foreshadowed by the sundering effect of the 2008 crisis on the Republican Party. It's no accident that the *bête noire* of the Hungarian supremo Viktor Orban is the international billionaire investor, business magnate and liberal philanthropist George Soros, who plays the role in today's Hungary that the figure of Goldstein plays in George Orwell's *1984*.

So yes, these are uncertain times. It may, of course, be, as Nicholas Taleb has suggested, that the real problem does not reside in the unreliability of the world but in our addiction to something we call 'normality'. In the 1980s, Taleb was a derivatives dealer, first in Wall Street, later on the Chicago Exchange. And he noticed something interesting: namely, that quite extreme market fluctuations seemed to occur much more frequently than most of his colleagues were prepared to accept. 'Most people,' he told an interviewer for the *Financial Times*, 'didn't realize that extreme events are constantly occurring.' Why not orient one's behaviour towards such events, rather than basing it upon a normality that may be illusory? He started to invest his own funds in extreme fluctuations, betting on the worst-case scenario. Two years later came the worst stock market crash since the Second World War. Taleb was twenty-seven, he had made a huge profit. He knew he would never have to work again. This is the kind of thing that doesn't happen to historians. Then he wrote a doctoral dissertation making sense of his experiences on the markets. Today he is professor of risk engineering at New York University.

In his 2007 bestseller *The Black Swan*, he attacks what he sees as the baneful influence of modern statistics. Statistically driven thought, he argues, is in thrall to the ideal of predictability and distributed probability. Of course, for birth and death rates and for other biometrical data, this assumption usually holds up well. The heights, life expectancy and nuptial ages of human beings really are distributed in a fairly predictable way; plot them and you get that Gaussian bell curve, the elegant symmetry of which makes us feel that the world is in good order.

But whereas biometric data tended to follow the contours of the bell curve, Taleb argued, the profile for financial markets was quite different, because they were not constrained by physical parameters but rather driven by the moods and psychic states of investors, their tendency to euphoria and collective panic, their lies and their delusions of grandeur. And the presence of these behavioural drivers in turn explained why financial markets were so unpredictable, so prone to extreme fluctuation.

What fascinated me about Nicolas Taleb's book was the notion that we are shaken by financial shocks only because we expect them not to happen and refuse to integrate them into our calculations. We were brainwashed by the Gaussian curve. Taleb compared us to the hapless turkeys on North American turkey farms. For many days, the farmer comes to her turkeys and provides them with plentiful food placed in easily accessible containers. Life is good for the turkey. Day by day, he gathers extensive and highly consistent – and also very reassuring – data suggesting that this food-bearing human will never do him any harm. Then comes Thanksgiving, the ultimate reality-check in the life of every American turkey.

If the financial markets are driven by the interplay of preferences, passions and fears, then how much more is this true of international politics? Of course, the stakes are higher in the politics of states. Because here it is often a question, as Carl Schmitt put it, of saying who is my friend and who is my enemy and of making decisions that, in their *ultima ratio*, are questions, not of profit and loss, but of life and death.

Today, as before 1914, we can see signs of a growing unpredictability in the system. Before 1914, the trust between the great powers was at a low point. The behaviour of governments was opaque, difficult to read. Even within alliances, levels of trust were too low to instil confidence in how any member of the alliance would behave in the event of a crisis. Even so, we do not know of any exchanges between heads of state in pre-1914 Europe that bear comparison with the remarkable tweet-battles between Kim Jong-un and Donald Trump in the winter of 2017.

What was striking about the crisis that followed was that the actors in question were not just responding to the problem of unpredictability, but actively cultivating it as a strategic asset. According to Eric-Julian Ballbach, who heads the research department on North Korea and International Security at the Institute for Korean Studies of the Free University in Berlin, unpredictability is 'part of the North Korean political strategy'. We still have next to no idea what goes on in the leadership circle around this man, who is one of the most opaque and internationally isolated personalities ever to represent any country in the history of international relations. But Kim Jong-un is seen – even within his own command structure – as more risk-friendly than his father, who was almost always at pains to prevent phases of escalation. And it doesn't look much different on the American side. 'We must become more unpredictable as a nation,' President Donald Trump told an audience during a campaign speech of April 2016. 'We must immediately become more unpredictable.'

To an extent, these outbursts were merely the expression of this president's special personality. But there may also be an element of conscious tactical manipulation. After all, Machiavelli wrote, it is 'sometimes a very wise thing to simulate madness'. Some political scientists in Washington have drawn parallels between Trump and the 'madman theory' of Richard Nixon. Nixon and his administration tried to make the leaders of hostile communist bloc states think Nixon was irrational and volatile. He explained it to his chief of staff, Bob Haldeman, in these words:

> I call it the Madman Theory, Bob. I want the North Vietnamese to believe I've reached the point where I might do anything to stop the war. We'll just slip the word to them that, 'for God's sake, you know Nixon is obsessed about communism. We can't restrain him when he's angry – and he has his hand on the "nuclear button"' and Ho Chi Minh himself will be in Paris in two days begging for peace.

Henry Kissinger was intimately involved in deploying this technique. Trump was an admirer of Nixon. And it is interesting to note that the first guest Trump invited to Trump Tower after his election, when he felt he needed an initiation into the arcana of foreign policy, was none other than – Henry Kissinger. There may perhaps be a scrap of comfort in the idea that at least some of the unpredictability is deliberately engineered, but it remains highly doubtful that the unpredictable behaviour of powerful actors, however contrived, will do anything to increase the stability of the system within which they operate.

The entire international arms control regime so laboriously pieced together in the 1980s and 90s is falling apart. Russia has installed a new and more potent generation of intermediate-range nuclear missiles aimed at European targets, in breach of the 1987 INF Treaty, and the US administration has published a 'Nuclear Posture Review' that loosens constraints on the tactical use of nuclear weapons. But more important in some ways than the rise of distrust and fear between blocs is the collapse of trust *within* the Western alliance. The collapse in trust between the Western states and Russia is scary, but the collapse in the cohesion of the transatlantic alliance is much more dangerous. In 1914, levels of trust were too low to instil confidence among alliance members in how any other member of the alliance would behave in the event of a crisis, meaning that some states accepted the risk of war for fear of having to fight at a later date, when their alliance might be less secure. The Russians feared the time would soon come when French support would no longer be on offer; the French feared that the growth of Russian power would encourage the decision-makers in St Petersburg to believe they could do without Paris. The Austrians feared losing the support of Germany, and nobody trusted Italy. This was arguably a greater source of risk than the paranoia that suffused relations between the two alliance blocs.

I want to close with a final thought. If you know what you are doing and you know why and to what ultimate end, then you will cope better with adversity. The shelves of airport bookshops are full of books by management gurus who will tell you that the capacity to invent and believe in a story about what you are and where you are headed can be crucial to the survival of a business in the face of challenging conditions. There was a time, I think, when the West was good at propagating such cohesion-enhancing narratives. They varied from country to country and across different political and social milieus, but there was an underlying story that most people in the Western political mainstream felt it possible to buy into. It was a story about becoming more modern, about the prosperity and ease that would come with economic growth, and about the universality of a specific liberal-democratic societal model that could be depended upon to bring blessings to all women and men.

Those stories no longer comfort us as they once did. Modernity has turned out to be dirty, unsustainable, choked with discarded plastics and heading for planetary catastrophe. Capitalism turned out (if we follow Piketty) to be generating asymmetries that threatened social cohesion. The German political scientist Wolfgang Streeck has compared modern capitalism to a terminally ill patient suffering from multiple incurable disorders, but whose moribund body is too large to be removed from the scene, or replaced by an alternative. (It's interesting how in this nightmarish picture, fears for the future of capitalism cross wires with anxieties about old-age care.) Its gradual death, Streeck predicts, will produce a long and painful period of cumulative decay: of intensifying frictions, of fragility and uncertainty. It's amazing how many books have appeared in the last three years with the word 'end' in the title: *The End of Politics, End of Liberal Democracy, The End of the Left, The End of the Right, How Democracy Ends* and so on. I don't want to endorse any of these scenarios, I just want to note them as symptomatic.

We needn't be too alarmed: in the 1520s, the religious reformers Martin Luther and Philipp Melanchthon thought the end of the world was nigh. When the end kept on not happening, they changed their minds and postponed it. The problem I am concerned with here is not the imminence of an *actual* end (which is another matter) but the death of the stories that gave us a future and proposed a means of acting in a politically efficacious manner. The effect of this narrative withdrawal is a besetting anxiety, an inability to replot our course after every disturbing incident.

That's why President Emmanuel Macron was right to remind Europeans in the speech he gave at the Sorbonne in September 2017 that Europe is still 'our horizon, that which gives us a future'. Macron went on to warn that if Europeans didn't address themselves to completing the unfinished building of the EU, the present would be submerged by the past. The message was addressed to the leaders and citizens of the European member states and focused on a particular geopolitical and institutional structure. But in connecting the exhaustion of the future with helplessness and inactivity in the present he made a point that we could profitably reflect on. We need to re-plot and re-occupy the future. Perhaps *that* is the problem to which we and our political leaders should address our attention as we contemplate a present marked by ever higher levels of unpredictability.

Notes

FROM PRUSSIA WITH LOVE

1. Richard van Dülmen, *The Society of the Enlightenment. The Rise of the Middle Class and Enlightenment Culture in Germany*, trans. Anthony Williams (Oxford, 1992), pp. 47–8; Ferdinand Runkel, *Geschichte der Freimaurerei in Deutschland* (3 vols.; Berlin, 1931–2), vol. 1, pp. 154–8.

2. Eduardo Mendieta, 'The Power of Religion in the Public Sphere', in id. and Jonathan Van Antwerpen (eds.), *The Power of Religion in the Public Sphere* (New York, 2011), pp. 1–14, here p. 2; Niamh Reilly, 'Introduction. Religion, Gender and the Public Sphere: Mapping the Terrain', in id. and Stacey Scriver (eds.), *Religion, Gender and Public Sphere* (London, 2014), pp. 1–17.

3. On the place of religion in the formation of a global public sphere, see Abigail Green and Vincent Viaene (eds.), *Religious Internationals in the Modern World: Globalization and Faith Communities since 1750* (Basingstoke, 2012).

4. On Habermas's 'anti-religious assumptions', see Craig Calhoun, *Habermas and the Public Sphere* (Cambridge, MA, 1992), pp. 35–6.

5. Jürgen Habermas, 'Religion in the Public Sphere: Cognitive Presuppositions for the "Public Use of Reason" by Religion and Secular Citizens', in Ciaran Cronin trans., id., *Between Naturalism and Religion. Philosophical Essays* (Cambridge, 2008), p. 131; id., 'Religion in the Public Sphere', *European Journal of Philosophy*, 14:1 (2006), pp. 1–25, esp. p. 20.

6. Christopher Clark, 'The Napoleonic Moment in Prussian Church Policy', in David Laven and Lucy Riall (eds.), *Napoleon's Legacy. Problems of Government in Restoration Europe* (Oxford, 2000), pp. 217–35, here p. 223; Christopher Clark, 'Confessional Policy and the Limits of State Action: Frederick William III and the Prussian Church Union 1817–1840', *Historical Journal*, 39 (1996), pp. 985–1004.

7. E. L. v. Gerlach, *Ernst Ludwig von Gerlach. Aufzeichnungen aus seinem Leben und Wirken 1795–1877*, ed. J. von Gerlach (Schwerin, 1903), pp. 132, 149–50.
8. Friedrich Wiegand, 'Eine Schwärmerbewegung in Hinterpommern vor hundert Jahren', *Deutsche Rundschau*, 189 (1921), pp. 323–36, here p. 333.
9. See for example Geheimes Staatsarchiv Berlin (GStA Berlin), HA I, Rep. 76 III, Sekt. 1, Abt. XIIIa, Nr 5, vol. 1.
10. Clark, 'The Napoleonic Moment in Prussian Church Policy'.
11. ' Die im Bezirk der Regierung zu Königsberg in Preussen befindlichen Vereine zu ausserkirchlichen Religionsübungen oder Erbauungsstunden zu 1822', GStA Berlin, HA I, Rep. 76 III, Sekt. 2, Abt. XVI, Nr 1, vol. 1, fols. 30–35.
12. Christopher Bayly, *The Birth of the Modern World 1780–1914* (Oxford, 2004), p. 147.
13. Frankfurt/Oder government to Rochow, Frankfurt/Oder, 9 June 1836, GStA Berlin, HA I, Rep. 76 III, Sekt. I, Abt., XIIIa, Nr. 5, vol. 2, Bl. 207–8.
14. Christopher Clark, 'Confessional Policy and the Limits of State Action: Frederick William III and the Prussian Church Union 1817–40', *The Historical Journal*, 39 (1996), pp. 985–1004.
15. 'Die Mukkerei – Eine Bezeichnung, welche [...] auch in der Jägersprache mit einem Bekannten von der Begattung des Hasengeschlechtes Gebrauchten Worte Synonym sein soll ...' Extrakt aus der *Kritischen Prediger-Bibliothek von Dr. Röhr*, 17/1 (1836), GStA Berlin, HA I, Rep. 76 III, Sekt. 2, Abt. XVI, Nr 4, vol. 1, fol. 238.
16. Hermann Olshausen, *Lehre und Leben des Königsberger Theosophen Joh. Heinrich Schönherr* (Leipzig, 1838), pp. 24–9.
17. Ibid., pp. 12–3; Dixon, *Spiritual Wives*, p. 118.
18. Olshausen, *Lehre und Leben des Königsberger Theosophen*, pp. 15–16; Dixon, *Spiritual Wives*, p. 122.
19. 'Die im Bezirk der Regierung zu Königsberg in Preussen befindlichen Vereine zu ausserkirchlichen Religionsübungen oder Erbauungsstunden zu 1822'.
20. William Hepworth Dixon, *Spiritual Wives* (London, 1868), p. 108.
21. Schön to Altenstein (Minister of Church Affairs), Königsberg, 7 August 1835, GStA Berlin, HA I, Rep. 76 III, Sekt. 2, Abt. XVI, Nr 4, vol. 1, fols. 1–4, here fol. 2; see also the tedious theological novel of 1823, widely viewed at the time as a caricature of Ebel and his disciples: Ludwig August Kähler, *Philagathos. Andeutungen über das Reich des Guten*.

Ein Beitrag zur einfachen Verständigung über Christlich-religiöse Wahrheit für denkende Freunde derselben (Königsberg, 1823).

22. Finkenstein to Zelina von Mirbach, Königsberg, 14 January 1835, transcribed in GStA Berlin, HA I, Rep. 76 III, Sekt. 2, Abt. XVI, Nr 4, vol. 1, fols. 5–6.

23. Diestel gives a full account of his reply to the charges against Ebel in 'Ausführliche Erklärung des Predigers Diestel über die dem Archidiakonus Dr. Ebel erkennbar gemachten Anschuldigungen', Königsberg, 15. Oktober 1835, GStA Berlin, HA I, Rep. 76 III, Sekt. 2, Abt. XVI, Nr 4, vol. 1, fols. 60–96.

24. Extrakt aus der *Kritischen Prediger-Bibliothek von Dr. Röhr*, 17/1 (1836), GStA Berlin, HA I, Rep. 76 III, Sekt. 2, Abt. XVI, Nr 4, vol. 1, fol. 238.

25. Friedrich Wilhelm III to Rochow and Altenstein , Berlin, 26 April 1836, GStA Berlin, HA I, Rep. 76 III, Sekt. 2, Abt. XVI, Nr 4, vol. 1, fols. 236–8.

26. On student rowdiness, see Dixon, *Spiritual Wives*, pp. 27–31; on lampoons, see Schön to Altenstein, Königsberg, 28 September 1835, GStA Berlin, HA I, Rep. 76 III, Sekt. 2, Abt. XVI, Nr 4, vol. 1.

27. For example, the *Elbinger Anzeigen* ran a piece describing Ebel as a self-proclaimed 'new Messiah' on 27 September 1835; see also, 'Zuverlässige Mittheilungen über Johann Heinrich Schönherrs Theosophie [. . .] sowie über die durch letztere Veranlassten sectiererischen Umtriebe zu Königsberg in Preussen', *Illgens Zeitschrift für historische Theologie* (1838); reports attacking Ebel and his associates appeared in the *Evangelische Kirchenzeitung* of 1836; on the public resonance of the case, see Kanitz Ernst Graf Kanitz, *Aufklärung nach Actenquellen über den 1835 bis 1842 zu Königsberg in Preussen geführten Religionsprozess für Welt- und Kirchengeschichte* (Basel and Ludwigsburg, 1862), pp. 128–44.

28. 'Unser Planet', *Blätter für Unterhaltung, Zeitgeschichte, Literatur, Kunst und Theater*, No. 70, Tuesday 22 March 1836, p. 275, cutting in HA I Rep. 76 III, Sekt 2. Abt. XVI, Nr 4, vol. 2.

29. 'Neuestes Leben und Treiben auf unserem Planeten. Königsberg, Anfang Februar 1836', *Unser Planet. Blätter für Unterhaltung, Zeitgeschichte, Literatur, Kunst und Theater*, no. 70, Tuesday 22 March 1836, p. 275, cutting in HA I Rep. 76 III, Sekt 2. Abt. XVI, Nr 4, vol. 2.

30. Extrakt aus der *Kritischen Prediger-Bibliothek von Dr. Röhr*, 17/1 (1836), GStA Berlin, HA I, Rep. 76 III, Sekt. 2, Abt. XVI, Nr 4, vol. 1, fol. 238.

31. Christopher Clark, *The Politics of Conversion. Missionary Protestantism and the Jews in Prussia, 1728–1941* (Oxford, 1995), p. 138.

32. 'Die im Bezirk der Regierung zu Königsberg in Preussen befindlichen Vereine zu ausserkirchlichen Religionsübungen oder Erbauungsstunden zu 1822', GStA Berlin, HA I, Rep. 76 III, Sekt. 2, Abt. XVI, Nr 1, vol. 1, fols. 30–35; on gendered and sexual themes in anti-Catholic discourse during the Culture Wars, see Michael B. Gross, *The War against Catholicism: Liberalism and the Anti-Catholic Imagination in Nineteenth-Century Germany* (Ann Arbor, 2004).

33. '... der Anblick des Nackten könne geschehen zur Lösung der Fantasie von ihren Bildern, zur Verwandlung des blinden Triebes in eine bewusste Neigung zur Gattin'. This is Diestel's own account of Ebel's teaching on the matter: Diestel to Consistorium, 15 and 16 October 1835, GStA Berlin, HA I, Rep. 76 III, Sekt. 2, Abt. XVI, Nr 4, vol. 1, fols. 54–59, here fol. 59.

34. 'In der Schilderung ist eine Anweisung zu unnatürlicher Überreizung des Körpers gegeben, die ich verabscheuen muss, und nicht empfohlen haben kann', Diestel to Consistorium, 15 and 16 October 1835, GStA Berlin, HA I, Rep. 76 III, Sekt. 2, Abt. XVI, Nr 4, vol. 1, fols. 54–9, here fol. 56.

35. GStA Berlin, HA I, Rep. 76 III, Sekt. 2, Abt. XVI, Nr 4b: Erkenntnis 1ster Instanz in der Untersuchungssache wider den Archidiakonus Dr Ebel und den Prediger Diestel in Königsberg Pr; eingereicht mittels Schreibens des Königlichen Kammergerichts hierselbst vom 15. August 1839, unnumbered folios.

36. The letter from Charlotte von Finkenstein is transcribed in Diestel to Consistorium, 'Ausführliche Erklärung des Predigers Diestel über die dem Archidiakonus Dr. Ebel erkennbar gemachten Anschuldigungen', Königsberg, 15 October 1835, GStA Berlin, HA I, Rep. 76 III, Sekt. 2, Abt. XVI, Nr 4, vol. 1, fols. 60–96; the letter is transcribed on fols. 81–84, here fol. 84.

37. This point is made in Diestel to Consistorium, 'Ausführliche Erklärung des Predigers Diestel über die dem Archidiakonus Dr. Ebel erkennbar gemachten Anschuldigungen', Königsberg, 15 October 1835, GStA Berlin, HA I, Rep. 76 III, Sekt. 2, Abt. XVI, Nr 4, vol. 1, fols. 60–96, here fol. 88.

38. Ebel to Ministry of Church Affairs, Königsberg, 12 October 1835, GStA Berlin, HA I, Rep. 76 III, Sekt. 2, Abt. XVI, Nr 4, vol. 1, fols. 23–5.

39. Deposition by Ebel, transcribed in GStA Berlin, HA I, Rep. 76 III, Sekt. 2, Abt. XVI, Nr 4b: Erkenntnis 1ster Instanz in der Untersuchungssache wider den Archidiakonus Dr Ebel und den Prediger Diestel in Königsberg Pr.; eingereicht mittels Schreibens des Königlichen Kammergerichts hierselbst vom 15. August 1839.

40. Schön to Altenstein, Königsberg, 7 August 1835, GstA Berlin, HA I, Rep. 76 III, Sekt. 2, Abt. XVI, Nr. 4, vol. 1, f. 1; the same point is made in Fink von Finkenstein to Zerlina von Mirbach, Königsberg, 14 January 1835, GstA, Rep. 76 III, Sekt. 2, Abt. XVI, Nr. 4, vol. 1, f. 6.
41. Kanitz, *Aufklärung nach Actenquellen*, p. 65.
42. Ibid., p. 285.
43. Ibid., pp. 286–7.
44. Schön to Altenstein, Königsberg, 7 August 1835, GStA Berlin, HA I, Rep. 76 III, Sekt. 2, Abt. XVI, Nr 4, vol. 4.
45. Kanitz, *Aufklärung nach Actenquellen*, p. 129.
46. See ibid., pp. 64–72, 160–66.
47. Heinrich Diestel and Johannes Ebel, *Verstand und Venunft im Bunde mit der Offenbarung Gottes. Zwei Abhandlungen* (Leipzig, 1837), a leaflet based on a statement of belief composed by the two preachers at the request of the consistory; on this feature of Ebel's work, see also Kanitz, *Aufklärung nach Actenquellen*, pp. 4–5, 354.
48. Diestel, Statement to the Consistorium, Königsberg, 15 October 1835, GStA Berlin, HA I, Rep. 76 III, Sekt. 2, Abt. XVI, Nr 4, vol. 1, fol. 67.
49. Ida von der Gröben to Minister Altenstein, Königberg, 18 October 1835, GStA Berlin, HA I, Rep. 76 III, Sekt. 2, Abt. XVI, Nr 4, vol. 1, fols. 38–44, here fol. 40.
50. On the supposed attractiveness of the group to women and 'effeminate males', see Finkenstein to Zelina von Mirbach, Königsberg, 14 January 1835, transcribed in GStA Berlin, HA I, Rep. 76 III, Sekt. 2, Abt. XVI, Nr 4, vol. 1, fol. 6.
51. Ida von der Gröben to Prince Wilhelm of Prussia, Königberg, 18 October 1835, GStA Berlin, HA I, Rep. 76 III, Sekt. 2, Abt. XVI, Nr 4, vol. 1, fols. 38–44, here fol. 41. Emphasis in original; the phrase relating to Ebel's pastorship is from 2 Corinthians 1: 24: 'Not for that we have dominion over your faith, but are helpers of your joy'; this was a stock theme in the sermons of the Awakened after 1815, see the inaugural sermon 'Der Diener des Evangeliums ist nicht Herr über euren Glauben sondern Gehülfe eurer Freude', held by the Awakened Elberfeld preacher Gottfried Daniel Krummacher on 11 February 1816, id, *Gottfr. Dan. Krummacher's gute Botschaft in fünfundvierzig Predigten*, ed. Emil Wilhelm Krummacher (Elberfeld, 1838). On the same theme, see his brother, the reformed theologian Friedrich Adolph Krummacher's, *Die christliche Volksschule im Bunde mit der Kirche* (Essen, 1825), p. 42.
52. Olshausen, *Lehre und Leben*, p. 20.

53. Siegfried August Kähler, *Dr Ludwig August Kähler. Mittheilungen über sein Leben und seine Schriften von seinem ältesten Sohne* (Königsberg, 1856), p. 142.

54. See, for example, the anonymous article by 'Lawyer' in Blätter für literarische Unterhaltung, 1833, no. 170, 171; Johannes Wilhelm Ebel and Georg Heinrich Diestel, *Zeugnis der Wahrheit. Zur Beseitigung der Olshausenschen Schrift: 'Lehre und Leben des Königsberger Theosophen Joh. Heinrich Schönherr'* (Leipzig, 1838); Ernst von Hahnefeld, *Ein Moment aus den 'Mittheilungen' des Consistorialrath Kähler über das 'Leben und die Schriften' seines Vaters, beleuchtet von E. v. Hanhnefeld* (Braunsberg, 1856), a brochure defending Ebel and his mentor; Ernst von Hahnefeld, *Die religiöse Bewegung zu Königsberg in Preussen in der ersten Hälfte des neunzehnten Jahrhunderts und die heutige Kirchengeschichte* (Braunsberg, 1858); Ida von der Gröben, *Die Liebe zur Wahrheit* (Stuttgart, 1850); G. H. Diestel, *Ein Zeugenverhör im Criminalprozesse gegen die Prediger Eben und Diestel mit der darüber laut gewordenen Publicität angestellt* (Basel, 1868); E. v. Kanitz, *Aufklärung nach Actenquellen über den 1835 bis 1842 zu Königsberg in Preussen gefürhten Religionsprozess* (Basel, 1862); E. v. Kanitz, *Ein Mahnwort zu Gunsten der Nachwelt, an die historische Literatur der Gegenwart* (Basel, 1868).

55. Schön to Altenstein, Königsberg, 7 August 1835, GStA Berlin, HA I, Rep. 76 III, Sekt. 2, Abt. XVI, Nr 4, vol. 1.

THE LIFE AND DEATH OF
COLONEL GENERAL BLASKOWITZ

1. See 'The Fatal German Duel. Lieut. Hildebrand, who slew Lieut. Blaskowitz, Sentenced to Two Years' Imprisonment', *New York Times*, 19 November 1901; also the editorial piece in *The Times*, 28 November 1901, p. 9, col. D.

2. The problem was that Blaskowitz was the youngest member of his class, with an Offizierspatent dated seven months later than his comrades. Promoting him with his age group would thus separate him from his classmates. Pastor Blaskowitz of Walterkehmen to Wilhelm II, 7 February 1902: petition requesting the 'Vorpatentierung' of Johannes Blaskowitz; same to Karl Dietrich Graf von Hülsen-Haeseler (adjutant-general to the Kaiser), 7 February 1902, in which the father mentions the death of his older son at the age of only twenty-five and notes that the fulfilment of his request would be 'ein Lichtblick in meinem unsagbaren

Herzenskummer', BA-MA Freiburg, Personalakte General-Oberst Blaskowitz, Pers. 6/20, fos. 7, 11.

3. See Gesuchsliste des Infanterie-Regiments von Grolman (1. Posenschen) Nr. 18, Osterode, 1 July 1912, signed v. Karger (Oberst and CiC of Regiment), et al., which requests, on Blaskowitz's behalf, 'transfer into one of the larger garrisons of the Grand Duchy of Baden on account of his daughter's illness and his own persistent inflammations of the ear and nose'. BA-MA Freiburg, Personalakte General-Oberst Blaskowitz, Pers. 6/20, fo. 24.

4. [General Gustav Seitz], 'Blaskowitz', in *Der Seehase. Nachrichtenblatt der Kameradschaft ehemaliger 114er and 14er*, No. 66 (Easter, 1955), [p. 4].

5. See, for example, Personnel report of 1 December 1913, which notes 'sein hervorstechendes körperliches Geschick' und seine Fähigkeiten als 'Reiter, Turner und Gewehrfechter', BA-MA Freiburg, Personalakte General-Oberst Blaskowitz, Pers. 6/20, fos. 6–7.

6. OB West (Oberkommando Hgr D) Beurteilung zum 1 May 1944, signed Rundstedt, Generalfeldmarschall Ob. d. Hgr. D und OB West, BA-MA Freiburg, Personalakte General-Oberst Blaskowitz, Pers. 6/20, fo. 66.

7. Hellmuth Stieff to his wife, Parade Ground Ohrdruf, 21 August 1932 in Horst Mühleisen (ed.), *Hellmuth Stieff: Briefe* (Berlin: Siedler, 1991), letter no. 36, p. 71; F. L. Cartsten, *The Reichswehr and Politics, 1918–1933* (Oxford: Clarendon Press, 1966), p. 374.

8. Hans Gies (Infantry General retd) to Anni Blaskowitz (B's daughter), Konstanz, 17 December 1965, BA-MA Freiburg, MSg 1/1814 Schriftwechsel von Hans Gies mit Kameraden u. Anna Blaskowitz, Presseartikel und Ausarbeitungen 1935–1967 (unfoliated).

9. Hans von Seeckt, 'Heer im Staat', in id., *Gedanken eines Soldaten* (Berlin: Verlag für Kulturpolitik, 1929), pp. 101–16, here p. 116.

10. Speech by Johannes Blaskowitz, Bommelsen cemetery, Sunday 17 March 1935 (copy), BA-MA Freiburg, MSg 1/1814.

11. Seitz, 'Blaskowitz', p. 4.

12. Nicolaus von Below, *Als Hitlers Adjutant 1937–1945* (Mainz: Von Hase und Koehler, 1980), p. 116.

13. Hanns Möller-Witten, 'Darstellung des Lebenslaufs von Blaskowitz', BA-MA Freiburg, MSg 1/1931.

14. Blaskowitz to Fischer (Reich Propaganda Chief), Prague, 14 May 1939, BA Berlin Lichterfelde, R 55/30181, Personalakten betr. Ebert, Karl Verwaltungsmann, Reichspropagandaamt Mark Brandenburg.

15. Major-General Erwin Jaenecke, 'Die Armee Blaskowitz im Polenfeldzug' (1939), [typescript], BA-MA Freiburg, RH 20-8/46, esp. fos. 1–2; see

also Friedrich-Christian Stahl, 'Blaskowitz', in Bernd Ottnad (ed.), *Badische Biographien*, New Series, vol. 2 (Stuttgart: W. Kohlhammer, 1987), pp. 41–4.

16. Richard Giziowski, *The Enigma of General Blaskowitz* (London: Leo Cooper, 1997), p. 147.

17. Ivo V. Giannini, Detailed Interrogation Report: Generaloberst Johannes Blaskowitz, special detention centre 'Ashcan', 28 July 1945, TNA WO 208/3154, p. 4.

18. Ibid.

19. Engel, diary entry of 18 November 1939, in Hildegard von Kotze (ed.), *Heeresadjutant bei Hitler 1938–1943. Aufzeichnungen des Majors Engel* (Stuttgart: Deutsche Verlags-Anstalt, 1974), p. 68.

20. Order of the Day of 26 October 1939, cited in Helmut Krausnick and Hans-Heinrich Wilhelm, *Die Truppe des Weltanschauungskrieges. Die Einsatzgruppen der Sicherheitspolizei und des SD 1938–1942* (Stuttgart: Deutsche Verlags-Anstalt, 1981), p. 96.

21. Stieff to his wife, Jüterbog, 10 October 1930, excerpted in Helmut Krausnick (ed.), 'Ausgewählte Briefe von Generalmajor Helmuth Stieff', *Vierteljahrshefte für Zeitgeschichte* 2/3 (1954), pp. 291–305, here pp. 295–6.

22. Same to same, Stuttgart, 12 August 1934, in Krausnick (ed.), 'Ausgewählte Briefe', pp. 297–8.

23. Same to same, Headquarters, 21 November 1939, in Krausnick (ed.), 'Ausgewählte Briefe', pp. 288–300, here p. 300.

24. Report of Supreme Commander East, Colonel General Blaskowitz to Army Supreme Command, Łódź, 27 November 1939, BA-MA Freiburg, N 104/3. Parts of this document are reprinted in Helmut Krausnick, Harold C. Deutsch and Hildegard von Kotze (eds.), *Helmuth Groscurth. Tagebücher eines Abwehroffiziers* (Stuttgart: Deutsche Verlags-Anstalt, 1970), doc. no. 43, pp. 426–7.

25. Kotze (ed.), *Heeresadjutant bei Hitler*, p. 68.

26. Thus Blaskowitz's account of the contents of the lost report during an interrogation by the American army on 28 July 1945, see Giziowski, *Enigma*, p. 179. But in view of the similarity between the three reports Blaskowitz is known to have submitted on police activities, the dates are uncertain and he may have confused the reports with each other.

27. For the text of Himmler's decree, which was formally secret but quickly became notorious, see 'Geheimerlass des Reichsführer-SS für die gesamte SS und Polizei' (28 October 1939), in Norbert Westenrieder, *'Deutsche Frauen und Mädchen!' Vom Alltagsleben, 1933–45* (Düsseldorf: Droste,

1984), p. 42. On the disapproval of many officers, see Groscurth, *Tagebücher eines Abwehroffiziers*, p. 78.

28. Krausnick, *Truppe des Weltanschauungskrieges*, p. 98.

29. Vortragsnotizen für Vortrag OberOst (Generaloberst Blaskowitz) beim Oberbefehlshaber des Heeres am 15.2.1940 in Spala (Abschrift), BA-MA Freiburg, RH 53-23/23.

30. Raul Hilberg, *The Destruction of the European Jews* (London: W. H. Allen, [1961]), p. 127.

31. Jochen Böhler, *Auftakt zum Vernichtungskrieg. Die Wehrmacht in Polen 1939* (Frankfurt am Main: Fischer Taschenbuch Verlag, 2006), p. 238; the same point is made in id., *Der Überfall. Deutschlands Krieg gegen Polen* (Frankfurt am Main: Eichborn, 2009), pp. 223–4.

32. Omer Bartov, 'Soldiers, Nazis and War in the Third Reich', *Journal of Modern History*, 63/1 (1991), pp. 44–60, here p. 57.

33. Vortragsnotizen für Vortrag OberOst, fo. 11.

34. Ibid., fos. 14, 11.

35. Ibid., fo. 11.

36. 'Nazis Admit "Firm" Polish Policy; Cardinal Sees National "Disaster"; Even General Blaskowitz Balks at Tactics Held Aimed at Virtual "Racial Extermination"', *New York Times*, 30 January 1940; see also 'Iron Hand in Poland', *The Times*, 31 January 1940, p. 7, col. A, which refers to Blaskowitz under the subtitle 'A General Objects'.

37. Vortragsnotizen für Vortrag OberOst, fo. 12.

38. Ibid., fo. 13.

39. Text of the speech by Pastor Schrader at Blaskowitz's funeral in Fallingbostel, 16 February 1948, BA-MA Freiburg, MSg 1/1814.

40. Hollidt to Krausnick, 5 August 1957, cited in Helmut Krausnick, 'Hitler und die Morde in Polen. Ein Beitrag zum Konflikt zwischen Heer und SS um die Verwaltung der besetzten Gebiete', *Vierteljahrshefte für Zeitgeschichte*, 11 (1963), pp. 196–209, here p. 204, n. 43.

41. Army Supreme Command to Commanders-in-Chief of Army Groups and to OberOst, 7 February 1940, cited in Krausnick and Wilhelm, *Die Truppe des Weltanschauungskrieges*, pp. 103–4.

42. Klaus-Jürgen Müller, 'Zur Vorgeschichte und Inhalt der Rede Himmlers vor der höheren Generalität am 13. März 1940 in Koblenz', *Vierteljahrshefte für Zeitgeschichte*, 18/1 (1970), pp. 95–120, esp. pp. 100–103, 106.

43. Ibid., p. 105.

44. Krausnick, 'Hitler und die Morde in Polen', p. 205.

45. Interrogation protocol, 25 October 1945, cited in Giziowski, *Enigma*, p. 211.

46. Ibid., p. 213.

47. Thus the impression recorded in the interim report by SS-Brigadeführer Berger, see Head of Erganzungsamt of the Waffen-SS, Tgb. Nr. 178/40 geh. An Reichsführer-SS and Head of German Police, Berlin, 25 April 1940, BA-MA Freiburg, RH 53-23/23, fo. 31.

48. Hermann Graml, 'Die Wehrmacht im Dritten Reich', *Vierteljahrshefte für Zeitgschichte*, 45/3 (1997), pp. 365–84, here p. 375.

49. Brauchitsch to Blaskowitz, HQ, 26 June 1940 (copy), BA-MA Freiburg, Pers 6/20, fo. 52.

50. Norman J. W. Goda, 'Black Marks: Hitler's Bribery of his Senior Officers during World War II', *Journal of Modern History*, 72/2 (2000), pp. 413–52

51. See Blaskowitz's training guidelines for units earmarked for service on the eastern front, Armeeoberkommando 1, 16 January 1942, BA-MA Freiburg, RH 20-1/109, fos. 25–7.

52. Blaskowitz to Colonel General Erwin Jaenecke (no location given), 15 September 1943, BA-MA Freiburg, N761/4.

53. Supreme Command 1st Army to commanding generals and divisional commands, 27 June 1941, signed Blaskowitz, BA-MA Freiburg, RH 20-1/100 (AOK I: Addenda to Activity Report Ia), vol. 1, fo. 12 (copy of copy).

54. Report of Supreme Commander East, Colonel General Blaskowitz, to Army Supreme Command, Łódź, 27 November 1939, BA-MA Freiburg, N 104/3.

55. Supreme Commander Army Group G to Commandant of H.V.St. 654 Toulouse (for forwarding to the regional prefects of Toulouse), secret, HQ, 17 June 1944, BA-MA Freiburg, RH 19 XII/3 (addendum 243), fo. 327.

56. On this measure and its later disavowal by OB West, see Peter Lieb, *Konventioneller Krieg oder NS-Weltanschauungskrieg? Kriegführung und Partisanenbekämpfung in Frankreich* (Munich: Oldenbourg, 2007), p. 392.

57. On Blaskowitz's impressive management of the withdrawals from southern France, see Joachim Ludewig, *Der deutsche Rückzug aus Frankreich 1944* (Freiburg: Rombach, 1994), esp. pp. 70, 73, 318.

58. See, for example, the discussion at Führer HQ on 27 January 1945 in H. Heiber (ed.), *Hitlers Lagebresprechungen. Die Protokollfragmente seiner militärischen Konferenzen 1942–1945* (Stuttgart: Deutsche Verlags-Anstalt, 1962), p. 855; also Ludewig, *Rückzug*, p. 319.

59. Letter to Anneliese Weitz (no location given), 17 February 1945, BA-MA Freiburg, MSg 1/2603.

60. Cited in W. Denis Winter and Shelagh Whitaker, *Rhineland. The Battle to End the War* (New York: St Martin's Press, 1989), p. 267.

61. Giziowski, *Enigma*, p. 403.

62. '10 Germans Executed by Blaskowitz', *The Times*, 18 May 1945, p. 4, col. B.

63. Kriegstagebuch (Army Daily Reports) Army Group G (Command Department), 21 July 1944.

64. On the political pressure on Blaskowitz to demonstrate conformity, see Lieb, Konventioneller Krieg oder NS-Weltanschauungskrieg?, p. 87; on the continuation of payments to Blaskowitz, see Goda, 'Black Marks'.

65. Appraisals: BA-MA Freiburg Personalakte General-Oberst Blaskowitz, Pers. 6/20, fos. 66, 67; on Blaskowitz's non-membership of the NSDAP, see his Personal Data Sheet of 15 October 1947, completed when he arrived at Nuremberg, which states under the rubric 'political history': 'As a professional soldier not a party member' BA – Aussenstelle Ludwigsburg, B 162/ Rep. 502 XA 13 and XA 155.

66. Friedrich Freiherr Hiller von Gaertringen (ed.), *Die Hassell-Tagebücher 1938–1944. Aufzeichnungen vom anderen Deutschland* (Berlin: Siedler, 1988), p. 365.

67. See, for example, the text of an interview conducted by a Mr Fred Kaufman – probably in the Steinlager Allendorf – on 17 October 1947 and the questionnaire requested by a Mr Walter H. Rapp on 17 November 1947, both in BA-MA Freiburg Personalakte General-Oberst Blaskowitz Pers. 6/20.

68. 'Anklageschrift gegen von Leeb und andere, hier gegen Generaloberst Blaskowitz' (copy), in BA-MA Freiburg, MSg 1/1814 Schriftwechsel von Hans Gies mit Kameraden u. Anna Blaskowitz, Presseartikel und Ausarbeitungen 1935–1967; the arrest of sixty French citizens in the course of 'counter-terrorist' actions near Nice is also reported in the War Diary of Army Group G, entry of 3 July 1944, BA-MA Freiburg, RH 19 XII/5, fo. 9.

69. See, for example, Heinz Mueller-Torgow to Hans Gies, Nuremberg, 20 January 1948; Hans Gies 'Eidesstattliche Erklärung zur Anklage gegen Gen.Obst. Blaskowitz'; Pastor Scriba, 'Bekundung [. . .] zur Benutzung und Vorlage als Beweismaterial beim Internationalem Gerichtshof im Justizpalast zu Nürnberg', 10 March 1948, excerpted in Gert Steuben, 'Wie sie starben. Todesfälle jener Jahre. So blieb er ohne Marschallsstab', *Das Neue Blatt*, 1953, p. 12, all in BA-MA Freiburg, MSg 1/1814.

70. Pastor Scriba, 'Bekundung [. . .] zur Benutzung und Vorlage als Beweismaterial beim Internationalem Gerichtshof im Justizpalast zu Nürnberg'.

71. Hans Müller-Torgow to Hans Gies, Nuremberg, 25 February 1948, BA-MA Freiburg, MSg 1/1814.

72. Letter from Blaskowitz (recipient unnamed), Nuremberg, 27 December 1947, cited in 'Porträts grosser Soldaten', *Kampftruppen* (June 1967) p. 94.

73. On this problem, see Frank Trommler, 'Between Normality and Resistance: Catastrophic Gradualism in Nazi Germany', *Journal of Modern History*, 64 (Supplement: Resistance against the Third Reich), (1992), pp. 82–101.

74. Martin Broszat, 'Resistenz und Widerstand: Eine Zwischenbilanz des Forschungsprojekts', in *Bayern in der NS-Zeit*, ed. M. Broszat et al. (4 vols., Munich: Oldenbourg, 1981), vol. 4, pp. 691–709, here p. 693; id., 'Zur Sozialgeschichte des deutschen Widerstandes', *Vierteljahrshefte für Zeitgeschichte*, 34 (1986), pp. 300–334.

75. Richard Löwenthal, 'Widerstand im totalen Staat', in Richard Löwenthal and Patrick von zur Mühlen (eds.), *Widerstand und Verweigerung in Deutschland, 1933–1945* (Berlin: Dietz, 1982), pp. 11–24.

76. On 'value-freedom' as a feature distinguishing mere *Resistenz* from resistance, see Klemens von Klemperer, '"What is the Law that Lies behind these Words?" Antigone's Question and the German Resistance Against Hitler', *Journal of Modern History*, 64 (Supplement: Resistance against the Third Reich), (1992), pp. 102–11.

77. Alf Lüdtke, 'The Appeal of Exterminating "Others": German Workers and the Limits of Resistance', in ibid., pp. 46–67, here p. 49.

78. See especially Richard Bosworth, *Mussolini's Italy. Life Under the Dictatorship, 1915–1945* (London: Allen Lane, 2005); id., *The Italian Dictatorship. Problems and Perspectives in the Interpretation of Mussolini and Fascism* (London, 1998); id., 'War, Totalitarianism and "Deep Belief" in Fascist Italy 1935–1943', *European History Quarterly*, 34/4 (2004), pp. 475–505; id., 'Everyday Mussolinism: Friends, Family, Locality and Violence in Fascist Italy', *Contemporary European History*, 14/1 (2005), pp. 23–43.

79. Ian Kershaw, *Popular Opinion and Political Dissent in the Third Reich: Bavaria, 1933–1945* (Oxford: Oxford University Press, 1983), p. 374.

Acknowledgements

'The Dream of Nebuchadnezzar' draws on material published in the essay 'Power' in Ulinka Rublack (ed.), *A Concise Companion to History* (OUP: Oxford, 2012). A version of 'Why Does a Battle Matter?' appeared in *Anglo-Norman Studies* XXXIX (Proceedings of the Battle Conference 2016). 'The Life and Death of Colonel General Blaskowitz' is a revised version of an essay published in Daniela Baratieri, Mark Edele and Giuseppe Finaldi (eds.), *Totalitarian Dictatorship: New Histories* (Routledge: New York, London, 2014). 'Psychograms from the Third Reich' is based on three review pieces for the *London Review of Books*. 'The Futures of War' is based on a review piece published in the *New York Review of Books*.